Campaign Finance Complexity

Campaign Finance Complexity

Before Campaigning Retain an Attorney

Mary Jo McGowan Shepherd

LEXINGTON BOOKS
Lanham • Boulder • New York • London

Published by Lexington Books
An imprint of The Rowman & Littlefield Publishing Group, Inc.
4501 Forbes Boulevard, Suite 200, Lanham, Maryland 20706
www.rowman.com

Unit A, Whitacre Mews, 26-34 Stannary Street, London SE11 4AB, United Kingdom

British Library Cataloguing in Publication Information Available

Library of Congress Cataloging-in-Publication Data

Names: McGowan Shepherd, Mary Jo, author.
Title: Campaign finance complexity : before campaigning retain an attorney / Mary Jo McGowan Shepherd.
Description: Lanham, Maryland : Lexington Books, 2018. | Includes bibliographical references and index.
Identifiers: LCCN 2017061428 (print) | LCCN 2017060803 (ebook) | ISBN 9781498535076 (Electronic) | ISBN 9781498535069 (cloth : alk. paper)
Subjects: LCSH: Campaign funds--Law and legislation--United States. | Election law--United States.
Classification: LCC KF4920 (print) | LCC KF4920 .M33 2018 (ebook) | DDC 342.73/078--dc23
LC record available at https://lccn.loc.gov/2017061428

∞ ™ The paper used in this publication meets the minimum requirements of American National Standard for Information Sciences Permanence of Paper for Printed Library Materials, ANSI/NISO Z39.48-1992.

Printed in the United States of America

Contents

List of Figures

List of Tables

Acknowledgments

Books do not happen on their own and this book is no different. I would like to gratefully acknowledge the support and help of all my colleagues and staff in the UNC Charlotte Department of Political Science and Public Administration. Their support and encouragement helped move this project forward. I especially would like to thank Martha Kropf, Suzanne Leland, Eric Heberlig, and John Szmer for their generous guidance over this process. Additionally, I want to thank UNC Charlotte's Project Mosaic, and Kailas Venkitasubramanian for their help and support with the data analysis. There are many others I wish to thank including the editors at Lexington Books who were generous and helpful with their guidance and feedback, and the anonymous peer reviewers, whose critical guidance made this book better. Finally, I thank my children, family, and friends for their long-lived support during the writing of this book.

Introduction

Consider a scenario in which a citizen of one of the fifty US states considers running for political office. We know there are many factors citizens take into consideration. When filing for office the citizen faces forms, filing fees, training classes, committee forms, and in some states candidacy petitions. Add to this the task of creating a campaign committee, strategizing, hiring a treasurer, and ensuring laws are upheld. All of this before the citizen officially becomes a candidate or even starts debating one issue. This steep learning curve is costly in terms of time and effort for an average citizen. An incumbent candidate considering reelection for the same seat faces a very different reality. The incumbent has already been through this and faces a much less costly campaign.

These albeit extreme options are choices faced by many individuals wanting to run for office today. The numerous regulations and rules created by campaign finance reforms enacted over the past few decades have created a complex regime that candidates face. As described in this book, some states have wide variation in complexity of campaign finance regulations. In some states candidates easily run for office. In other states, candidates have a difficult regulatory environment and spend countless hours filling out paperwork, forms, and complying with rules. This book studies the realities of this situation and answers questions such as: Are the regulations complex? In states with complex statutes, do fewer candidates run for office? Why would any legislator write regulations that are more complex in a democratic system in which the purported goal is to encourage citizens to run for office? The inspiration for this book (and the title) came from a joke Raymond La Raja[1] wrote that the Bipartisan Campaign Reform Act, or BCRA, really stood for Before Campaigning Retain an Attorney. La Raja's joke highlights the fact that running for office is complex, so complex that candidates might need an attorney or professional help to ensure compliance with all the rules and regulations. Because federal laws are very similar across the United States, this analysis uses the natural variation found in state campaign statutes to test this theory.

The above complex scenario happens more often than expected according to candidate interviews. Some candidates describe the process of running for office as a series of hurdles they have to jump over in order to get to run for office. Often candidates must seek professional help in order to have a viable chance of running for office. The importance of understanding how the candidacy process affects individuals cannot be underestimated. We must understand if there are serious impediments to individuals who actually would like to run for office but do not. Constraints may prevent the democratization goal of campaign finance legislation from actualization.

Understanding the constraining process, the constraints, and the potential effects of the constraints is the goal of this book. In chapter 1, the book first looks at institutions as a theoretical basis for the book. Rules and regulations as institutions are the front line on campaign finance. Understanding how institutions have the ability to constrain individuals is key to understanding how campaign finance institutions may constrain potential candidates. Institutions often work to constrain other institutions. The possibility that institutions or rules and regulations constrain individual choices to run for office exists.

When institutions constrain other institutions or individuals there are a variety of ways in which they utilize this behavior. From institutional structure to administrative procedures, one institution tries to create a beneficial outcome for their own institution. Scholars measure constraint as the number of agencies created to implement a statute, the administrative procedures with which bureaucrats must comply, or the ambiguity or specificity of the statute language. Adding to the constraint literature this book creates another way to measure institutions using the idea of complexity. The more complex an institution, the more difficult it should be for other actors to comply with or implement. Complexity theory uses a whole systems approach to analyze an entire system versus analyzing particular smaller factors within a system. This book utilizes this approach by analyzing the campaign finance statutes (chapter 3) governing campaign behaviors to get a whole systems picture understanding of what candidates face. By using the statute language, it is possible to measure if the statutes are complex.

As detailed in chapter 2, complexity is the time and effort required to learn and comply with a statute's rules and regulations. The burden emplaced on candidates creates the situation described above where a candidate must learn a myriad of rules and regulations and then learn how to comply with the regime in order to run a campaign. Candidates face learning costs, compliance costs, and potentially psychological costs to comply with the rules and regulations. Rules and regulations create an administrative burden for candidates. The burden creates additional time and effort necessary for compliance. Together, the rules and the burden create a complex system requiring more time and effort to run for office. Additionally different candidate types face different burdens. Novice candidates may require professional or legal help to aide their navigation and compliance of the campaign finance system. Individuals new to the elections system must climb a steep learning curve. Incumbents previously climbed this curve, but have the experience and knowledge to navigate the complex system. The complexity of the campaign finance system creates a real cost for candidates, but it also creates an opportunity cost where they spend money on legal or other professional help that could be spent campaigning.

The complexity of the statutes requires measurement. Chapter 4 describes how plain language metrics can facilitate measurement of complexity. If a statute has more rules and regulations, it would be longer in length than statutes with fewer rules and regulations. Word count is a long-used measure of statute constraint. However, length is not the only valid factor because the nature of the language itself can add complexity. This study uses both the word count and the grade reading level to measure statute complexity. Grade reading level allows us a measure of how hard it is for an average citizen to read and understand what they are reading. This makes it an appropriate measure for campaign finance statutes as average citizens need to read and understand the statutes before seeking to run for political office.

To test the idea of using language on campaign finance statutes, I look at how and if campaign finance rules are complex and formulate a way to measure complexity. An experiment conducted with university undergraduate students tests the hypothesis that campaign finance legislation is complex using statutory language. Language is not just about words but about the ability of an individual to read, comprehend what they have read, and to use what they have read to make decisions about their lives. The experiment tests how individuals understand and react to a complex and a plain language statute from North Carolina.

The book analyzes and measures the campaign finance statutes from all fifty states and uses the plain language idea, tested in chapter 5, to measure contribution limits, candidacy requirements, and campaign finance definition statutes. The plain language data test how candidates react in states with more or less complex rules. Results are analyzed and policy implications discussed in chapter 8 and the conclusion.

NOTE

1. "Will the BCRA Strengthen the Political System? Negative: BCRA Is Not Improving the Political System," *Journal of Policy Analysis and Management* 24, no. 3 (2005).

Chapter One

Institutional Theory

Institutional design theory has evolved over time to two different focal points, one political and one economic in nature. On the political side, theorists look at how one institution affects another institution. For example, scholars look at how legislatures affect bureaucracies or the judicial branch. Some institutional research focuses on institutional constraints such as rules or institution structure. Other institutional research focuses on the language of legislation in terms of ambiguity or clarity. The other focal point is economic in nature. Institutions are seen in the context of principal agent theory or transaction costs. If "policy makes politics"; institutions also make politics. Policies are a type of institution and the effect of their construction affects individuals. This book studies if that affect happens, and if so how does it occur? Taking campaign finance policy as the institution of choice, the book looks at how the design of the policy affects individuals' choices to participate in the political process.

Institutions create rules, and rules create institutions. Rules and regulations play a large role in policy creation and implementation. They give guidance to administrators on how to handle day-to-day situations. Rules set standards and guidelines and generally create a situation in which democracies can treat every person the same way. While institutions create rules, rules themselves become institutions with regular features, both formal and informal. Rules translate values or goals into actions; they are stable and normalized over time. As time goes on rules produce regulations and more rules. The additional layers build up and become intertwined and may have intended and unintended consequences. As the consequences occur, the rules create a burden for administrators and those to whom the rules apply. The burden creates the need for additional transaction costs such as learning, compliance, or psychological costs. The rule situation becomes one of increasing costs, scope, and burden. All of this I term the complexity of the regulatory rule regime.

Campaign finance is an interesting policy because it may have different effects when applied to either legislators or citizens. As an institution, campaign finance has direct effects on individuals and their manner and ability to run for office. From contribution limits to disclosure reports, individuals must comply with this institution. In the campaign finance literature there are many different treatments of the institution of campaign finance (see chapter 3). Some scholars study policy effects on voter turnout, war chests, and incumbency advantages. Scholars have looked at it many different ways. Raymond LaRaja joked about the Bipartisan Campaign Reform Act or BCRA that it really stands for Before Campaigning Retain an Attorney.[1] While this is a funny joke, it also leads to questions about the direction of campaign finance studies. Campaign finance studies look at many factors but there may be a different way to look at campaign finance that other scholars have missed. This different component is complexity of the law. If the law is complex, it may create constraints in the form of increased transaction costs for potential candidates. This increased complexity may deter candidates from running for office. The goal of this book is to look at campaign finance in this different way. In order to analyze this question, this chapter looks how institutional design theory applies to campaign finance.

Scholars have many different definitions of institutions that muddy the water and can make it difficult to understand why a particular entity is an institution. A foundational understanding of institutions is necessary to analysis. A definition, widely accepted by the field, helps ensure scholars are studying similar entities. Otherwise, scholars would compare differing entities and will be unable to generalize across institutions. Even though scholars do not agree on one definition of what constitutes an institution, several general definitions are available. Each definition provides valuable insight into institutions and ways to study them.

One widely quoted definition is from March and Olsen who define institutions as a "collection of interrelated rules and routines that define appropriate actions in terms of relations between roles and situations. The process involves determining what the situation is, what role is being fulfilled, and what obligation of that role in that situation is."[2] This definition tends more toward defining an institution as individual behavior or as simply a set of rules to follow. This is valid considering institutions are human creations. However, we have to consider how the individual acts in more collective environments such as legislatures. March and Olsen consider institutions as a process of determining a situation. This seems to assume that the actor doing the determination is within the institution. That actor might be confronting a situation and need to determine what the standard operating procedures are and what the actor's next steps—according to the rules—might be. If that actor however, is exogenous to the institution, but is required to act in accordance with the institution's rules, the actor fails to have the ability to determine the situation. The actor in this case, is in a coerced position. Rather than having the ability to determine next steps and their role in the process, the actor—because they are outside the rule making—is forced to adhere to rules not of their own making. As shown in chapter 3 on campaign finance reform, the rules and regulations of this institution are just this type of situation, where the rules are made without reference to those outside of the system.

Peters[3] criticizes March and Olsen's definition for its vague definition of "appropriate," its normative interpretation of what rules are, and the assumption that rules are uniform in nature. "[A]ppropriateness of action" and "role obligation" are also dissatisfying because they *assume* that individuals will act within the boundaries set by an institution.[4] It also assumes that individuals will conform to the obligations of their role. The assumption may be that the individuals act in the interest of society. What if they do not? What if those individuals in the role of legislators, act in their own interests instead of the interests of society? Are they able to create an institution that has a self-interested benefit? This book looks not at the obligatory role of legislators, but rather at the effect of legislative action in creating potentially complex legislation that may deter candidates from running. These would be self-interested rules and regulations.

Institutions have particular elements according to Peters. First institutions should have structural features that are formal or informal. These structural features should have predictable "patterned interactions" among individuals or groups of individuals. Campaign finance fits this structural requirement because it has formal features such as goals that intend to make the system less corrupt and disclosure requirements that aim to open the institution to public scrutiny. The formal campaign finance rules such as candidate requirements to run for office and contribution requirements are widely studied structural features. Less studied are the collective impact of all the campaigning rules. With a multitude of rules to follow, costs of running for office may increase as discussed later in chapter 2. Campaign finance also has informal features such as the peer and media pressure candidates feel that ensures compliance. Candidates face enormous pressure from other candidates to comply with the letter of the law. Even small indiscretions can trigger an ethics investigation with the resulting publicity and potential reputational loss. Informally candidates are expected to conform to certain behaviors and participate in the same types of events from year to year. There are informal rules regarding how much money candidates should raise. Informal violations can cost candidates. Consider John Kerry's windsurfing pictures, or George W. Bush's lack of elocution.

Stability over time is another characteristic of institutions. Peters's example is a coffee klatch. If you meet a friend for coffee once or twice, that is not an institution, but if you set up a specific date and time to continue meeting friends for coffee, that becomes an institution. Campaign finance does this because even though some particular details of the law have changed over time, the general goals are the same and most of the law's major components have stayed the same. These include requiring disclosure, setting contribution or spending limits. While the limits themselves might change over time or vary by state, the limits are still part of most states' laws. While most states' laws are stable over time, there is variance between states. As demonstrated in chapter 7, this variance is demonstrated by the complexity of the statute language. Overall, the statutes have remained remarkably stable over time.

An institution must also affect individual behavior. In campaign finance, we know that contribution limits might change how much an individual contributes or to whom they contribute, therefore campaign finance law is constraining individual choices. What this book seeks to investigate is if the complexity of campaign finance regulations constrains a candidate's decision to run or not run for office. If this choice is constrained it would be contrary to the stated goals of the institution. Society generally wants more participation and not less. The final characteristic that Peters lists is that there should be some set of shared values and meaning among members of the institution. This also exists in campaign finance, as there are very clearly stated and well-known goals such as reducing corruption or the appearance thereof, and reducing the amount of money in elections. Ultimately, the goals of honest and fair elections are shared.

Elinor Ostrom expands the definition of institutions to include "rules, norms, and strategies adopted by individuals operating within or across organizations."[5] She defines rules in two ways, rules-in-use and rules-in-form. Rules-in-form are those that are written down and proscribed as the standard operating procedures, the regulations that individuals within an institution must follow. These are similar to Peters's formal rules, or March and Olsen's appropriate actions. Rules-in-use are the "do's and don'ts you learn on the ground."[6] The rules-in-use are the day-to-day behaviors to which Peters's refers when he describes the coffee klatch. In campaign finance, the rules-in-form are the statutes and regulations set out for candidates in the law, while rules-in-use are the informal pressures or expectations for compliance by candidates. The same issue exists for rules in form as for March and Olsen's institution definition. These definitions are endogenous to the institution. They are created to describe the behavior of the institution and not to describe the behavior of an institution on another actor.

Similar to Peters's shared values, Ostrom also defines institutions in terms of norms or strategies. Norms are the "shared prescriptions that are to be enforced by participants themselves through internally and externally imposed costs and inducements."[7] These norms in campaign finance statutes revolve around mutual adherence to the statutes because of the external costs such as non-reelection, accusations of corruption if candidates fail to comply. The strategies to which Ostrom refers are "regularized plans that individuals make within the structure of incentives produced by rules, norms, and expectations of the likely behavior of others in a situation affected by relevant physical and material conditions.[8] These strategies are particularly relevant for this book because the book assumes strategizing by legislators—conscious or unconscious—to alter the behavior of others running for election by making legislation that is more complex with which candidates must comply. Interestingly, Ostrom's strategies could be applied exogenous to an institution. Candidates could create strategies within the structure of the campaign finance regulatory structure to comply (or not comply) with the rules given the material costs imposed by the rules. At least this definition gives candidates the possibility of making their own choice within the confines of the institution.

These rules, norms, strategies are particularly relevant because this study assumes strategizing by legislators—conscious or unconscious—to alter the behavior of others running for election by making legislation that is more complex with which candidates must comply. "Actors may use their political authority . . . to change the rules (both formal institutions and various public policies) designed to enhance their power."[9] As noted above, the assumption is that candidates' norms center on mutual adherence to the statutes. If candidates do not adhere to the rules, there are external costs such as non-reelection or accusations of corruption. Thus, the opportunity exists for incumbents to create constraints using the campaign finance laws. Such a constraint may be found in the language of campaign finance legislation. Crawford and Ostrom define this ability to constrain as an institutional statement that combines rules, strategies, and norms. The institutional statement "refers to a shared linguistic constraint or opportunity that prescribes, permits, or advises actions or outcomes for actors (both individual and corporate)."[10] It is this linguistic constraint or opportunity used by legislators that may constrain the behavior of potential or actual challengers.

Another important part of Elinor Ostrom's institutions definition is her categorization of decision making into three tiers—constitutional, collective choice, and operational. Ostrom defines the operational tier as "where actors interact in light of incentives they face to generate outcomes directly in the world."[11] This book assumes that legislators have incentives to make campaign finance statutes in a particular fashion in order to generate the desired outcomes in elections. Legislators face an incentive to increase or protect their election chances by disincentivizing others from running. Thus, campaign finance fits well in Ostrom's operational tier. I do not test in this book the incentives of legislators, but rather I test the effect on potential candidates as discussed in chapters 6, 7, and 8 of this book.

Political Institutionalism

One question this book considers is whether institutions can be constrained and if so how? Political institutionalism literature indicates that institutions not only can be constrained, they often are. This is relevant because this study is arguing that the institution of campaign finance may be a constraint on individual behavior. If legislators can make campaign finance statutes constraining on potential candidates it may help increase the probability of winning the next election or decrease the probability of facing a challenger. First, we need to understand how institutions constrain other institutions and individual behavior. I look at two ways: Procedures or rules as constraints and the structure of an agency or organization that may lead to constraints.

Procedures/Rules as Constraints

Institutional rules and procedures constrain behavior. In some way one institutional actor wishes to prevent another institutional actor from taking an action. It may be that rules are cultural where congressmen are usually polite when speaking from the floor or formal rules such as when and how to introduce a bill or amendment.[12] Regardless of type, the idea is to prevent chaos and promote stability in an institution. Without rules, actors would be able to run amok and do whatever pleased them. Rules prevent this chaos and allow the work of the institution to ensue. However, rules can also go too far if rules prevent individuals or institutions from acting in the democratic interest. Rules are powerful tools to direct outcomes and looking at how rules affect actors' behavior helps us understand the power of the rules to affect outcomes.

There is a long debate over how rules affect others as tools of power. Lukes[13] cites Bachrach and Baretz[14] when discussing rules as both visible and invisible. Visible rules help us see the manifestation of power, but there are invisible rules in place that "prevent conflict from arising in the first place." Visible or tangible rules are rules that we know and from which we can see and measure effects. Visible rules such as contribution limits, and candidacy requirements enable us to see and measure the effects of these rules and their power on very tangible outcomes such as participation rates or contribution quantities. Invisible rules prevent us from tangibly observing or measuring the effects of one actor on another, but a collection of rules such as the entire campaign finance institution could be considered an invisible rule regime. The effects of this invisible rule regime are not often measured because they are difficult to quantify. One contribution of this book is to attempt to measure this regime through language. As discussed in the next chapter, complexity theorists look at the entirety of a system rather than just the component parts. Using language to look at campaign finance as a collection of rules and regulations helps us understand the impact of the whole on candidate decisions.

Visible rules are written into the statutory code for any piece of legislation. The statutes as shown in later chapters are written using language that may be easy or difficult to understand. Just as important as a single statute or regulation, the cumulative effect of a section of the statute constitutes any number of rules. This body of statutes or invisible rule regime fits the definition of an institution. It is a set of rules or norms that represent shared values that are stable over time. This institution of campaign finance is what this book tests for its effect on candidate decisions. To test this we must understand how rules constrain.

Studying tools used to constrain is important to understand the implications of the constraint. One tool for constraint is to implement administrative procedures that allow legislatures to tell bureaucrats exactly how to go about implementation.[15] The legislatures can be very specific in order to prevent bureaucrats from having discretion on policy implementation. Legislatures might want to maintain control over policy because bureaucrats are closer to the policy via implementation than legislators are. Issuing specific procedures minimizes the control that bureaucrats have, and maximizes control for legislators. Specifically McNollgast hypothesizes much of administrative law is written for the purpose of helping elected politicians retain control of policy making. Legislators use administrative law to retain control of public policy over bureaucrats,[16] so why would they not also use administrative law to retain control over their jobs? Campaign finance administration may be written by legislators in order to ensure that they control their positions in government. This is the fox in control of the henhouse scenario. Potential candidates have little recourse to protest this law because they are outside government and have little recourse for feedback.

Legislators articulate very clear rules but often rules can be ambiguous. Unclear rules may serve two ends. First ambiguous rules help in the event of unforeseen or distasteful outcomes. Legislators can tweak the rules to accommodate desired results. Legislators make statutory changes altering the status quo potentially to favor themselves.[17] Legislators might not have all the necessary information, which Shepsle and Weingast[18] call the "uncertainty postulate,"[19] to make policy reach certain goals. Therefore, the policy might be vague in order to allow legislators to tweak it ex post. The "legislators do not know the precise relationship between the instruments they select and the outcomes subsequently produced."[20] In other words, legislators make policy with no real understanding of how it is going to turn out. An important question here is why? What is the motivation of the legislators? Most scholars posit that legislators do this in order to maintain control over the policy outcomes. It is quite possibly accidental also, but it could also be that legislators make policy with uncertain outcomes on purpose. The cost of gaining the correct information in order to make effective policy might be too high. The cost involves gaining the correct data on who the legislation affects. Legislators must determine the intended and unintended outcomes of the legislation. Unless a legislator takes the time to pay this price, the legislation will end up with uncertain outcomes that a legislator can control ex post through oversight.

A second purposeful rationale for making the legislation vague is to ensure a certain outcome. If the cost to the legislator for making effective policy is high in terms of data, efforts and so on, what if the cost of effective policy also costs him his job? If a legislator makes effective campaign finance policy with which all citizens comprehend and comply, this might mean a legislator would face a challenger. If a legislator could make policy ambiguous, it puts the transaction costs[21] of learning the policy on the challenger. This would be a rational choice for that legislator to make legislation that potentially increases the probability of his reelection. The challenger pays the cost of figuring out the legislation if written vaguely. Arthur cites this phenomenon discussing elections as public goods: "A public good is having competitive elections. It's generally hard to limit consumption of a public good, or we want it to be hard to limit because we want more competitive elections and we want people to run for office. However, at the same time we put rules in place to make it harder to run—we constrict the political market."[22]

An important distinction is made between rules and burdens in the public administration literature on administrative burden. Rules are administrative tools that may or may not add burdens or costs upon implementation. "Burdens are seen as distinct from rules, pointing instead to costs that individuals experience in their interactions with the state."[23] This distinction is important to point out here. The question of complexity or administrative burden is taken up in the following chapter. For this book, rules are institutions emplaced by legislators or administrators on candidates running for office. Whether the rules create a burden remains to be determined.[24]

If legislators can put the cost of learning on the challenger, it is problematic for democratic elections because challengers may not be able to participate as effectively. It is important to understand whether or not legislators actually succeed in changing the rules or whether it is just a strategy without success. Shepsle and Weingast try to answer the question of whether or not the constraints actually work in practice. They refute McKelvey and Ordeshook's[25] argument that rules constrain legislators only so long as individuals find the constraints useful. Arguing that coalitions of legislators are able to pass legislation without evading the rules, McKelvey and Ordeshook argue this means that the rules are insufficient to overcome the transaction costs to the legislators. Legislators follow the rules but are able to manipulate the system in such a way to get their legislation passed. Because of this,

McKelvey and Ordeshook think that rules do not matter. Rules can be "modified or bypassed" in order to achieve the desired outcome.[26]

Far from bypassing the rules, Shepsle and Weingast disagree and argue that rules do matter because incentives may be insufficient to overcome the transaction costs of overcoming the rules. In other words, it is too expensive to overcome the rules, therefore legislators stick with them.[27] There is some evidence of rule adherence and rules enhancing the legislative process. What if the stakes are so high that overcoming the transaction costs is worth the effort? If the stakes are your job, your livelihood, and your reputation then you might think it worth the effort to manipulate the rules in order to win reelection. Endersby[28] tests rules for methods and rules for conduct in congressional committees based on Shepsle and Weingast's disagreement with McKelvey and Ordeshook. Endersby tests this idea and finds that rules "do effect outcomes of political choices. . . . If the majority players in a game wish to avoid a theoretical or equilibrium outcome and if they have the incentives and the resources to do so, they will."[29] It is clear that there are rules and the rules generally do matter. Even if they did not legislators are still going to find a way. The take-away from this is that rules in general do constrain legislator's behavior. Additionally, rules may be used by legislators to constrain others' behavior. Legislators might be able to create rules that constrain challengers from running for office.

In other words if there is a will, there is a way. If legislators want to manipulate the constraints and have the will to do so, they will be able to avoid them. The question is whether they have the will to do so. Their desire for reelection[30] establishes that legislators would have the will to overcome the rules and procedures in campaign finance. Shepsle and Weingast, Endersby, McNollgast and McKelvey and Ordeshook all study if the rules are constraining enough for a legislator to have the will and desire to overcome them. In other words, is the hurdle high enough that it prevents legislators from overcoming it? Another way of studying this is to determine if legislators themselves can build the hurdle high enough to constrain others. Can they prevent or constrain other citizens from challenging their reelection chances through the campaign finance institutions? Shepsle and Weingast say, "Procedures will prove more binding and less susceptible to evasion when the costs of negotiating, policing, and enforcing agreements to circumvent procedural restrictions are high."[31] When the transaction costs are high, it is difficult to evade the rules. If legislators can make the transaction costs for seeking office high enough, it may be difficult for challengers to overcome.

McKelvey and Ordeshook and Shepsle and Weingast argue that the rules/institutions are important to understanding the outcomes of policy. The rules mandate the way policy is implemented, thus mandating policy outputs. Legislators make rules that set up the campaign finance policy institution. The campaign finance rules and regulations can be changed or altered to meet the policy needs of legislators. In order to maintain their office, they must at least publicly choose to adopt constraining rules.[32] They adopt policies to regulate campaign finance in response to the public's demand for clean elections. However, because they are the ones making the rules, they can make them in such a way as to ensure a specific outcome. What outcome would a politician seek other than reelection? Thus, politicians should be able to make the rules of campaign finance that benefit themselves and their reelection prospects. The politicians cannot simply evade the rules otherwise they would be guilty of violating campaign finance rules and their reelection chances would decline.

Structural Constraints

Constraints can also become part of the legislative process through the structure of bureaucracies. Scholars argue that legislatures constrain bureaucracies in a variety of ways to ensure control. This is relevant because the legislature writes campaign finance regulations that election bureaucracies implement and administer around the country. In the same way, legislatures might use rules and regulations to constrain actions, legislatures might use the bureaucracy to constrain challengers. While this is not as relevant to this book as rules, bureaucratic constraint may lead to policy complexity which is another facet of complexity in general.

Can legislatures actually constrain bureaucracies? Moe[33] looks at this issue and concludes that yes, legislatures use their power to set up burcaucratic structure to constrain bureaucrats. Moe[34] looks at the structure within institutions and finds that structure is determinant of outcomes. Interest groups lobby legislators, legislators then structure bureaucracies so that interest groups' interests are protected. Protecting interest groups helps legislators protect their incumbency because the interest groups will help favorable legislators stay in office. If legislators are likely to promote interests of their constituencies through bureaucratic structure, might they not also want to protect their own interests similarly. Moe[35] studies legislators' desire to change or tweak bureaucrats' ability to make policy when their interests change. However, all legislators want to be reelected—so this interest never changes. Legislature might want to structure the election law and thus the bureaucracy in such a way as to make policy more complex in order to ensure victory or vice versa, make policy more complex to ensure challengers defeat.

Macey[36] focuses on congressional control of bureaucracies. Politicians in Congress establish agencies that put measures in place that reduce the likelihood of future changes. The goal of legislators is to constrain the agency. They do this using agency structure. For example, Congress might structure an agency in such a way that the agency either covers one or many interest groups, thereby setting up competition within or between agencies for resources. Legislators want to control the discretion and authority that bureaucrats have in order to maintain control for the long term. The long term might entail the legislator being out of office, so control can be set up for the future and not only the present. A good example of this has recently occurred in North Carolina. For decades, the NC Board of Elections (NC BOE) was run by Democrats. Republicans used to have a saying that "Democrats make election rules to elect Democrats." The understanding was that the longevity of Democrats in power in NC was in part because Democrats ran the NC BOE.

More than one agency structuring policy is another method of constraint. Kathleen Bawn[37] focuses on how statutes written by legislators constrain bureaucrats. Using the typology created by McCubbins, Noll, and Weingast[38] and Moe,[39] she lays out the procedures to constrain bureaucrats. These include requiring at least two agencies to collaborate on decision making. The idea here is that when more than one agency gets involved in making a regulation on some activity, the agencies will constrain the discretion of the agency or activity being regulated. This is an idea also supported by Hammond and Knott.[40] Legislators can require an agency to perform to a specific research agenda in order to constrain behavior. Legislators can specify what types of information can and cannot be used in the making of regulations in order to ensure that regulator's behavior is constrained. Legislators can simply limit the scope of regulatory authority for an agency and finally legislators can put a due date on regulations so that if the agency fails to meet the date, the legislators revisit the regulation at a later time. Johnson[41] shows on the flip side that bureaucrats involved with designing an institution are able to use the design process to benefit themselves. All of these constraining behaviors by legislators are meant to increase control over the bureaucracy by the legislators. Procedures change or mandate the way the bureaucracy is structured and managed thereby ensuring that legislatures have control over the agency.[42]

According to Calvert, McCubbins, and Weingast[43] elections may have an impact on how institutional preferences are managed. Some scholars argue that bureaucrats operate without much constraint from elected legislators because the legislators have to worry about reelection, whereas bureaucrats do not. The other view is that bureaucratic agency policies are constrained by legislators because of the way in which procedures are structured. The actions of the legislators determine policy outcomes because the choice of outcomes is traceable to the preferences of legislators. The appointment of bureaucrats directly relates to the preferences of legislators. Thus, policy choices relate as well because whoever is making the policy choice was the preferred appointment of a legislator or executive branch politician. They were the ones with the preference first.[44]

It is clear that legislatures can structure bureaucracies in such a way as to ensure specific policy outcomes they favor. In doing so, they help their reelection prospects because of support from the interest groups benefiting from the favorable policy. They may also help their reelection prospects by structuring the bureaucracies to help themselves and hinder challengers. As challengers navigate the ins and outs of an election bureaucracy, incumbents should already be familiar with the agencies because of previous experience, but also because they may have been the ones to structure the election agency.

Economic Institutionalism

As discussed above, institutional entities use political rules or structures to constrain other institutions and possibly individuals' behavior. The economic realm of institutionalism focuses on many factors such as transaction costs and the principal/agent problem. It is theorized that transaction costs constrain the choices that potential candidates have by raising the cost of running for office. The costs are defined below. The principal/agent problem is less obvious and is treated minimally here as the focus is on transaction costs.

The Principal/Agent Issue

Scholars have clearly found that a principal/agent relationship exists between legislators and bureaucrats. Legislators try to control bureaucrats based on the structure of agencies, vague or ambiguous legislation. That relationship is not under examination here, but rather the idea of a principal/agent relationship is applied to legislators controlling challengers by manipulating the structure of campaign finance legislation.

This relationship between legislators and bureaucrats is understood in the principal/agent context.[45] Legislatively politicians set up principal/agent type controls to ensure legislators maintain control over bureaucrats. As this theory develops however, the agents are able to provide feedback and negotiate with the principals.[46] In campaign finance regulations, if we consider the agents being controlled as the candidates, the feedback mechanisms can be missing because the candidates/challengers have no way to give feedback or complain to their principals—the bureaucracy/legislators.[47] The candidate—especially a novice candidate—has little recourse to challenge the regulation or they face the possibility of losing elections. The candidates also face a higher compliance cost than legislators. Legislators have already successfully run for office and gone through the learning curve, new candidates have yet to pay this learning price. The possibility exists for legislators to make rules more difficult for potential challengers.

Legislators want to constrain bureaucrats' behavior so that legislators can maintain control over policy. The argument here is that legislators should also want to constrain challengers to maintain control over their seat. Scholars typically fall into three camps regarding how bureaucrats are controlled. First bureaucrats might not be affected by legislation at all and thus have total control over policy implementation. Second, bureaucrats are mostly controlled by legislators and thus bureaucrats have little control over implementation. A third camp is somewhere in the middle of the first two meaning that bureaucrats have some but not total control over implementation.[48] In two of the three scenarios, legislators have the ability to constrain bureaucrats to some extent. Most of this control that legislators have over bureaucrats stems from information problems. Bureaucrats have the information on how to implement legislation that legislators might not have. The uncertainty postulate states when legislators are uncertain about policy outcomes they make policy vague so that they will be able to circle back and tweak the policy when the outcomes are negative.[49] Here we understand that legislators can both constrain because they might have information others do not have, and they can constrain at different points in the policy-making process. They can constrain either ex post or ex ante. This book is not testing when the constraint happens, but rather if it happens at all.

Applying this same logic to candidates and challengers, candidates/incumbent legislators have asymmetric information regarding campaign finance laws than challengers. Inherently incumbents have an advantage of "knowing the ropes" of campaign finance law. However, if we take this a step further and understand that those same incumbents were the writers of the legislation, we can see that they are able to control the outcome of the policy. If incumbents are legislators, and challengers are synonymous with bureaucrats this is a simple principal/agent problem where the principal/incumbent/legislator is able to control the agent/challenger/bureaucrat through the administrative procedures written into the law.

Principal/agent control might test better by studying the complexity of the policy via the structure of campaign finance policies. A principal/agent relationship could use the change in campaign finance regulations over time, which is beyond the scope of this work. This book studies the complexity of campaign finance by looking at another aspect of economic institutionalism—transaction costs.

Transaction Costs

The idea of transaction costs in campaign finance legislation is the increase in time, effort, and learning required ensuring compliance with the statutes. If the legislation is more complex it might require a potential candidate to hire a lawyer or other professional in order to make sure that the candidate does not violate the statute. If the statute is written in more complex language, this transaction cost might be higher than if the statute is written in less complex language. In other words, the complex statute would take longer to read, be harder to comprehend, and may require candidates to take additional time or effort to ensure understanding of the statute.

The transaction cost approach generally sees institutions as reducing transaction costs by reducing difficulties in decision making and interactions. "Transaction costs analysis can be used to design programs in ways that make changes away from the status quo more expensive in transaction terms, thus locking in the preferences of the designers."[50] Legislators are able to maintain the status quo, which in this argument would be maintaining their legislative seat, by creating higher costs of entry into the legislature. The idea is that if it costs more to run for office because you have to hire a professional in order to understand the legislation, you may not run. The transaction cost for this study is the language itself. Idiomatically we know that time is money. If challengers must spend more time to learn the complexity of campaign finance, it may put them at a disadvantage when running for office against an incumbent legislator. This disadvantage is covered more in the next chapter and in the chapter on candidate decisions. Lee covers this topic very well and breaks the cost components down into direct cost and the opportunity costs of complying with regulations. He states:

> No doubt petitioning requirement imposes a direct cost on candidates, which is the amount of effort and resources (labor and monetary) expended on collecting signatures. Not all potential candidates will be able to bear this cost, either blocking unsuccessful attempts or discouraging attempts. All else equal, as the number of signatures increases, the likelihood of seeing any third candidates decreases. There is also the opportunity cost of the requirement.[51]

The opportunity cost means the efforts to collect signatures takes time away from more valuable campaign activities and leaves the challenger in a deficit. In particular, a novice candidate will have a hard time learning and then complying with the signature requirements. In the qualitative interviews originally conducted for this research, one candidate mentioned the petition requirements stating that:

> The big headache is campaign petitions. You have to get signatures in your district and polling places. You need to get the data ahead of time [on how and who to petition] because getting the data from the state takes 4–5 weeks and then you have 3–4 weeks to get the petitions done. You have to educate people on why they're signing the petition. Incumbency has its advantages.[52]

An important caveat with the costs of campaigning is that most of the literature looks only at signature petitions and not at a holistic picture of the costs of running for office. This book attempts by looking at the statutes as a whole, to measure the big picture or the entire context in which a potential candidate may find themselves.

Transaction costs increase time, effort, and learning of the statutes or hiring of professionals to ensure compliance with the law. If the statutes are so complex that they require more time to understand then complexity may be a type of transaction cost added onto candidates running for office. If challengers must spend more time to learn the complexity of campaign finance, it may put them at a disadvantage when running for office against an incumbent legislator. This book suggests one way to measure this complexity is to use the language of the statute.

Measuring complexity of legislation using language is not new. Complexity of legislative language is generally studied in context of the constraint literature. These studies look at how one institution constrains another using the language within the law or regulatory system. Some studies use word count as a constraining factor in legislation. This is relevant to a study of complexity because if legislation can be constraining to bureaucrats, it may also be a constraint on "regular" citizens. Huber, Shipan and Pfahler[53] posit that the legislature would put constraints in legislation when it does not trust the bureaucracy. Huber et al.[54] use the word count feature in the Microsoft Word program. This measure is simple and very objective. The researcher simply enters the text into MS word and then specifies "word count." Huber et al. use word count as a way to measure statutory constraint because logically the more words in a bill, the more detailed and thus constraining it might be. This measure is reliable because it takes all the Medicaid legislation in all fifty states and examines the word count of that legislation. Even though there are some other factors involved in this analysis, the result is that legislation is being used to constrain bureaucrats.[55] This study argues that if legislators can constrain bureaucrats, they may be able to write legislation that could possibly constrain their electoral opponents also.

Constraint is not the only function of language. It may also add in transaction costs. Transaction costs are the cost of learning or making ones way up the learning curve. If you are an incumbent, you have already paid the transaction costs of learning how to run for office. If you are a challenger, you have yet to pay this cost. The cost can be steep depending on the laws for your state. Incumbents can write the law in such a way as to not only constrain the law's outcome, but also in such a way that makes it difficult to understand and comply with the law. If the law is difficult to understand, it takes time for challengers to grasp the meaning of the law's provisions. This time constraint takes away from raising money or campaigning. Further, if the challenger fears reprisals from failure to understand and comply with the law, they may choose (or be required) to hire a lawyer, treasurer, and so forth, in order to ensure compliance all of which adds time and hence costs.

Applying Peters's definition of transaction costs to the language of campaign finance it may be possible to design campaign finance statutes in such a way as to make the statutes more difficult for challengers to understand. If the statutes were harder to comprehend then the statutes would be harder in compliance terms and might require challengers to hire professionals to ensure compliance.

Individuals running for political office face challenges. One challenge is to navigate the campaign finance system in order to maximize their ability to raise funds and campaign. That ability to use their time wisely can be compromised if they must spend additional time learning and comprehending the campaign finance legislation. This adds transaction costs to a legislator's attempt at running for office. Adding to that cost may be the de facto requirement of candidates to hire professionals in order to help them navigate the system.

Legislator Motivations

Incumbent legislators may be creating a campaign finance system that adds transaction costs to challengers in order to help incumbents maintain their seats. This study is not arguing the legislators do this consciously but as part of their ability to structure legislation, over time complexity may be added to the campaign system that has the effect of increasing costs to challengers.

The two main goals of campaign finance are reducing corruption and increasing participation in the electoral system. Ignoring the corruption goal as beyond the current scope, this book focuses on the goal of increased participation. Campaign finance statutes intend to broaden the base from which contributions originate, and increase the number of people participating in the system. Creating an election system in which the people have confidence should inspire greater candidate participation. However, a legislator's main goal is reelection,[56] which stands in opposition to the increased participation goal for campaign finance policy. A legislator's goal of reelection should mean that they want less participation. More participation means more competition for the legislator's seat. Mayhew describes the activities in which legislators engage in order to ensure reelection. These include credit claiming, advertising, and position taking. Mayhew is clear that "what a congressman has to try to do is to insure that in primary and general elections the resource balance (with all other deployed resources finally translated into votes) favors himself rather than somebody else."[57] Clearly, legislators are motivated to ensure that the legislative environment is conducive to, at the very least, maintenance of their seat and, at the most, a situation in which participation is minimized.

The ambition present in legislators combines with a status quo maintenance position to give legislators both the opportunity and motive to keep their seats and their majority status in the legislature. This comports with the theory that "if there is value to be gained through politics, persons will invest resources in efforts to capture this value"[58] and self-interested individuals, groups, or industries seek regulation as a means to serve their own private interests. Campaign costs are supposedly one reason for campaign finance reform, but if the regulations emplaced are the tool by which candidates protect their seat the goal of the reform is in jeopardy.

Evidence from campaign finance studies have shown different effects of contribution limits on electoral outcomes. These are discussed in full in chapter 3. However, one recent study[59] looked at state campaign finance limits and found that when contribution limits were in place, the margin of victory for incumbents was smaller. The Stratmann et al. article goes further and finds that the effect of the contribution limits was smaller for the legislator who passed the limits and that those same legislators were not subject to increased competition.[60] At least in some studies it is clear that legislators can and do try to constrain their competition through legislation.

The problem for this policy antagonism is that campaign finance policy impedes democracy when citizens' choices are constrained. According to Powell, "high quality democracy is sustained when institutional arrangements provide incentives supporting each of the major linkages of responsiveness."[61] Democracy is enhanced when democratic institutions foster responsiveness of legislators.

Two of the subversions that break the chain are lack of information and constraints. If citizens fail to have accurate information, they cannot make accurate electoral choices. Following the same logic down a different path, if candidates have higher transaction costs for accurate information they cannot make accurate choices on how and if to run for election. "Constraints that the larger policy-making setting can impose on even the most sincere officeholders may also impede responsiveness"[62] indicates that when constraints are placed on officeholders they may not be as responsive to constituents. Again, following similar logic down the electoral path, the constraints may be emplaced by the officeholder in order to impede responsiveness. Legislators may not want to open the electoral system; instead, they want it less responsive in order to maintain their seat. Powell goes on to say that, fairly low barriers to entry of new parties should help to keep the party system attentive to what citizens want. Substituting candidates for parties, we can see that low barriers might allow citizens to have different electoral choices/candidates. High barriers to entry in the form of higher transaction costs for challengers might lead to fewer candidates running for office.

CONCLUSION

Institutions can be on a high-level, such as the legislature, and as street-level as a campaign regulation. Campaign finance regulations are the formal and informal institutional rules that govern individual candidate behavior. Institutions have consequences. Institutions are long understood to have various effects on policy and policy makers. The way in which institutions are structured affects the outcome of policy making. Institutions are able to constrain other institutions and individuals in a variety of ways from the structure of an agency, to the type of written language of the statute. Constraint happens at every level of government and between all the governmental institutions. The question is can legislators create institutional rules that constrain other candidates? Moreover, are those rules created in a complex fashion in order to create that constraint? This chapter answers the first part of that question; the next chapter answers the complexity question.

NOTES

1. Michael Malbin, Anthony Corrado, and Raymond La Raja, "Will the Bipartisan Campaign Reform Act of 2002 Strengthen the Political System?" *Journal of Policy Analysis and Management* 24, no. 3 (2005).
2. James G. March and Johan P. Olsen, *Rediscovering Institutions* (New York: Free Press, 1989).
3. B. Guy Peters, *Institutional Theory in Political Science* (New York: The Continuum International Publishing Group, 2012).
4. Ibid.
5. Elinor Ostrom, "Institutional Rational Choice: An Assessment of the Institutional Analysis and Development Framework," in *Theories of the Policy Process*, ed. Paul Sabatier (Cambridge: Westview Press, 2007), 23.
6. Ibid.
7. Ibid.
8. Ibid.
9. Paul Pierson, "Increasing Returns, Path Dependence, and the Study of Politics," *American Political Science Review* 94, no. 2 (2000): 259.
10. Sue E.S. Crawford and Elinor Ostrom, "A Grammar of Institutions," *American Political Science Association* 89, no. 3 (1995): 583.
11. Ostrom, "Institutional Rational Choice: An Assessment of the Institutional Analysis and Development Framework," 27.
12. Eric Uslaner, *The Decline in Comity in Congress* (The University of Michigan Press, 1993).
13. Roy L. Heidelberg, "The Power of Knowing the Rules," *American Review of Public Administration* 46, no. 6 (2016); S. Lukes, *Power: A Radical View* (New York, NY: Palgrave Macmillan, 2005).
14. P. Bachrach and M. S. Baretz, "Decisions and Nondecisions: An Analytical Framework," *American Political Science Review* 57 (1963).
15. Mathew McCubbins, Roger Noll, and Barry Weingast, "Administrative Procedures as Instruments of Political Control," *Journal of Law, Economics and Organization* 3 (1987).
16. Ibid.
17. John Ferejohn and Charles Shipan, "Congressional Influence on Bureaucracy," *Journal of Law, Economics, and Organization* 6, Special Issue (1990).

18. "Positive Theories of Congressional Institutions," *Legislative Studies Quarterly* 19, no. 2 (1994).
19. When legislators are uncertain about policy outcomes they make policy vague to allow for tweaking ex post if outcomes are negative.
20. Shepsle and Weingast, "Positive Theories of Congressional Institutions," 159.
21. Transaction costs are defined below.
22. Pierson, "Increasing Returns, Path Dependence, and the Study of Politics," 258.
23. Donald Moynihan, Pamela Herd, and Hope Harvey, "Administrative Burden: Learning, Psychological, and Compliance Costs in Citizen-State Interactions," *Journal of Public Administration Research and Theory* 25 (2014): 45.
24. Elaboration on the distinction between rules and burdens is covered in chapter 2 on complexity.
25. Richard D. McKelvey and Peter C. Ordeshook, "An Experimental Study of the Effects of Procedural Rules on Committee Behavior," *The Journal of Politics* 46, no. 1 (1984).
26. Ibid., 201.
27. Kenneth A. Shepsle and Barry R. Weingast, "When Do Rules of Procedure Matter?"
28. James W. Endersby, "Rules of Method and Rules of Conduct: An Experimental Study on Two Types of Procedure and Committee Behavior," *Journal of Politics* 55, no. 1 (1993).
29. Ibid., 232.
30. David R. Mayhew, *Congress: The Electoral Connection* (New Haven, CT: Yale University, 1974).
31. Shepsle and Weingast, "Positive Theories of Congressional Institutions," 215.
32. Ibid.
33. Terry Moe, "Politics and the Theory of Organizations," *Journal of Law, Economics, and Organization* 7, no. Special Issue (1991); "Political Institutions: The Neglected Side of the Story," *Journal of Law, Economics and Organization* 6 (Special Issue 1990).
34. "Political Institutions: The Neglected Side of the Story."
35. Ibid.
36. Jonathan R. Macey, "Organizational Design and Political Control of the Administrative Agencies," ibid. 8, no. 1 (1992).
37. Kathleen Bawn, "Choosing Strategies to Control the Bureaucracy: Statutory Constraints, Oversight, and the Committee System," *Journal of Law, Eocnomics, and Organization* 13, no. 1 (1997).
38. McCubbins, Noll, and Weingast, "Adminsitrative Procedures as Instruments of Political Control."
39. Terry Moe, "The Politics of Bureaucratic Structure," in *Can the Government Govern?* (Washington, DC: The Brookings Institute, 1989).
40. Thomas H. Hammond and Jack H. Knott, "Who Controls the Bureaucracy?: Presidential Power, Congressional Dominance, Legal Constraints, and Bureaucratic Autonomy in a Model of Multi-Institutional Policy-Making Author," *Journal of Law, Economics, and Organization* 12, no. 1 (1996).
41. Tana Johnson, "Institutional Design and Bureaucrats' Impact on Political Control," *Journal of Politics* 75, no. 1 (2013).
42. McCubbins, Noll, and Weingast, "Adminsitrative Procedures as Instruments of Political Control."
43. Randall L. Calvert, Matthew D. McCubbins, and Barry R. Weingast, "A Theory of Political Control and Agency Discretion," *American Journal of Political Science* 33, no. 3 (1989).
44. Ibid.
45. Barry R. Wiengast, "The Congressional-Bureaucratic System: A Principal Agent Perspective (with Applications to the Sec)," *Public Choice* 44, no. 1 (1984).
46. Gary J. Miller, "The Political Evolution of Principal-Agent Models," *Annual Review of Political Science* 8 (2005).
47. Feedback loops are discussed in chapter 2 on complexity.
48. John D. Huber and Charles R. Shipan, "The Costs of Control: Legislators, Agencies, and Transaction Costs," *Legislative Studies Quarterly* (2000).

49. Shepsle and Weingast, "When Do Rules of Procedure Matter?."
50. Peters, *Institutional Theory in Political Science*, 49.
51. Daniel J. Lee, "Taking the Good with the Bad: Cross-Cutting Effects of Ballot-Access Requirements on Third Party Electoral Success," *American Politics Research* 40, no. 2 (2012).
52. QI4, ed. Mary Jo McGowan Shepherd(2014).
53. John Huber, Charles R. Shipan, and Madelaine Pfahler, "Legislatures and Statutory Control of Bureaucracy," *American Journal of Political Science* 45, no. 2 (2001).
54. Ibid.
55. Ibid.
56. Mayhew, *Congress: The Electoral Connection.*
57. Ibid., 43.
58. James M. Buchanan, "Politics without Romance," *Policy* 19, no. 3 (2003).
59. Thomas Stratmann and Francisco J. Aparicio-Castillo, "Competition Policy for Elections: Do Campaign Contribution Limits Matter?," *Public Choice* 127 (2006).
60. Ibid.
61. Richard T. Powell, "The Impact of Term Limits on the Candidacy Decisions of State Legislators in US House Elections," *Legislative Studies Quarterly* 25, no. 4 (2000).
62. Ibid.

Chapter Two

Complexity of Legislation

Studies of legislation generally focus on implementation, outcomes, or inputs to the structure and composition of legislation. Even studies looking at complex legislation focus on the implementation environment or the technical nature of the laws. Complexity as a constraint or deterrent on the outcome of a policy is different. Complex legislation or statutes as a whole entity require looking at the big picture of legislation to determine the legislation's effects on outcomes.

This chapter looks at the different ways scholars have grappled with the concept of complexity. Even though the concept evolved over time and people have a general idea of what it means idiomatically, there does not appear to be consensus on what it actually means in operation. A good definition of complexity gives scholars another factor with which to analyze legislation and the policy process. Throughout the literature, there are a number of factors that scholars relate to complexity. These include complex language as studied by Plain Language scholars; content including technical factors such as scientific and financial terminology; the steps in the decision-making process of legislators creates a more complex piece of legislation and finally the number of required actions for fulfilling legislation goals creates a cost component to complexity.

However, to my knowledge, complexity has not been studied with respect to how it might damage the purported goals for a piece of legislation. Does complexity reduce the effectiveness of laws if those to whom they apply cannot understand them? This chapter reviews past tools to measure complexity and introduces a complexity measure. Measuring campaign finance rules for complexity is important because we want individuals to comply with the laws. Campaign finance rules might affect candidates in two theoretical ways. One is that candidates want to obey the law and therefore their behavior might be constrained, and the second is that candidates might misunderstand the legislation if it is complex.

COMPLEXITY THEORY

Complexity theory as it pertains to the social sciences is under development. As a theory or methodology there are few studies in the social sciences using complexity. Initially studies on complexity theory came from the physical sciences where whole systems are carefully measured and connections evaluated. Social science use of complexity theory is . . . for lack of a better word . . . complex. Where the physical sciences are concrete and grounded in measurable facts, social science research is not permanent and focuses on relationships rather than proven facts. Finding a relationship between a complex policy component and an outcome requires an understanding of what complexity is. Complexity theory is useful to the social sciences by creating a paradigm in which scholars can study an entire system at once. Applications of complexity theory to public policy and public administration are expanding. Scholars are using the flexibility and dynamic nature of complexity theory to evaluate similarly flexible and changing policy process systems.

In this chapter, complexity theory is a backdrop for this study of complexity in campaign finance systems. Using complexity theory serves as a framing device to understand that campaign finance is a multifaceted system. Campaign finance is a much-studied subject however; there are still facets of the system that need attention. The campaign finance regulatory system and its effects on individual decisions to run for office is one such facet. Complexity theory, because of its attempt to look at whole systems is relevant to try to understand this relationship. Furthermore, complexity theory builds the foundation for using a complexity variable to measure the campaign finance regulatory regime.

Complexity theory's slow application to the policy process uses different constructions to describe the relationship between complexity and policy. Complexity policy's use by Klijn and by Geyer and Rihani demonstrate its use in policy contexts. Using strains such as complex adaptive systems, chaos theory, and path dependency, these scholars continue applying complexity theory to policy. Robert Geyer and Samir Rihani detail the use of complexity theory into the public policy realm in their book *Complexity and Public Policy.*[1]

The idea that the complexity of the physical sciences is measurable and systematic translates into public policy by using ideas of whole systems, self-organizing mechanisms, order, reductionism, feedback, and determinism. Using these paradigms creates a policy system in which humans are able to gain enough knowledge to create some order out of our environment, use that order to measure predictability with an end in mind. The idea of order and measurement is challenged throughout the past century (or longer) in a long running debate over the ability to control and measure life. According to complexity theorists, the idea of structured measurement quickly falls apart when faced with factors that are uncontrollable or immeasurable. Campaign finance is one policy using reductionism to measure complex parts of the system for predictability and determinism. Determining if particular parts of the system have negative or positive effects on candidates' ability to raise contributions or on vote totals is important. Measuring the effect of the whole system is also important to understand if candidates are deterred from running. Candidates face an entire system of rules and regulations when deciding to run for office. They do not just face one part but a multifaceted regulatory system which, if disregarded can derail a campaign.

Whole Systems of Complexity

The idea of partial order means that in some policies there can be both orderly and chaotic behaviors. In campaign finance, the system intends to be orderly using rules and regulations to produce predictable processes for all candidates and campaign donors. However, because of the possibility of diverse outcomes between incumbents and challengers, there is a chaotic component of the policy where order may not be controlled. Likewise, not all phenomena in campaign finance are reducible to indices or simple variables. This book uses the whole system of campaign finance to analyze a whole system outcome. Using the plain language structure as detailed in chapters 4 and 5, allows a look at the entire system at once rather than particular elements of the campaign finance system.

Throughout the past century, in the debate of order versus chaos in the policy process, the idea of chaos, or organized chaos, starts to gain precedence. With garbage can models of the policy process, and advocacy coalition networks, policy scholars are trying to explain how public policies are made and the process of policy-making moves toward explaining the stages or parts of the policy process.[2] The policy process and the policies implemented are part of a larger system of institutions, rules, and behavior. Often we are looking only at simple parts of a system instead of the whole. We are beginning to have the capability to look at the whole using more advanced computer analysis and bigger data. This complexity approach also moves social science away from reducing variable relationships to the most reductionist form in order to measure them more efficiently.[3] In light of this movement, I attempt to look at the larger system of campaign finance by looking at the whole statute using plain language metrics. The whole statute includes provisions on campaign contributions as a whole system of regulation. This is still reductionist to a certain extent, but it also tries to encompass a bigger picture of the administrative burden emplaced on candidates. Using complexity theory helps us understand how this method can be valid and effective.

Campaign finance studies tend to look at the different factors affecting different parts of the electoral system. Looking at the whole system allows a look at how an entire institution affects an outcome variable. Haynes uses complexity as a methodology promoting it as "a new approach to the consideration of policy structures and actors/agents that respects the complex interaction between these elements."[4] Understanding the interaction between how campaign finance policies are structured and how that structure affects citizens' decisions to run for public office is an important relationship to understand. It is the complex nature or the whole system of rules and regulations that citizens face. It is not just one rule; it is a multiplicity of rules that create a complex system. Haynes concludes that public policy evaluation needs "a whole systems analysis"[5] which this book uses by looking at the campaign finance statute as a whole. Teisman and Klijn[6] liken this to analyzing an entire film versus analyzing the plot or scenery separately. Looking at a complete picture of the candidates' situation as they decide to run for office allows a more comprehensive look at how complexity affects their decisions.

This context is important to complex systems. The situation, which may be constantly changing, affects the policy process. Agents must adapt to a constantly changing context in order to meet end goals. By looking at how the entire contribution statute affects individual decisions to run for office enables determination of whether the entire campaign finance regime has an effect versus looking at smaller parts of the system. This is important because as rules and regulations accumulate over time, what seemed like a good idea at first may morph into something unintentionally constraining. If that is the case, we need to know if this is happening.

Campaign finance regulations are more than just one factor affecting candidate decisions as discussed in chapter 6. This book looks at the whole statute for candidate campaign contributions and not just one part of the statute. While it is very important to look at discrete factors such as union contributions, or how much a candidate can donate to their own campaign, it is also important to understand the cumulative effect of all the rules and regulations written over time. Indices tally the effect of multiple factors, but even indices are simple numbers used as a proxy for a count of factors affecting decisions. Using the statute as a whole allows study of what candidates actually face when deciding to run for office. This also gives a more robust idea of complexity.

Using complexity theory to study an entire political system is useful to understand the effect of a system or policy on other variables or outcomes. Understanding the collective effect of the campaign finance system on individual's choices to run for office means understanding what candidates face as they decide to run for office. As discussed in the chapter on campaign finance, there are many factors involved in the campaign finance system. As those factors accumulate, they increase the burden on individuals seeking to run for public office. It is important to understand this burden, its measurement, and its effect on citizen decisions.

Adapting complexity theory to public policy is not straightforward, nor are scholars in agreement about how to apply complexity. Teisman and Klijn[7] describe those factors on which scientists do agree, such as complex phenomena, as dynamic in nature. The dynamism of complex systems stems from the idea that complex phenomena are evolving, may, or may not be non-linear, and changeable.

Feedback Loops

Getting feedback from candidates on the potential constraint of the campaign finance system would be useful and is an important component of complexity theory. However, the feedback loop may be nonexistent in campaign finance. Complexity theory stresses the need and importance of feedback loops as important parts of a complex system. Feedback loops allow policy adjustments making processes and policies more effective and efficient. The more complex, the more feedback and interactions you might elicit. Importantly, feedback creates changes in policy decisions coming from end users. Seemingly, potential candidates have little opportunity for giving feedback on their experiences running for office. Candidates who have run unsuccessfully or potential candidates who have thought about running but chose not to, are not subject to many studies regarding their campaigns (or lack of campaigns). Because of this, there is little feedback on how cumbersome it may be on individuals to run for office. We do know that candidates cite family pressure, time issues, and finances as among top reasons why they chose not to run for office. However, we have not yet studied whether the campaign finance regime as a whole has an effect on candidate decisions.

Paul Cairney makes the point that complexity theory is generally a corollary of punctuated equilibrium theory a la Baumgartner and Jones, and so forth. The idea that negative and positive feedback from policy choices makes for longer or shorter policy change windows, respectively, is interesting. The campaign finance feedback loop is beyond the scope of this book, but initially it appears that there is a bottom-up feedback loop that may be nonexistent or ignored. In normal policy loops, given a policy choice, when there is enough negative feedback it will create the necessary threshold to create a policy change. For example, Samsung eventually got enough negative feedback (that was also emotionally charged feedback) from bottom level consumers to create change in their battery policies. On the contrary, in campaign finance, without networks of like-minded potential candidates there is never enough critical mass to create change in campaign finance regulations. Potential candidates or everyday citizens rarely form an interest group, protest, or have complaints heard about the campaign finance system. Even if a candidate had issues with the campaign finance system and vowed to fix it if in office; once he is in office that candidate has a stake in not fixing the system in order to create a barrier to entry for future challengers.

Self-Organizing Mechanisms

A significant feature of complex systems is self-organizing networks or capacities. Organizing individuals into networks of like-interested citizens can be easy if citizens all have the same policy goals or outcome in mind. Aside from the collective goods willingness to pay issue, citizens will unite to push their agenda. The number of interest groups and political parties supports this idea. Political actors also organize into issue networks and advocacy coalitions in a similar manner. According to complexity theorists, this organization might stem from the endogenous or exogenous forces acting on actors. Whether a change comes from within or without an administrative agency, actors might organize to work toward a reform goal or to change a policy procedure. Similarly, citizens often organize when factors from inside or outside their policy issue change. Regardless of whether they are citizens or government workers, most will join other individuals sharing the same goals to change a policy.

The citizens who self-organize may have similar goals, but what if there are disincentives to organize? Candidates lack incentives to self-organize. Regardless of whether the factors are endogenous or exogenous, candidates are unlikely to unite even if they have similar policy goals. One of the potential reasons for the lack of feedback from potential candidates is the lack of self-organizing mechanisms among candidates. Obviously being a political candidate is a very competitive endeavor which precludes the formation of potential candidates grouping together to help one another run for office or grouping together to protest campaign finance rules and regulations. The public policy idea of self-organizing networks of folks responding to government policy changes fails to work in campaigns. In most policy issues, people respond to policy choices by creating their own coping mechanism in the form of self-organizing networks. Citizens reach out to others in similar situations and are able to cope with the government policy or policy change. By coping, they are then able to implement the policy but might implement using adapted rules. You can imagine a budget analyst getting a policy change from superiors, talking it over with coworkers, reaching out to a network of budget analysts and deciding the "right" way to implement this change. In many cases, this would be acceptable or even desirable if we want our bureaucrats to be adaptable to real world situations. The problem is when the government's policies apply to everyday citizens; they do not have a readily available network of people with which they can confer. There is no one with which to confer and decide how they are going to apply the law to themselves. This is likely the case for campaign finance regulations. Because so few individuals actually choose to run for office, everyday citizens do not have an available pool of other individuals with which to create this self-organizing network. Thus, the individuals are stuck with a policy that may or may not work for them. In the case of campaign finance regulations, they are additionally stuck with complying or their reputation and their chance of winning office diminishes. Individuals wanting to run for office would seem ideally motivated people to self-organize networks in order to create outcomes that are more rational. However, because the networks are not naturally occurring this is unlikely.

In addition, the complexity theory focus on street-level bureaucrats allows bureaucrats to adopt "rules of thumb" or routines allowing them to implement government policy successfully. Because of a lack of an organizing network, individuals do not have this luxury. Street-level individuals are unable to establish, let alone adopt "rules of thumb" because of the risks described above. Individuals choosing to run for office do not have routines because running for office is an occasional activity. Candidates comply with regulations to file for office one time in a one- to two-year period. This increases the likelihood of street-level individuals not knowing or understanding complex campaign finance regulations. It also increases the likelihood that more knowledgeable individuals—that is, previous candidates or incumbents—would have an advantage over first-time candidates. Novice candidates might seek professional help to avoid the reputational or electoral risks in running for office.

These factors may also explain why individuals interviewed for this book almost all sought some type of help in running for office. Many candidates sought help through mentors or candidate school type organizations. The individuals who sought this information knew they were at a disadvantage to other individuals and wanted to increase the probability of winning and reduce the risk to their reputation from making campaign finance mistakes.

Thinking about complexity from both the theoretical systems viewpoint and from the content viewpoint, it seems we have statutes that may have different effects for different users. For incumbents who have been through an election cycle their learning curve is extremely short or nonexistent. They have already learned how to run for office and therefore have few learning costs or a reduced administrative burden. Novice candidates are in the opposite position. They will have to learn all the rules—whether formal or informal—and novice candidates will have increased costs compared to incumbents. Furthermore, candidates are unlikely to unite to help one another or to report negative effects of a campaign finance burden given the context in which the candidate is running for office. All of these factors combine to create a difficult regulatory system for potential candidates.

ADMINISTRATIVE BURDEN—POLICY MAKING BY OTHER MEANS? OR, CAMPAIGNING BY OTHER MEANS?

Complex systems theory is one way of looking at the idea of complexity. Adding to the complexity idea is the concept of costs or burdens borne by different actors within the campaign systems. Incumbents have a very different environment and context in which they run for office when compared to potential challengers such as everyday citizens. Incumbents have already learned how to run for office, they have filled out the forms on previous attempts, and they have a likely list of campaign donors. Challengers, especially novice challengers, have none of this. They must start up the process from scratch and learn as they go.

Measuring the burden borne by candidates is a difficult task. The public administration idea of administrative burden is a tool to evaluate the costs of the campaign finance system. The administrative burdens of running for office include learning the rules of how to run, complying with the rules and regulations, and the psychological effects of taking a risk and running for office. The crux of the burden is the rules and regulations that encompass running for office.

The previous chapter discussed the idea of rules. Discussing rules as an institution is different from discussing the effect of rules. Institutionally, rule creation seeks to make institutions more efficient or effective. They are supposed to create norms of behavior, normal operating procedures, or an equal playing field. Problems arise when rules have unintended or collateral consequences. Defining or measuring the point at which rules start to have unintended consequences is difficult and ambiguous. The public administration red tape literature alludes to this when those scholars try to figure out when rules and regulations go from being green tape to red tape.[8]

Specific end goals need specific rule creation and implementation. We have rules for simple ends such as speed limits, or there are rules for more ambitious goals such as financial regulation and the Dodd-Frank law. Regardless of what the original goal of a rule is, sometimes circumstances change the effect of the rules creating unintended or intended consequences. Rules may become burdensome over time, but the burden of rules is the ultimate outcome of the rules' effect. The intervening outputs such as complexity drive how or if a rule becomes burdensome. Burdens are created when rules create additional learning, compliance, or psychological costs to a process or situation. Additional costs though are not enough for rules to be complex. Complexity must also create a situation in which there are differing applications of the rules or differing outcomes from the rules. There is an administrative effect of the rules on the outcomes of an individual's experience. Complexity for this book is the costs—learning, compliance, and psychological costs—of the rules when applied to candidates running for office. It remains to be seen if the outcomes are different. The concepts are borrowed from Moynihan, Herd, and Harvey's[9] work on administrative burden but add in a way to measure the costs using word counts and reading comprehension in the chapter on plain language.

The administrative burden of rules discussed below borrows heavily from the public administration literature. Public administration is at the forefront of studying administrative burden.

Learning Administrative Burdens

The cost of learning the rules is a focus of this book. Candidates who have previously run for office have climbed the learning curve and know the rules and regulations surrounding campaign finance. New or potential candidates do not have this knowledge yet and will have to spend time learning the ropes instead of campaigning. This creates a drag on their campaign where the newer candidates are playing catch up with the incumbents. Learning costs accrue when candidates must gather the information necessary to run for office.[10] Candidates have to gather information on filing forms, candidacy requirements, contribution requirements, treasurer and other official requirements, and the list goes on. Moynihan et al. state that administrative burdens are "Typically opaque and often poorly understood by public or most political actors."[11] This directly applies to candidates running for office. In almost all elections, there is an incumbent who has learned how to run, and there is a less experienced citizen who does not understand all the rules and regulations of running for office. There are many rules passed by the legislature or implemented by the executive branch that are unclear to citizens. Moynihan et al. cite studies in which potential social welfare recipients are unaware of requirements to qualify for benefits and that the lack of understanding may exacerbate other variables such as distance, education, and language.[12]

If potential social welfare recipients miss out on benefits given a lack of understanding of program rules and regulations, running for office might also be missing out on potential candidates. Qualitative interviews done for this book suggest that learning to run was a fairly difficult task. Candidates remarked on the difficulty of determining what and who qualified to sign a candidacy petition, figuring out how to fill out forms correctly in order to avoid potentially risky errors, and navigating the rules of how much money candidates could accept for any one donation. The campaign regulations experiment conducted and analyzed in chapter 5 illustrates the difficulties potential candidates have with learning and comprehending the campaign finance statutes.

Compliance Costs of Administrative Burdens

In addition to the difficulty learning rules and regulations potential candidates must also deal with costs of complying (or failing to comply) with campaign finance regulations. Compliance costs are typically associated with the need to fill out forms and the work or man-hours required fulfilling these requirements. Bozeman[13] calls these compliance costs red tape. Red tape is understood as formal rules and constraints or unnecessary procedures that end up creating delays.[14] Alternatively, an increase in red tape is seen as producing a "corresponding reduction in benefits provided to clients."[15] The concept of compliance costs is implicit in the literature on ballot access regulations—specifically the regulatory cost of complying with the need to collect a certain number of signatures to get on the ballot. Much of the literature on ballot access looks at the effect on third party or independent candidacies. Lee[16] separates the two phases of election cycles by looking separately at the first phase—getting on the ballot; and the second phase—getting enough votes to be elected. While Lee still looks at third party candidacies, he studies the effect of the petition signature requirement in terms of the costs imposed on candidates. As noted in the previous chapter, the petitioning requirement in many states imposes a direct cost on candidates. It is expensive not only to collect the signatures but also to ensure that the signatures are valid and comply with your state's regulations. This is a seemingly significant drawback to novice candidates. Lee separates the costs into direct and opportunity costs. The opportunity costs include the time away from campaigning that a candidate must spend on petitions and complying with the regulatory system of campaign finance.

While much of the red tape literature focuses on the various definitions, the administrative burden literature puts a lot of focus on determining compliance costs. Compliance costs indicate that the rules and regulations are explicit and measurable. However, if as Moynihan quotes from Lineberry, administrative burdens create "policymaking by other means," there may be implicit rules and regulations at work here also. Bozeman alludes to this as the internal and external effects of red tape. Internal effects relate to managerial constraints on internal actors versus external effects on actors in other agencies. Yet, this fails to incorporate the effects on everyday citizens. Citizens are also potential actors in the political system and as demonstrated by the welfare take-up literature (see below), sometimes citizens fail to participate because of complicated rules and regulations.

When legislators pass campaign finance legislation, it may go beyond policy making by other means and potentially stretch to campaigning by other means. This idea is not explicitly tested in this book; it is assumed that legislators have the rationale to create a complex campaign finance regulatory regime (see chapter 1). Indeed Drometer and Rincke test for barriers to entry created by legislators seeking to prevent challengers from entering the race.[17] Drometer and Rincke test that endogenous institutional barriers may be put in place to limit competition from election challengers. They find that when competition increases in races (they primarily look at gubernatorial races in the United States) barriers to entry tighten over time. They measure the costs as the number of signatures required for ballot access petitions. Over time, they conclude that when an extra candidate comes into the race the subsequent increase in signature requirements can increase by more than 7,300 signatures. They conclude that:

> If competition by such candidates increases, the political system dominated by the major parties tends to respond by setting barriers to entry. This finding is consistent with the view that the major parties (or state governments and legislatures dominated by them) use ballot access provisions to protect their current position in a quasi-duopolistic system of political parties.[18]

As described above, compliance costs include the campaign requirements for forms and personnel. In campaigning for office, there is an additional burden of the risk of noncompliance. If an everyday citizen fails to comply with the forms for college financial aid, they risk losing benefits. Additionally, candidates face the risk of losing their reputation if or when an opponent exploits their compliance failure as campaign fraud or malfeasance.

Psychological Costs of Administrative Burdens

Psychological costs include the idea that citizens might not participate in social or political programs because the rules and regulations are so complex they make citizens feel inferior and unworthy of benefits. For example, if the college financial aid form is so cumbersome a less educated citizen might feel the costs outweigh the benefits of finishing the form. Much of the psychological effects are studied with respect to social welfare programs. Moynihan and Herd,[19] and Moynihan et al.[20] study citizens' wait times to meet with administrators, means tested versus universal access regulations, and various other administrative burdens. These burdens generally indicate that as the burdens are increased, the participation rates decrease; whereas if the burdens decrease participation increases. Moynihan and Herd's look at Wisconsin's Medicaid policies and find additionally that political party affects the burden put in place. It is therefore reasonable to speculate that if democrats and republicans use administrative tools to increase or decrease participation in social policies, legislators in general might use the same type of tool to decrease participation or competition in elections.

If everyday citizens can be constrained from applying for or participating in social and political benefits, it makes sense that potential candidates might also be additionally burdened. We know that potential candidates tend to be strategic and risk averse. If we add on the burden of compliance, learning, and psychological effects—why would anyone ever run? Kaufmann and Feeney[21] find that when a stakeholder perceives a rule having a positive outcome, the stakeholder sees less red tape and vice versa. Kaufmann and Feeney use vignettes consisting of two dimensions and demonstrating university course registration. One dimension is procedural length and the second is procedural outcome. Length has two possible perceptions—long and short, while outcome is positive and negative. The study outcomes indicate that when facing a realistic situation such as course registration, individuals facing more difficult burdens psychologically perceive a negative outcome prior to even attempting the task.

In elections, candidates—because they are strategic—may view the outcome realistically. This is unknown without empirical testing, but it is possible to hypothesize that candidates who are more risk averse might view the rules and regulations of the campaign as more burdensome because they are facing an unknown outcome. Incumbents' outcome is more assured and they can therefore face the regulatory system with more confidence. Candidates that wait for the right opportunity would view the burden as lower, but that leaves the rest of the elections without a challenger.

Burden Outcomes

The crux of the burden literature is the effect of the burden on policy outcomes. Most of the literature thus far focuses on participation rates in social and political policies. Moynihan et al. find:

> There is little doubt that, within the area of social policy at least, administrative burdens have material impacts on whether individuals receive public services. Policy feedback research further suggests that the experience of burdensome processes undermines political efficacy and civic participation. There is therefore a strong theoretical and empirical basis to understand how the experience of policy implementation matters to citizens in these and other ways, and in a wider variety of policy areas than has been studied thus far.[22]

For example, the take-up rates of welfare policies[23] find that with increasing amounts of burden or costs, take-up rates for social policies decrease. Many of the burden changes are political in nature[24] with differing political parties changing the structure of the burden. Newer studies focus on the political effects of burden. Jacobs and Matthews[25] find that when citizens lack confidence in leaders' ability to deliver goods the citizen's support for policies declines. While not directly testing the same concept this lends support to the idea of psychological effects of burdens.[26] If citizens lack confidence in legislators' ability to govern, the citizens will doubt whether the policy will be delivered. If elites are able to deliver on goods, everyday citizens might think that running for office is only for elites because elites can easily overcome the burdens. Moynihan and Herd[27] study the outcomes for democracy more directly. They look at both social policies and voting or political policies to measure the burden on citizens. Moynihan and Herd state, "Policies are the primary means by which citizens experience the state. They empower some groups, and discourage others."[28] The effect here is that when burdens are put in place on citizens' choices, those burdens inherently differentiate between respondents. This book assumes that differentiation is—if not intentional[29] —accidental insofar as legislators have a rational motivation to create a burden for future challengers. Whether or not this disadvantages one group over another is a future research agenda. The current ballot access literature would suggest that challengers are burdened by different administrative costs than incumbents leading to fewer challengers.[30] Currently we need to understand if there is a constraint on participation. The research on burdens indicates that there is. Burdens affect citizens' ability to participate in their government effectively. This lack of participation affects our democracy in ways different from social welfare policies. If citizens bear too high a burden to run for office, our democratic processes are diminished by not having the best individuals represent us in government.

COMPLEXITY AND CONTENT

So far, this chapter looks at how complexity is structured using complexity theory and administrative burden. Both of these paradigms give us a more robust understanding of how a system can be complex. Complexity is neither a well-defined nor well-examined area in terms of legislation reaching legislative goals. There have been some studies of complexity in legislation, but many of those studies pertain to how legislators use complexity to control bureaucrats, who implement legislation; or judges who interpret it; and not upon "regular" citizens who might be affected by the legislation. So how can we know if legislation is complex or if it creates a burden for individuals? One way is to look at the content and language of the rules and regulations.

Complexity theory is most often applied to systems, especially computer systems or in organizational literature. It has applications to political science and has been used in public administration literature. Teisman and Klijn[31] liken complexity theory to the difference between looking at static photos and a moving film. The photos only show one view of a situation, where the film can illustrate a bigger—more complex- situation. Because complexity theory can show the bigger picture, we can study how factors change either over time or in different contexts. For example, we can study how campaign finance regulations are more or less complex in different states by comparing their language or component parts.

The content of legislation is an obvious factor in affecting whether or not legislation is complex. What is not so obvious is how to define what is or is not complex content. Based on the literature this is difficult to do because the concept is a subjective measure. What is complex to one person may not be to another. Some scholars have tried to put some meaning behind the idea of complex content. Krepel[32] does a convincing job of this. Krepel examines education policies to understand the factors affecting whether or not a policy is complex. Krepel wants to determine "how content characteristics and environmental conditions affect policy maker perceptions of complexity" and "what characteristics of policy proposals are perceived as being more or less complex."[33] The study done by Krepel used a national survey. The survey used three vignettes presented to the legislators and then asked them a series of questions on the vignettes. Each vignette contained a description of state legislation on education policy. The state legislators were asked to analyze the education policy to see if the legislators judged it complex or not. The first vignette contained policy that had simple content and inactive environment. The second vignette had two forms: A—complex content and inactive environment, and B—simple content and active environment. The third vignette had both complex content and active environment.

In this study, Krepel uses definitions of complexity culled together from previous studies. The definitions fall into the three categories, content, environment, and content and environment together. Content of legislation that is deemed complex contains "multiple subtopics, the use of technical, specialized concepts or language, and novelty."[34] The other category, environment (or environmental conditions) is defined as legislation containing conflict, cost certainty, ambiguity and availability of information."[35] The third category combines content and environment. The study found that when analyzed alone, there was no difference between the effects of content or environment complexity characteristics on the policy proposals. Krepel concludes that when legislators deem a policy proposal complex, it is a function of both content and environment together (his third category) and not just one variable alone. The second finding of the study was that the perceived complexity of the policy proposals increased as both the content and environment characteristics increased in the vignettes. Krepel concludes that the more content and environment characteristics, the more complex the policy will be.

Hamm[36] treats content differently and considers a description of what complex content looks like. Hamm considers complex legislation to be longer than most legislation. Hamm analyzes various pieces of legislation and finds complex legislation requires extensive information, and professional staff to help the legislative committee members get the information that they require. This extensive information creates bills that are longer. Hamm measures this by counting the number of lines in a bill. Hamm also measures the legislation's scope of impact. Hamm defines scope as "the number of people who would seem to be affected directly by a piece of legislation."[37] If a greater number of people are affected by the legislation then its scope is increased and it may be more complex. A piece of legislation that only affects a small group of people or a small local area would be less complex than a piece of legislation that covers every American or has a large economic impact. While the number of lines concept is intriguing, it seems outdated given our ability to change font sizes, spacing between lines, and so forth. It also fails to control for amendments, earmarks, and other extraneous parts of a piece of legislation that, because they are not germane, fail to increase or decrease the complexity of policy legislation.

Technical considerations included in the content of legislation are part of how Gormley[38] rates various pieces of legislation as either complex or salient. For Gormley, a technically complex issue is one that raises factual questions that cannot be answered by generalists or laypersons. The question or problem would need to be answered by an expert. Only an expert with in-depth knowledge of the regulations would be able to administer and implement them. Rinquist, Worsham, and Eisner[39] agree with Gormley that complexity includes technical complexity while also including procedural complexity. Technical complexity is the degree to which specialized technical knowledge is necessary to craft effective policy solutions or understand the policy area. The technical experts would need to be able to understand the technical considerations of the law, but it is not clear if others (citizens) would understand them. In order to analyze who is able to understand and possibly administer regulations we need a more precise definition of technical considerations. Procedural complexity is covered below in decision making. Both studies technical considerations are important but are still subjective and related to the knowledge of the writer of the legislation and not to the user. These studies assume complexity important as a constraining tool or as a way to measure control of one governmental branch over the other. It is just as important to determine whether complexity affects every day citizens as it does other governmental actors.

Continuing with technical issues in legislation, Sabatier and Whiteman see policy information as having technical factors. Technical factors are the contents of the proposed policy and how the policy may affect society. These authors looked through legislation to determine which pieces of legislation had technical components and which did not. They defined a bill that has technical considerations as one that deals with scientific or engineering information and might have socioeconomic impacts beyond the local area.[40] Relatedly, a scientific factor "relates the results of an empirical investigation of specifically defined variables."[41] Mooney investigated the written notes and correspondence of legislators to see what information they were gathering on a piece of legislation. If they used empirical evidence, it was considered hard science. The impacts of the policy are similar to Hamm's discussion of policy scope. Complexity is not only the technical considerations but also the scope of the policy. If the policy touches or affects a large part of the country or a large proportion of state residents then that policy may be more complex in order to encompass the diversity of needs of that population. If a policy only affects a small and homogenous segment of the population, it is considered a simpler policy. It is possible that campaign finance reform would fall into the less complex policy because it would only affect a small segment of the population that is considering running for office. However, there is the possibility that the population would be larger if the policy were less complex. In other words, if the policy were easier to understand and comply with, then more folks might run for office, thus increasing the population covered by the legislation. The effects of legislation are not always direct. The scope of campaign finance legislation might affect directly only the handful of individuals who actually run for office, but the electoral outcomes affect the entire population. Scope varies depending on how it is defined.

Complexity involves more than just complex or technical information. It also involves *how* that information is used in making policy. The use of policy information or knowledge revolves around how decisions are made by legislators. They choose which information to use and when. In doing so, they are able to make policy affecting citizens' lives that may cover a continuum from simple to complex policy. Making these decisions involves gathering the information, and going through the policy process to make a decision. Covered below are the areas of how legislators get the information needed, how legislators make decisions, and how those decisions affect citizens.

Policy complexity sometimes refers to the steps in the policy process. Each step along the policy process provides legislators and bureaucrats the opportunity to add complexity by including additional components, restrictions, and regulations to a policy proposal. Politicians considering a complex issue often look to bureaucrats for expertise and bureaucrats may dominate the implementation of the policy.[42] Issue networks work together to help craft policy choices, but while this is happening additional complexity may be baked into the policy. It is understandable that politicians cannot be experts on everything and therefore seek help from those who are experts. Politicians pay an information cost to bureaucrats for help constructing legislation. Politicians pay for the expert help by giving up some coercion over the bureaucrats. Theoretically, if politicians need help understanding these policy choices how much more difficult is it for an average citizen trying to adhere to the laws? Average citizens have a tacit understanding of some laws but campaign finance is much more specific by targeting a subset of the population. That subset is also only subject to the laws when they run. An everyday person would have three options to comply with the regulations. One would be to spend a large amount of time and incur a large cost in order to gain a basic understanding of the complexities of a regulation. Most everyday people would not have this time and would therefore resort to their second option—turn to an expert in order to avoid some of the burden and to ensure compliance with the regulation. The third option is to give up. One candidate who was interviewed said that as a lawyer he felt he had a "leg up" on his competition. He said he "didn't know the . . . code off the top of his head but if he needed to look something up it wouldn't be hard. If you were an average person you would need help."[43] Hiring a professional is a cost incurred, so either with or without an expert, this regulation has burdened the everyday person in some way. In the same way, Congress is burdened with finding information from bureaucrats especially on complex issues. The literature is clear that when Congress must seek informational help from bureaucrats, and Congress deems the bureaucrats as the experts this is when they try to put constraints on the bureaucrats.[44] The important point here is that there is an information cost involved in creating this legislation. One party has all the information and the other party does not and must seek it out, at a cost to themselves. Legislators have an election incentive to pass the information costs to the citizen requiring citizens pay the cost of understanding the legislation. The steps in the policy process and the information gathered along the way has the potential to create complexity or additional costs to citizens.

Once legislators gather information they use it to make policy decisions. Kingdon focuses on the actual decision steps that legislators take. He is not focusing on the result of their decisions but on how they make the decisions on legislation. This is the procedural complexity discussed by Ringquist, Worsham, and Eisner.[45] This is important because when legislators are going through the process of making decisions; it can become more complicated according to Kingdon. Legislators make a series of decision-rules, and at each rule is the potential for legislation to be created. If a legislator applies a decision rule and says "yes," this is the final product for this legislation and this is a relatively simple decision according to Kingdon. When the decision rule is applied and the legislator says "no"; they are in essence saying that they need more information because this legislation is complex. Therefore, the number of decision steps that a legislator makes is part of what makes the legislation more complex. Intuitively one can think of the types of legislation to which this may apply, from earmarks to comprehensive reform bills. Earmarks, in this context, are not complex. They barely have attention paid to them; they involve few decision steps (because they are not voted on individually) and rarely are controversial or debatable. If one considers comprehensive pieces of legislation such the McCain-Feingold act, one can intuitively understand the complexity involved by asking how many steps did this take.

Kingdon is correct that the decision process reflects the complexity of the bill itself.

Kingdon continues a discussion of policy dimensions. In this discussion, congressmen come to the decision process with attitudinal mechanisms and political actors, such as their party and constituency that direct their decision making. If the legislator follows their party, the relevance of the legislation is usually focused on government management decisions, if considering their constituency the relevance is usually on legislation regarding civil liberties. The question here is what happens when a legislator looks to the party on a management decision such as campaign finance, but ends up unintentionally affecting his constituents' civil rights—such as the ability to participate in the political process? The procedural justice literature touches on this idea also. The study contends that when citizens are not involved in making procedural regulations that those regulations lack legitimacy.[46] If citizens are deterred from participation in the legislative system, it also affects the legitimacy of the law. Even if a law, such as campaign finance, aims to protect the electoral system, how can it work properly if citizens are prevented or deterred from participating in the system if it is too complex with which to comply?

Legislative Constraints

Earlier in this chapter, an assumption is made that incumbents might have a willingness to create a complicated institution. This section details if legislators can do this by using language to create constraints on actors.

Institutional design studies how an institution's design and organization affects policy outcomes. Much of this literature focuses on how institutions affect bureaucrats and policy implementers. Kathleen Bawn[47] focuses on how statutes written by legislators constrain bureaucrats. Using the typology created by McCubbins, Noll, and Weingast and by Moe, she lays out the procedures to constrain bureaucrats. These include requiring at least two agencies to collaborate on decision making. The idea here is that when more than one agency gets involved in making a regulation on some activity, the agencies will constrain the discretion of the agency or the regulated activity. Legislators can require an agency to perform to a specific research agenda in order to constrain behavior. Legislators can specify what types of information can and cannot be used in the making of regulations in order to ensure that the regulator's behavior is constrained. Legislators can simply limit the scope of regulatory authority for an agency and finally legislators can put a due date on regulations so that if the agency fails to meet the date, the legislators revisit the regulation later. All of these constraining behaviors by legislators are meant to increase control over the bureaucracy by the legislators. Using a variety of tools legislators are able to impose constraints on actors. The addition of these constraints adds words and linguistic complexity into the statute. The greater the number of constraining factors must use more language to articulate that constraint. Therefore, it is logical to use language as a measure of constraint or complexity.

Using language to measure constraint is found in political science and policy literature. Scholars have studied how legislatures use decisions to constrain actors, in particular, the bureaucracy. These studies have used word count as a constraining factor in legislation. This is relevant to a study of complexity because if legislation can be constraining to bureaucrats, it may also be a constraint on "regular" citizens. For example, Huber, Shipan, and Pfahler[48] analyze states' Medicaid laws to see if legislatures were able to put statutory constraints on the bureaucracy. The authors posit that legislatures would do this when legislatures do not trust the bureaucracy. Huber et al. use the word count feature in the Microsoft Word program. The researcher simply enters the text into MS word and then specifies "word count." Huber et al. argue that word count is a way to measure statutory constraint because the more words in a bill, the more detailed and thus constraining it is. Huber et al. collected all the words related to Medicaid across all fifty states in an effort to establish that word count is a valid measure of constraint. They find:

> Longer bills increase constraints on the agency. When designing a new children's health initiative to be part of the Medicaid program, for example, it takes a great many more words for the legislature to specify who is to be covered, what sorts of enrollment techniques should be used, which procedures should be followed, and so on, than it does to simply ask the agency to "do something" without providing any additional instructions. Long bills with lots of words tend to specify these details, while short bills do not. More words imply more precise instructions to the agency, and thus less discretion.[49]

Even though there are other factors involved in this analysis, the result is that the quantity of words may constrain bureaucrats. If bureaucrats can be constrained by legislation, then regular citizens could also be constrained by legislation. Citizens may be even more constrained because they had no input into the creation of the legislation nor may they have any prior knowledge of the legislation. To study the creation of administrative burdens, Moynihan, Herd, Ribgy[50] look at Medicaid burdens by studying the content of Medicaid applications in all fifty states and developing a coding instrument that includes a word count. They also used each state's interview requirements and reapplication policies for Medicaid.

While Huber et al. analyze bureaucrats; Randazzo, Waterman, and Fine[51] and Randazzo[52] examine judicial constraints. They theorize that Congress writes legislation that is either vague or detailed. If it is detailed then it would constrain the behavior of judges and they would have no leeway to interpret the law. However, if the law is vague, this allows for little restraint on the judges and they can interpret the law as they want. Randazzo et al. utilize word count but see word count as inadequate to measure constraint because of the "noise associated with a raw count and the considerable skewness of the measure."[53] They therefore take the natural log of the word count for each statute to operationalize statutory constraint. They find that there is evidence of judicial constraint found in the legislation that Congress passes.

Word count is an interesting way to measure complexity and it is referenced in the earlier literature as well because the length of the legislation can signify technical difficulties of the legislation that need to be explained and new solutions that have to be spelled out. It may also signify conflict if the different viewpoints debating the legislation have put incentives for their members in the bill. A possible problem with word count solutions is that it may not capture the essence of what makes a law or regulation complex. Just counting words (or logs of the number of words) misses the syntax and nuances in written language. By missing these, it is logical to assume word counts also miss complexity. Nonetheless, word count is important to consider because of its past use in the policy literature and its simplicity. It is included as a measure of this book's complexity introduced in chapter 5.

There are other key language measures of complexity besides word count. Most analyses of language or constraints consider institutions in terms of how political actors are affected, but Kimball and Kropf[54] examine voters. Kimball and Kropf's research on ballot design from the 2002 presidential election brings to light another potential method for analyzing complexity. Although ballot design is very different from legislation it is the language function the authors use here that is helpful. The authors look at ballot design to figure out why there are under-recorded votes on the ballots. The authors analyzed the graphical elements of the ballot design including location of the instructions, readability of the instructions, and layout of the candidates on the ballot, how the candidate's names appear on the ballot, and so forth. The authors create an overall index of ballot features that counts the number of simplifying or complicating features on each ballot. "Readability describes the ease of processing the information content of written words."[55] The grade level feature is a categorical variable so the authors coded it into low (4th–8th grade), medium (9th–11th) grade and high (12th grade and above). This allows the variable to be added to the index. The higher the score the more difficult it is to read the document.

This measure is relevant for campaign finance regulations because if they could be analyzed based on their readability it could be determined if they were difficult to read. If found to be difficult, it might be another factor that contributes to the complexity of campaign finance legislation. Kimball and Kropf operationalized voting instructions using the Flesch-Kincaid measure and grade levels. Using these same measures of grade level and readability could capture how complex the legislation is regarding everything from filing forms to contribution limits in campaign finance reform. It may also be able to capture the technical aspects of the law. For example, if the reading level of the regulation/law was on a graduate school level, it could mean that the regulation/law is extremely complex. If the reading level of a regulation is on the eighth grade level, it could signify a less complex law.

Complexity and Campaign Finance Reform

Complexity is difficult to define. Including such different aspects as costs of compliance, language, policy process, and constraints makes it difficult to include all factors in a study of complexity. In some cases, legislation might make the process of complying with a law more complex (i.e., doing one's taxes) versus understanding a law (i.e., Dodd-Frank). The focus for this book is on the language and understanding of the law. The process is different in each state making the language a natural tool with which to measure complexity across the states. Using plain language creates a more robust measure of complexity than word counts alone and plain language allows capture of the learning and compliance costs inherent in regulations. A candidate must learn and understand the regulations in order to comply. This process takes time that candidates must take away from the campaign trail. The time spent learning and complying is different for novice versus incumbent candidates.

The literature is clear that the content of legislation is an important determinant of whether a piece of legislation is complex. Underlying the language are the factors of that content that can really determine if legislation is complex. These factors include scientific, engineering, or financial factors, the scope of the policy including the socioeconomic impacts, the geographic impacts (whether it is national or local) and whether the legislation needs interpretation and/or help from an expert before implementation. There are so many factors that legislation is—for lack of a better term—complex to measure.

Using these content factors would be helpful, but it would be nearly impossible to include all of them into a measure of legislation. In order to simplify and standardize the measurement, I use the legislative language in this book. Language or word count alone is insufficient to capture complexity given that raw word counts may fail to capture the essence of complexity in a rule or regulation. After reviewing campaign finance legislation in chapter 3, chapter 4 reviews the efforts of the plain language movement to measure different linguistic components of language.

NOTES

1. Robert Geyer and Samir Rihani, *Complexity and Public Policy* (New York: Routledge, 2010).

2. Paul A. Sabatier and Christopher M. Weible, *Theories of the Policy Process*, ed. Paul A. Sabatier and Christopher M. Weible (Boulder, CO: Avalon Publishing, 2014).

3. David Colander and Roland Kupers, *Complexity and the Art of Public Policy: Solving Society's Problems from the Bottom Up* (Prineton, NJ: Princeton University Press, 2014).

4. Philip Haynes, "Complexity Theory and Evaluation in Public Management," *Public Management Review* 10, no. 3 (2008): 402.

5. Ibid., 417.

6. Geert R. Teisman and Eric-Hans Klijn, "Complexity Theory and Public Management," ibid.

7. Ibid.

8. Barry Bozeman, "A Theory of Government "Red Tape," *Journal of Public Administration Research and Theory: J-PART* 3, no. 3 (1993).

9. Donald Moynihan, Pamela Herd, and Hope Harvey, "Adminsitrative Burden: Learning, Psychological, and Compilance Costs in Citizen-State Interactions," *Journal of Public Adminsitration Research and Theory* 25 (2014).

10. Ibid.

11. Ibid., 43.

12. Ibid.; James J. Heckman and Jeffrey A. Smith, "The Determinants of Participation in a Social Program: Evidence from a Prototypical Job Training Program," *Journal of Labor Economics* 22, no. 2 (2004).

13. Bozeman, "A Theory of Government 'Red Tape.'"

14. Ibid.

15. Patrick G. Scott and Sanjay K. Pandey, "The Influence of Red Tape on Bureaucratic Behavior: An Experimental Simulation," *Journal of Policy Analysis and Management* 19, no. 4 (2000): 615.

16. Daniel J. Lee, "Taking the Good with the Bad: Cross-Cutting Effects of Ballot-Access Requirements on Third Party Electoral Success," *American Politics Research* 40, no. 2 (2012).

17. Marcus Drometer and Johannes Rincke, "Electoral Competition and Endogenous Barriers to Entry," *European Journal of Political Economy* 34 (2013).

18. Ibid., 261.

19. Donald Moynihan and Pamela Herd, "Red Tape and Democracy: How Rules Affect Citizens Rights," *The American Review of Public Administration* 40, no. 6 (2010).

20. Moynihan, Herd, and Harvey, "Adminsitrative Burden: Learning, Psychological, and Compilance Costs in Citizen-State Interactions."

21. Wesley Kaufmann and Mary K. Feeney, "Effect of Outcome Favourability on Red Tape Perceptions," *Public Administration* 92, no. 1 (2014).

22. Moynihan, Herd, and Harvey, "Adminsitrative Burden: Learning, Psychological, and Compilance Costs in Citizen-State Interactions," 63.

23. Barbara Wolfe and Scott Scrivner, "The Devil May Be in the Details: How the Characteristics of Schip Programs Affect Take-Up," *Journal of Policy Analysis and Management* 24, no. 3 (2005). Wojciech Kopczuk and Cristian Pop-Eleches, "Electronic Filing, Tax Preparers and Participation in the Earned Income Tax Credit," Journal of Public Economics 91 (2007).

24. Moynihan, Herd, and Harvey, "Adminsitrative Burden: Learning, Psychological, and Compilance Costs in Citizen-State Interactions."

25. "Policy Attitudes in Institutional Context: Rules, Uncertainty, and the Mass Politics of Public Investment," *American Journal of Political Science* 61, no. 1 (2017).

26. Kory Kroft, "Takeup, Social Multipliers and Optimal Social Insurance," *Journal of Public Economics* 92 (2008).

27. Moynihan and Herd, "Red Tape and Democracy: How Rules Affect Citizens Rights."

28. Ibid., 654.

29. See Drometer and Rincke, "Electoral Competition and Endogenous Barriers to Entry." for an empirical study on the intentional use of barriers to entry for candidates (also discussed in chapter 1).

30. Much of the ballot access literature pertains to third party or independent candidates. Here I argue that regardless of party, different candidates face different barriers when deciding whether to run for office.

31. Teisman and Klijn, "Complexity Theory and Public Management."
32. Thomas Krepel, "The Characteristics of Complex Policy Proposals," *Planning & Changing* (1986).
33. Ibid., 48.
34. Ibid.
35. Ibid.
36. Keith E. Hamm, "U.S. State Legislative Committee Decisions: Similar Results in Different Settings," *Legislative Studies Quarterly* 5, no. 1 (1980).
37. Ibid., 38.
38. William T Gormley Jr, "Regulatory Issue Networks in a Federal System," *Polity* 18, no. 4 (1986).
39. Evan J. Ringquist, Jeff Worsham, and Marc Allen Eisner, "Salience, Complexity, and the Legislative Direction of Regulatory Bureaucracies," *Journal of Public Administration Research and Theory* 13, no. 2 (2003).
40. Paul Sabatier and David Whiteman, "Legislative Decision Making and Substantive Policy Information: Models of Information Flow," *Legislative Studies Quarterly* (1985): 417 FN9.
41. Christopher Z Mooney, "Putting It on Paper: The Content of Written Information Used in State Lawmaking," *American Politics Quarterly* 20, no. 3 (1992).
42. Matthew Eshbaugh-Soha, "The Conditioning Effects of Policy Salience and Complexity on American Political Institutions," *The Policy Studies Journal* 34, no. 2 (2006).
43. QI4, ed. Mary Jo McGowan Shepherd (2014).
44. Bruce Bimber, "Information as a Factor in Congressional Politics," *Legislative Studies Quarterly* (1991).
45. Ringquist, Worsham, and Eisner, "Salience, Complexity, and the Legislative Direction of Regulatory Bureaucracies."
46. David L Markell, "Understanding Citizen Perspectives on Government Decision Making Processes as a Way to Improve the Administrative State," *Environmental Law* (2006).
47. Kathleen Bawn, "Choosing Strategies to Control the Bureaucracy: Statutory Constraints, Oversight, and the Committee System," *Journal of Law, Economics, & Organization* 13, no. 1 (1997).
48. John Huber, Charles R Shipan, and Madelaine Pfahler, "Legislatures and Statutory Control of Bureaucracy," *American Journal of Political Science* 45, no. 2 (2001).
49. Ibid., 336–37.
50. Donald P. Moynihan, Pamela Herd, and Elizabeth Ribgy, "Policymaking by Other Means: Do States Use Adminsitrative Barriers to Limit Access to Medicaid?," *Administration & Society* 48, no. 4 (2016).
51. Krik A. Randazzo, Richard W. Waterman, and Jeffrey A. Fine, "Checking the Federal Courts: The Impact of Congressional Statutes on Judicial Behavior," *The Journal of Politics* 68, no. 4 (2006).
52. Kirk A. Randazzo, "Statutory Constraint on the Seventh Circuit: Examining Congressional Influence," *Southern Illinois University Law Journal* 32 (2008).
53. Randazzo, Waterman, and Fine, "Checking the Federal Courts: The Impact of Congressional Statutes on Judicial Behavior," 1101.
54. David C. Kimball et al., "The Policy Views of Partisan Election Officials," *UC Irvine Law Review* 551 (2013).
55. Ibid., 513.

Chapter Three

Campaign Finance Reform

Campaign finance reform in the American states has been either a steady progression of independent legislation or a representation of legislation passed by the federal government. Some of the same themes are covered in both the states' and the federal government's efforts to reform the campaign system. This chapter reviews the campaign finance reform legislation in an effort to set the stage for the way in which this same legislation is studied in the next chapters. State campaign finance laws are studied in this book as a way to maximize scholarly leverage. Many studies of campaign finance reforms contribute to our understanding of how campaign finance reform efforts affect institutions or individuals. Here campaign finance is studied as a holistic complex institution. This chapter reviews campaign finance studies and the tools of campaign finance reform. The chapter also investigates how campaign finance is an institution that is an amalgamation of rules and regulations. Using the variation of campaign finance regulations by state creates a complexity variable measuring the rules and regulations of the system as a whole.

A System of Reforms

A look at state campaign finance reform must start with a look at the federal reforms because it is from the federal government that the states take many ideas and models of reform.[1] From the Tillman Act of 1907 to the Bi-Partisan Campaign Finance Reform Act (BCRA) or McCain-Feingold bill of 2002, most campaign finance has come through the federal government. The first laws were passed by Congress in the 1880s in an effort to reform corrupt civil service practices such as soliciting campaign contributions in public buildings, or disallowing political assessments[2] as a requirement for employment. The Civil Service Reform Act of 1883 passed and states quickly followed suit, with New York, Massachusetts, and Pennsylvania passing their own versions. While most of these acts dealt with civil service reform, the Tillman Act of 1907 prohibited corporations from contributing funds to candidates for federal office. Again, the states followed with thirty-two also outlawing this practice by 1932.

David Schultz explains, "the role of money in politics at the state level is increasingly coming to resemble . . . federal campaigns and elections."[3] The question is how did states get to this point? The literature on federal campaign finance reforms generally sets the reform movement into two phases. The first is the post-Watergate era and second is the 1980s when the reform movement changed to encompass equalization efforts. These same eras are found in the literature on state campaign finance reform efforts.[4] The states focused on regulating or restricting "big donors" in the past but by the 1990's focused on equalizing political power. By the time that the Bipartisan Campaign Finance Reform Act was passed in 2002 most states had similar types of policies that reflected the federal reform movement toward restricting or regulating special interests. Three other types of reform were also articulated: one—to reduce the costs of elections, two—reduce the importance of any single donor by keeping contribution limits low and three—force candidates to find contributions from a larger base number of donors.

The early campaign finance reform efforts in the post-Watergate era focused mainly on the candidate. The goals of reform were to ensure that the atypical or unusual donation was avoided. This effort disallowed single, large donations from one contributor to one candidate in order to avoid the possibility of corruption.[5] To do this, the early reforms focused on listing all contributors over a certain amount to ensure that candidates could resist pressure to take large donations as these would be made public. The reforms also disallowed anonymous contributions. The candidates had to report all contributions and expenditures before and after both election cycles (primary and general election). The focus in this early era was just on the candidate's activities. The reformers wanted to highlight where the donations were coming from and to whom they were going. These are the early efforts at disclosure requirements. There was no emphasis on interest groups, political parties or the like.[6]

With increases in campaign spending and an increase in the number and variety of actors in campaigns, the reform effort shifted in the 1980s. Interest groups, lobbyists and Political Action Committees (PACs) were increasingly involved in campaign activities. Instead of focusing on the unusual campaign contribution to an individual candidate, the reform focus shifted to regulating the normal, typical campaign behavior of all candidates.[7] The reforms increased the reporting requirements of candidates' campaigns and put in place more stringent contribution limits. These limits were also expanded to include interest groups, political parties, and corporations. New restrictions encompassed new behaviors such as loans to candidates, transfers between campaigns, payoff of campaign debts, and disclosure requirements for interest groups.[8] These new restrictions generally fell into three general goals. The first goal is to reduce the cost of elections. This is generally done by putting in place spending and contribution limits. The second goal is to reduce the importance of a single contributor. This is similar to the post-Watergate reforms but here we have the reduction in contribution limits to make sure that "fat cat" donors are limited. The third goal is broaden the base on contributors so that any potential influence is dispersed.[9]

The 1980s reform was followed by numerous attempts to change and progress the reform on both the federal and state level. Most of these attempts were unsuccessful although there were some small changes in various states. Scott Harshberger and Edwin Davis[10] recount the numerous attempts at introducing and passing campaign finance legislation throughout the 1980s and 1990s. What are interesting in these attempts are the incremental changes and additions to legislation over this time period. There were initial pieces of legislation that included bans or limits on PAC money, then an aggregate limit on PAC contributions. There were pieces of legislation introduced and passed by Congress with the knowledge that President Bush would veto the legislation. Ultimately, there was no major piece of legislation passed to change or overhaul the campaign finance system. Thus, the status quo remains virtually unchanged until the passage of the Bipartisan Campaign Reform Act of 2002.[11]

How the campaign finance regulations vary through the states is important to the understanding of how those reforms affect the elections within those states. This understanding may lead us to find where policy reforms are having a positive or negative effect and point to appropriate policy solutions. Today, however, little consensus regarding the effects of campaign finance reform is found among scholars.

So why should we look at the states instead of just looking at the federal government? Thompson and Moncrief[12] offer some insight into why the states should be studied. First, they point out that more and more policy is devolving to the states making them more important decision makers in the policy arena. State legislatures are making important policy decisions therefore, we should know more about how they are being elected. Second, states' policies matter to their citizens and since the elections often are held every two years, therefore we should know more about the role campaign finance plays in their election. Third, since the states copy much of the campaign finance regulations and policies from the federal government we should look to see if what has been learned at the federal level applies to the states. Because of these reasons the states are important actors when it comes to policy and elections therefore we need to know what is affecting the state elections. It also is the state's responsibility for creating the rules and regulations governing the majority of elections, since federal law regulates federal candidates, such as those for president and Congress. State laws still govern all state and local elections and there are more of these elections than elections within states for federal candidates. According to Thompson and Moncrief, there are thousands of state elections per year. Therefore, the state election laws generally regulate more elections than federal election laws. Because of the sheer number of elections, the general move to implement more policy in states and their traditional governance of the state electoral systems it is important to understand the factors affecting campaign finance reform in the states.

Campaign finance reform theoretically consists of two major goals: the reduction of corruption or the appearance thereof in the political system and creating a system in which more citizens are able to participate. This second goal is known throughout the literature as democratization. Democratization entails more participation from citizens in the form of more people able to run for office and more people contributing to campaigns. The reform efforts have used various tools to reach these two goals. These tools include contribution limits, spending limits, public finance of elections and disclosure requirements. These tools have been examined for their effect on the goals of campaign finance reform. This examination is detailed below. The reader will note that while valuable strides have been made in this scholarship, no scholars have examined the unintended consequences of the statutes purportedly created to increase democracy.

Reform Tools

One of the reform tools used to meet the goals of campaign finance reform is campaign contribution limits. The rationale is that if contribution size were limited, politicians would need to seek out a larger volume of smaller contributions in order to make up the monetary difference for their campaign coffers. By seeking out more contributions, they would contact more potential contributors and thus more people would be contributing to campaigns. The idea is that more people contributing spreads out the democratic effect of the reform. In addition, contribution limits are intended to reduce overall spending by candidates by making fund-raising more difficult.[13]

The public's perception is that there is too much money in campaigns.[14] Thompson and Moncrief's[15] analysis of contribution limits shows that the reasons for this perception vary from just the vast amount of money being collected, to the idea among the public that this money must be in return for some type of *quid pro quo* situation. If political action committees (PACs) are giving a lot of the money then the public assumes that the PACs must be receiving something in return. Thus, there is a perception of corruption even if the public cannot pinpoint it. Thompson and Moncrief argue that much of this perception filters down from the national stage and national corruption scandals until there is the assumption of corruption at the state and local level. Contribution limits are enacted as an attempt to try to reduce the amount of money in campaigns with the thought that if there are fewer contributions, there will be less corruption or the appearance thereof. The other potential advantage of campaign finance is to reduce the appearance of impropriety on the part of politicians accepting "big" donations from a small group of donors. If they can no longer contribute the "big" donations, then the appearance of impropriety is minimized, and the system is more open, the people trust the system more and therefore it is more democratic.

The democratization goal of campaign reforms is to increase the number of contributors. The number of contributors by donor type is one way of looking at donor behavior. Some donors are particularistic donors. Particularistic donors are those that want to influence a particular or narrowly defined policy, while universalistic donors want to influence policy on a more broad or ideological basis. Eom and Gross study the different donor types by analyzing campaign donations in 58 gubernatorial election cycles in forty-two states over the 1990–2000 time period. Because of the variation in state data and collection methods for the data and because most states only require data to be collected over a certain threshold, the authors are only looking at contributions and contributors over the threshold amounts. The authors find that the contribution limits tend to result in a lower average dollar amount per contributor and this finding is carried through no matter the type of contributor. However, the authors also point out that there was no evidence to support the idea that there would be an increase in the number of universalistic donors. Even though there was a decrease in the dollar amount of the contributions, there was not an increase in the number of universalistic donors and a decrease in particularistic donors.[16] Still the authors think that the democratization goal is upheld because with a decrease in the dollar amount of the contributions—which was one of the reform goals—this will lead to the *possibility* of an increase in the number of contributors in the future. One could also argue the opposite that the evidence showing no increase in the universalistic donors could mean that the reform failed to increase the number of donors; in reality therefore; there may be no democratization effect because more citizens did not participate in the process.

As Eom and Gross find that the average dollar amount is reduced, their work does not indicate that the number of donors is increased, nor do they look at the number of candidates running. This is covered more comprehensively in chapter 3 on candidate decisions. However, it is important to note that some scholars have found that more challengers are likely to emerge when contribution limits are in place[17] supporting the idea that the reforms do democratize the system. Hamm and Hogan use an index of campaign restrictions in their analysis. This additive index sums the number of sources from which candidates can receive contributions. Other studies also indicate that with contribution limits in place more candidates would positively decide to run[18] while other studies concluded that the race itself would be more competitive.[19]

Other studies find that contribution limits neither increase the number of candidates nor the quantity or amount of contributions.[20] No doubt the debate will continue. This book pursues a different theoretical angle of measuring contribution limits. Instead of creating an index or conducting a survey of candidates, the language of contribution legislation is used to create a measure of complexity. This method is used to determine the candidate participation rate in all fifty states. Looking at the campaign finance regulatory system as a whole system means evaluation of the effect of many rules and regulations on candidate choice. Rather than just look at one type of rule or regulation, this book studies the complex systematic burden candidates face.

Another proposed reform of campaign finance is to reduce spending in campaigns. Reduced spending allows more challengers to enter the race while also ameliorating the public's view that there is too much money in elections. The intent of spending limits is to hamper incumbents from outspending challengers by creating a level playing field or equal opportunity for both candidate types. The scholarship on spending limits is mixed because there are so many factors that could affect spending. Hogan[21] analyzes campaign spending factors in the states by examining campaign data for candidates from both parties facing an opposition in the general election in twenty-seven states in 1994.[22] The candidate level factors that affected spending relate to whether the seat is held by an incumbent or if it is an open seat. As Hogan states most of these types of seats attract more campaign money because donors want their money to go to someone with a good chance of winning. The district level factors such as primary competition increases spending simply because the candidate has to compete in at least two election cycles; therefore, we should expect an increase in spending. The same can be said of partisan competition. Where candidates' parties are closely matched, spending by the candidates will increase in their effort to win. Hogan concludes that the spending levels are affected by the reform laws, but the spending is also affected largely by candidate characteristics (challenger/incumbent) and district level factors (primary competition, partisan competition). Hogan ultimately finds that campaign finance laws are only moderately successful at limiting spending by candidates.[23]

Gross, Goidel and Shields[24] also find a varied outcome when they studied candidate campaign spending limits in gubernatorial elections from 1978–1997. The goal of the spending limits was to create parity among candidates. Spending limits worked in some cases but it depended on candidate type, partisanship, and the level of the restrictions. They also find that the limits do not affect challenger spending but that an increase in limits will increase incumbent spending. There was no real parity created between the candidates. If the goal was to increase the fund-raising burden on challengers, this too failed to restrict spending. The authors failed to find evidence that a spending limit inhibited incumbent or challenger spending and in fact, the limits could actually create greater disparity between the candidates. So here also the burden is increased on the candidates but has little effect on the actual goal of the legislation. Hogan's[25] analysis would agree with Gross, Goidel, and Shields because he finds that war chests—the amount of money saved ahead of an election cycle for campaign reelection accounts—are a deterrent to challengers. Hogan appraised the candidate level information on over 1,300 incumbents from eight states for a presidential and mid-term election.[26] Even if the deterrent effect of war chests is reduced by the attractiveness of the seat, it still shows that money can inhibit challengers from running for office. Therefore, while one of the goals of campaign finance reform is to reduce the amount of money in elections, the results appear mixed with scholars finding such a variation in factors as to make an overall assessment of the results unclear. Spending limits do seem to have some effect on the electoral process however, it is not conclusive yet as to whether these effects would create a more level playing field and induce more candidates to join the electoral process.

Spending limits have also had limited success because of court cases in which campaign spending is seen as free speech.[27] Because of the court's rulings however, spending limits cannot be mandatory but are often voluntary and are tied to an agreement by the candidate to accept public financing. Therefore many states have turned to public financing. If the candidate accepts the public financing, then he or she agrees to limit his or her spending during the electoral cycles. Some scholars[28] find that public financing can often act as an incentive or an aid for candidates to run for office. La Raja surveyed candidates in local elections in Connecticut, Massachusetts, and Rhode Island to analyze what made the candidates likely to move from local to state elections. He posits that the funding of a campaign is often a serious obstacle for potential candidates considering a run. He found candidates, who run in races where the fund-raising obstacle is in place either because the candidate dislikes fund-raising or who do not have access to funding, benefit from public financing. Furthermore, La Raja also found that candidates who have a high level of political ambition tend to benefit from public funding because they are more willing to take advantage of the funds. La Raja's contention is that public funding may be a valuable reform tool because it is likely to help change the skill set found in candidates by allowing candidates who are not good at fund-raising to have a chance at running for office. Overall, public financing is one option that does seem to reduce barriers to run for office. However, these programs must remain optional as a result of various court decisions and therefore their effectiveness is limited. As an aid to candidate challengers who had access to public financing benefited from its use because they were able to spend less than candidates who did not have access to public financing.[29]

Public disclosure of both contributions and expenditures is the least controversial of the reform efforts. Even though there are wide variations in how the data are collected, most states require reporting of the data in some way. The disclosure requirement was intended to increase political accountability and transparency in the electoral process. This openness should allow for any corruption or any contributions from questionable sources to be investigated or at least disclosed to the public prior to the election. There is, however, little apparent evidence that this is the case. Gross and Goidel discuss that they previously found[30] no evidence that elections are more competitive or that there is less corruption. They surmise that as voters learn more about how and from where contributions are obtained, they are less engaged and elections are less competitive. This seems to be a case where sometimes too much information can be a bad thing because the public is disgusted the more they learn about how much money is in campaigns.

Christopher Witko originally created an index of campaign regulation stringency which was then updated with his coauthors through 2012.[31] The stringency index is a terrific tool to measure the restrictions on various aspects of campaign finance regulations in each of the fifty US states. The stringency index measures contribution limits, disclosure requirements, and public financing regulations for each state. These three requirements are each used to create a sub-index with one point for each requirement. Witko then created a composite index from each of the sub-indices. Witko uses the index to measure factors affecting increased stringency in the states. Factors such as government ideology and legislative professionalism factor prominently in the index. Interestingly, the index shows that the self-interested nature of state legislators does not increase the stringency of state campaign finance laws. State legislators "almost reflexively resist campaign finance reform."[32] However, as Witko explains it would depend on the current state context for campaign finance regulations. In states where the campaign finance regulations are already expensive, legislators may leave the regulatory system alone because they are content with the restrictions. The incumbents have already learned the regulations and they know how to comply with the statutes. Incumbents may know how difficult the regulations are and leave them in place as a barrier to entry for challengers.

Witko's index serves as a robust tool to measure the stringency of campaign finance regulations. What is missing, however, is how those regulations affect novice candidates who are starting to make decisions on if they will run for office. That is the gap that this book seeks to fill. There are no data on potential candidates and the costs of learning to run for office. This book also seeks to fill this gap using the experimental method detailed in chapter 5 on plain language. Measuring the statute language contributes to the idea of stringency indices by adding in a learning element for the statute.[33]

As seen above, the goals of the reform have been to make the campaign process more democratic and to increase participation in the electoral process—both by reducing barriers for challengers and broadening the base of contributors. The reforms aimed at reducing corruption in campaign finance want to make it more open and accountable. By making the system more transparent, the reforms allow the public to see where the money comes from and where it goes. The goal of this transparency is to increase the public's confidence in the system and thus increase its democratic nature. Contribution limits are intended to have the dual effect of limiting the amount of money in campaigns thus allowing a more level playing field for challengers; and limiting the amount of "big" donors and spreading the contributions to a wider base in order to allow more, smaller contributors to participate.[34] Public financing should allow for more participation by challengers by decreasing the deterrent of incumbent war chests. Ultimately, all of the reforms were aimed at increasing the number of candidates by decreasing barriers, decreasing corruption by increasing transparency, and making the system more democratic by spreading the accessibility of the campaign process to more citizens.

Clearly, no reform has become the silver bullet with which to reform campaign finance. La Raja points out that the laws themselves have become complicated and the campaign finance regulations have become a barrier in themselves. While La Raja was looking at the Bi-Partisan Campaign Finance Reform Act, much of his assessment can also be applied to the states because the states' legislation is modeled on the national legislation. While scholars have explored the effects of money in the system, scholars have yet to explore the complexity problem as applied to campaign finance. This book studies whether the state campaign finance legislation has become so complex that candidates cannot always understand it and it thus becomes a barrier in the form of increased transaction costs in running for office.

As La Raja jokes, BCRA has come to mean Before Campaigning Retain an Attorney. This may be a joke, but it illustrates why the question of complexity on the effectiveness of reform are important to study. Scholars and policy makers alike are beginning to realize the ways in which the complexity of legislation affects legislative outcomes.

This book studies only the contribution limits on campaign finance reforms in an effort to study these limits in a different context. Rather than looking at contribution limits in terms of how many incumbents versus challengers or voter turnout, it is important to understand if the contribution legislation is itself a barrier to entry for candidates seeking office. The goals of the contribution limits were to lower the bar to allow more entry into the political process by leveling the playing field in such a way that average citizens would be able to participate.

Learning Campaign Finance Rules

The goals of campaign finance are laudable. Making our democratic system safe from corruption and fraud is important to ensure that citizens have confidence that their vote counts and that they are electing people on a collective basis. We want to ensure that anyone can run for office. The potential problem is with all those rules and regulations it may be that only those who have the time and money to spend learning how to run, will be able to run for office. A quick look at my local county's election website on how to become a candidate reveals that an individual would need to learn what a candidate committee is, how to set one up, who needs to be on that committee, the need for a treasurer, and how and when to appoint a treasurer. Treasurers in my state (North Carolina) must go through mandatory in-person training. That is just a quick look and then there are the forms to fill out, and tasks to complete—the statement of organization, the certification of the treasurer, the certification of financial accounts, the designation of committee funds.

In preparation for writing this book, interviews of actual and potential candidates were conducted from around the United States. These individuals either considered running or had run for office. The general finding of the interviews was that these individuals found the campaign finance system difficult.

One respondent said in the future he would consider town council positions and possibly the state senate but not higher office because of the cost of running. He stated, "It costs a lot of money to run." His training to run for office consisted of previous training through his state's Election Law Enforcement Commission to be a campaign treasurer because he wanted to know and understand the laws. He considers his campaign to have been "easier because he had experience in campaigns." Regarding the campaign rules, he stated, "It's complicated to see if anyone is violating the laws, but has the effect of shutting out smaller candidates. It's really a pain—more time and effort than just running. You have financing, tracking, and dates to file. You want checks or less than $300 because it's the least amount of work."[35]

If novice candidates have to choose between the amount of work required and a specific donation amount, this candidate's experience is that they chose the least amount of work. Experienced candidates or incumbents may be in a better position to complete the paperwork because they have learned the rules through their experiences. The incumbents would then be in a better position to accept higher dollar amount contributions leaving novice candidates in a less advantageous position.

Campaign Compliance

Compliance with campaign finance regulations can be a difficult task for candidates. The difference between incumbent or experienced candidates and novice candidates points to differing effects for each candidate type. Since the original goal of campaign finance was, in part, to increase participation in the electoral system, the unintended consequences of the campaign finance red tape means that candidates face a burden that is hard to master and may be deterred from running for office. Learning how to run for office is hard and time-consuming. As noted above there are myriad forms to fill out, training classes to take, speeches to write and master delivery of, fund-raising to organize, bank accounts to manage and the list goes on.

From the qualitative interviews done for this book, it was clear that some candidates got help from previous candidates for office or through election schools and groups geared to helping candidates run. If the candidates did not have help running, they ran their campaign on their own, managing a difficult process as best as they were able to do. One previous candidate interviewed stated "Filing for office was difficult. Getting support from and finding people who had done it before was hard. Getting reliable advice was very hard. Getting on the ballot was easy and only required a petition or a $50 fee." The candidate "expected to raise about $10k to be competitive, if he could get $20k that would be ridiculous."[36] He ended up getting about $8k. In his district, there were about twenty thousand people in a transient community having both college and military folks moving in and out. Getting contributions from individuals without a permanent stake in the community was difficult. Lacking support from his party or other leadership made it more difficult for this candidate.

Using the qualitative interviews to understand the burden candidates face is instructive regarding the learning necessary to run for office. One candidate interviewed was a lawyer. When asked if being a lawyer helped in his run for office, he replied "Yes, in the sense that I had a leg up on opponents. I don't know the code on top of my head, but the average person would need help." When registering as a candidate, the respondent set up an LLC, then a committee and got a treasurer. He added that he did not think his opponent had done this. "It was frustrating the amount of time to find info about when filing is due. . . . The declaration of financial interest statement negatively impacts people's decisions to run."[37] His experience as a lawyer helped him navigate the paperwork and allowed him to take the extra step of creating an LLC, which is not necessary, but gave him some extra protection in financing and reporting requirements.

The qualitative interviews were also illustrative as to what happens when campaign finance regulations are made easier to navigate. One respondent said that to run for office in his state requires a $250 fee. “You can find this information on the Secretary of State’s office website. The site was cleaned up five years ago and makes it easy to find information on how to run. It’s like a ‘running for dummies’ website. The paperwork etc. is easy. The hard part is the retail politics in the state. You have to raise money and spend the time to run for statewide office.”[38] This indicates that when states make it easier to navigate the campaign finance regulations, candidates have an easier compliance burden and candidates have more time to spend on actual campaigning rather than on paperwork.

Even though one proposed solution for the campaign finance system is public financing, it does not appear to be a cure all. A respondent to the qualitative interviews stated that his state has public financing for state representatives and other state offices. According to respondent, this “makes it easier to run because you don’t really have to raise money. You do have to raise 150 donations of $5–$100 and raise $5,000 total to qualify for state public funding.” The respondent feels this is “great for more fair elections and great for our democracy. Even though it is easier to raise the campaign money, candidates have to file many reports. In addition, supporters have to file reports also. “If you donate even $5 to a candidate, you have to file your own report. “It’s a big pain,” says respondent. “I didn't have to raise ‘a lot’ of money but each election cycle I raise approximately $1,000–$2,000 for the slate.” “The citizen election process is a pain but the efforts are worth it in order to ensure transparency.” When asked how a novice would fare in this process respondent said, “It can be a slow process; therefore you need to have the right motivation to do it.”[39]

Psychological Costs

The psychological costs of social welfare programs involve the feelings of inferiority that citizens feel when they consider the costs of the time and effort to apply for welfare benefits. Scholars have found that when citizens feel the costs outweigh the benefits, the individuals are less likely to apply for and get those benefits.[40] Additionally, the time spent waiting to apply for the benefits in a social welfare office may be a deterrent.[41] Adding to the psychological costs when citizens perceive the likelihood of success to be low, they view the administrative burden of applying to be higher than if they view the likelihood of success to be high.[42]

We know that some candidates are more risk averse than others. Certainly, candidates facing an incumbent face a more daunting challenge than those facing an open seat, or a weak opponent. It makes sense that candidates who perceive the likelihood of success may view the administrative burdens of running for office as higher when facing such formidable opponents. If we add together the general risk aversion, plus a formidable opponent, running for office becomes even more daunting. One candidate interviewed is now a campaign manager. Coming from this different perspective, he stated that his job as a campaign consultant is easier now. He is no longer under attack and can just watch the strategy play out. "The hard part is finding people to run for office because the risks of being in front of people is big. People are afraid of humiliation of messing up and business owners fear losing business."[43] Scholars know that the aversion to risk is difficult for many candidates. What is new here is the additional administrative burden and the psychological effects it may have on candidates considering a run for office.

Campaign Finance Rules and Regulations

As discussed throughout this chapter, campaign finance studies look at rules mostly in the particularistic sense. Contribution limits effect donors or possibly challengers, but rarely considers the whole system. Hamm and Hogan do create an index that is a close proxy for a systematic approach. As discussed in the chapter on complexity theory, the whole system is important because campaign finance systems are dynamically evolving over time. As demonstrated above, campaign finance systems evolve over time in response to different factors such as corruption, changing perceptions, or government reforms. Regardless of why the changes occur, the changes happen and often the rules and regulations adopted are accumulated over time with little consideration of the effect of the whole on candidates. The changeable nature of campaign finance may also be non-linear. We see reforms passed, then court cases challenge and change those reforms, bringing what was conceived as a linear and predictable system into a non-linear and unpredictable environment of regulations. Campaign finance context changes depending on whether a citizen is a challenging candidate or an incumbent legislator. A challenger has a different outlook and context for campaign finance regulations that they face when running for office. They face a complex system of rules and regulations that they must overcome to run for office successfully. They face risks in terms of reputation, time, and finances while overcoming these hurdles. An incumbent faces a different context because they are more familiar with the campaign finance regulations. They are repeat candidates and as such enjoy an advantage of learned experience. The legislators making the rules can self-organize to create rules and regulations that may constrict challengers. Even legislators from different parties should be likely to band together to constrain or deter challengers. Challengers or novice candidates—as noted in the previous chapter—have no such self-organizing mechanism. As a whole, campaign finance consists of contribution limits, spending limits, and public financing. Adding to the campaign system are ballot access restrictions covered in the chapter on candidate decisions. All of these factors impact candidates, but contribution limits and candidacy requirements affect candidates at the point as they decide to run or not to run for public office. Spending limits only affect candidates once they have managed to navigate the hurdles of becoming a candidate. Because of this, spending limits are not included in the book analysis. What is included are those campaign finance rules and regulations that affect candidates as they are making decisions to run for office. While it is very important to look at discrete factors such as union contributions, or how much a candidate can donate to their own campaign, it is also important to understand the cumulative effect of all the rules and regulations written over time. Indices have been used to tally up the effect of multiple factors, but even indices are simple numbers used as a proxy for a count of factors affecting decisions. Using the statute as a whole allows study of what candidates actually face when deciding to run for office. This also gives a more robust idea of complexity. The next chapter on plain language lays out a way of measuring language for complexity using the number of words and the grade reading levels.

NOTES

1. Donald A. Gross and Robert K. Goidel, *The States of Campaign Finance Reform* (Columbus: The Ohio State University, 2003).
2. Political assessments were required political donations given to candidates by public sector employees as a condition of employment.
3. David Schultz, "States and Campaign Finance Reform," *National Civic Review* 91, no. 2 (2002): 205.
4. Michael J. Malbin and Thomas L. Gais, *The Day after Reform: Sobering Campaign Finance Lessons from the American States* (Albany, NY: Rockefeller Institute Press, 1998); Gross and Goidel, *The States of Campaign Finance Reform*.
5. Scott Harshberger and Edwin Davis, "Federal Campaign Finance Reform: The Long and Winding Road," *National Civic Review* 90, no. 2 (2001).
6. Malbin and Gais, *The Day after Reform: Sobering Campaign Finance Lessons from the American States*.
7. Ibid.
8. Ibid.
9. Gross and Goidel, *The States of Campaign Finance Reform*.
10. Harshberger and Davis, "Federal Campaign Finance Reform: The Long and Winding Road."
11. Ibid.
12. Joel Thompson and Gary F. Moncrief, "Exploring the 'Lost World' of Campaign Finance," in *Campaign Finance in State Legislative Elections*, ed. Joel A. Thompson and Gary F. Moncrief (Washington, DC: Congressional Quarterly Inc., 1998).
13. Kihong Eom and Donald A Gross, "Democratization Effects of Campaign Contribution Limits in Gubernatorial Elections," *Party Politics* 13, no. 6 (2007).
14. Thompson and Moncrief, "Exploring the 'Lost World' of Campaign Finance."
15. Ibid.
16. Eom and Gross, "Democratization Effects of Campaign Contribution Limits in Gubernatorial Elections."

17. Keith E. Hamm and Robert E. Hogan, "Campaign Finance Laws and Candidacy Decisions in State Legislative Elections," *Political Research Quarterly* 61, no. 3 (2008).

18. L. Sandy Maisel and Walter J. Stone, "Determinants of Candidate Emergence in US House Elections: An Exploratory Study," *Legislative Studies Quarterly* 22, no. 1 (1997).

19. Thomas Stratmann and Francisco J. Aparicio-Castillo, "Competition Policy for Elections: Do Campaign Contribution Limits Matter?," *Public Choice* 127 (2006).

20. D. P. Green, and Krasno, J. S., "Salvation of the Spendthrift Incumbent: Reestimating the Effects of Campaign Spending in House Elections," *American Journal of Political Science* 32, no. 4 (1988); B. A. Abrams and R. F. Settle, "Campaign-Finance Reform: A Public Choice Perspective," *Public Choice* 120, no. 3/4 (2004); Eom and Gross, "Democratization Effects of Campaign Contribution Limits in Gubernatorial Elections."

21. R. E. Hogan, "The Costs of Representation in State Legislatures: Explaining Variations in Campaign Spending," *Social Science Quarterly* 81, no. 4 (2000).

22. With the exception of five states from other years. See Hogan (2000) for more complete information.

23. Hogan, "The Costs of Representation in State Legislatures: Explaining Variations in Campaign Spending."

24. Donald A. Gross, Robert K. Goidel, and Todd G. Shields, "State Campaign Finance Regulations and Electoral Competition," *American Politics Research* 30, no. 2 (2002).

25. Robert E. Hogan, "Campaign War Chests and Challenger Emergence in State Legislative Elections," *Political Research Quarterly* 54 (2001).

26. The states were Idaho, Illinois, Indiana, Massachusetts, Michigan, Minnesota, Oregon, and Tennessee. He used the election years 1994 and 1996 for all states except Massachusetts where 1996 and 1998 were used.

27. *Buckley V. Valeo*, (1976).

28. K. Bardwell, "Campaign Finance Laws and the Competition for Spending in Gubernatorial Elections," *Social Science Quarterly* 84, no. 4 (2003); Raymond J. La Raja, *Small Change: Money, Political Parties, and Campaign Finance Reform* (Ann Arbor: University of Michigan Press, 2008).

29. According to the National Conference on State Legislatures twenty-five states have public financing of elections. National Conference of State Legislatures, "NCSL" in *National Conference of State Legislatures*. Public financing (PF) is not included in this analysis because in order to qualify for it in states with partial public financing, you have to raise funds (just like other non-PF candidates) in order to get the PF. Looking on the data on NCSL.org only one state (Maine) has clean elections in which the candidates do not have to raise any money to qualify. The rest of the states have qualifications to get the PF. Omitting PF is justified for this analysis because candidates with PF would still have to go through the same processes to raise money as candidates without PF. Public financing should be included in future analysis.

30. The authors cite their previous work in Gross, Goidel and Shields, *Money Matters*. Robert K. Goidel, Robert August Gross, and Todd G. Shields, *Money Matters: Consequences of Campaign Finance Reform in US House Elections* (Lanham, MD: Rowman & Littlefield, 1999).

31. Christopher Witko, "Measuring the Stringency of State Campaign Finance Regulation," *State Politics and Policy Quarterly* 5, no. 3 (2005); "Explaining Increases in the Stringency of State Campaign Finance Regulation, 1993–2002," *State Politics & Policy Quarterly* 7, no. 4 (2007); Christopher Kulesza, Christopher Witko, and Eric Waltenburg, "Reform Interrupted? State Innovation, Court Decisions, and the Past and Future of Campaign Finance Reform in the States," *Election Law Journal* 2 (2016).

32. Witko, "Explaining Increases in the Stringency of State Campaign Finance Regulation, 1993–2002," 372.

33. As a robustness check on the analysis presented in the second half of this book, Christopher Witko kindly allowed me to compare the plain language measure with the stringency index. I found no difference in the study results using either the stringency index or my plain language measure. The plain language measure adds to this field of study by analyzing the whole system of campaign finance regulations.

34. Eom and Gross, "Democratization Effects of Campaign Contribution Limits in Gubernatorial Elections."
35. QI5, ed. Mary Jo McGowan Shepherd (2016).
36. QI12, ed. Mary Jo McGowan Shepherd (2014).
37. QI13, ed. Mary Jo McGowan Shepherd (2014).
38. QI7, ed. Mary Jo McGowan Shepherd (2016).
39. QI6, ed. Mary Jo McGowan Shepherd (2016).
40. Donald Moynihan and Pamela Herd, "Red Tape and Democracy: How Rules Affect Citizens Rights," *The American Review of Public Administration* 40, no. 6 (2010).
41. Donald Moynihan, Pamela Herd, and Hope Harvey, "Administrative Burden: Learning, Psychological, and Compliance Costs in Citizen-State Interactions," *Journal of Public Administration Research and Theory* 25 (2014).
42. Wesley Kaufmann and Mary K. Feeney, "Effect of Outcome Favourability on Red Tape Perceptions," *Public Administration* 92, no. 1 (2014).
43. QI11, ed. Mary Jo McGowan Shepherd (2014).

Chapter Four

Plain Language Theory

The previous chapter on complexity laid out the theoretical basis for how scholars conceptualize complexity. Variously this concept is called administrative burden, rules, or costs. Rules and regulations add time and compliance costs to policy processes. The added time and effort to comply creates a policy burden. In an effort to capture the burden and costs of the rules and regulations, I call this concept complexity. The rules and regulations are the substance of complexity, while the compliance, learning and psychological costs are the implementation costs of the policy to the user. Burdens or rules have been measured in a variety of ways such as indices. Legislative constraints are measured using word counts or language ambiguity. This book uses a measure, namely language, to capture the entirety of the regulatory constraint that candidates face when contemplating a run for office. This measure combines the idea of a whole system of rules and regulations by measuring them using language. Using language enables a quantitative way to measure complexity that goes beyond just the number of words but stretches this idea to include the usability of the language and the statutes.

One candidate interviewed for this book said, "Someone just off streets wouldn't be able to run [in my state]. You need to be a researcher to do it right." This quote is illustrative of the phenomena this book tries to understand. Some states' regulations make it very easy to run for office while other states make it more complex. In order to understand the difference between the statutes and to understand what it means to be "complex" a measure of complexity is required. Few empirical tests of language are available to aid understanding of what complexity means linguistically. This chapter uses plain language tools to help understand the comprehension and usability of statutes.

Language and the Law

Legal language complexity is nothing new. As Gibbons[1] relates, language is used in the law to increase precision and specificity. The need to be precise in the law is important to clarify meaning and intent. Regardless, the very precision makes the language of the law more complex. Gibbons points out that this conundrum has been well known and even satirized by authors such as Jonathan Swift and Charles Dickens.[2] Some states have rules and regulations on top of rules and regulations to fix problems or clarify meanings. This mish-mash of statutory regulations makes it difficult for the everyday citizen to understand the law's intent. The utility of specificity may be lost as regulations pile up. As the regulatory system becomes more and more opaque, it requires specialized help to navigate the meaning of the rules.

When rules and regulations necessitate professional help to clarify meaning, there may be a power discrepancy between those who know the rules and those who do not. Maley notes this disequilibrium particularly in the courtroom. Lawyers and judges enjoy an unequal understanding of the law over defendants or citizens in courtrooms.[3] Lawyers and judges respond that their language must be precise in order to guarantee that they are not legislating or enforcing the law; they are only interpreting and applying the law.

The tension between the precise, specific language and interpretation and understanding of that language is ongoing. The tension produces an unequal power relationship between the government agents and the citizens on whom the law is applied. This power relationship opens the door for legislators to shape legislation in ways that make it easier or more difficult to implement and comply. Campaign finance legislation is no different and I would argue a likely candidate for legislators to create a complex system. Language that is more complex creates an inequality between legislators and those on whom the law is intended—in this case potential candidates. As I showed in previous chapters, legislators have used legislation to create this power imbalance. The question for this book, and this chapter, is how to use language to measure the complexity of a statute.

Plain Language Theory

This chapter describes the theory of using plain language to measure the complexity of language. It is important to look at how to measure language because the debate over clarity in writing and comprehension of language stretches over time. In the past twenty years, a new dimension emerged in the form of the debate over the use of "plain language." The proponents of this movement argue that language must be understood if it is to be language at all, otherwise it is just letters or words strung together. Language must be comprehensible and usable in order to be language. Understanding the law is the first step in the ability to use the law effectively.

Plain language is a movement by scholars of different fields to make the transmission of information through language easier and more successful for end users. It involves changing various written media such as documents, pamphlets, charts, graphs, and articles into more easily understood documents so that the user or reader can use the information contained in the media more quickly and effectively. One of the most prominent advocates for Plain Language is Dr. Joseph Kimble who became an early cheerleader for the effort and maintains a Plain Language website.[4] The website's definition for plain language is "communication your audience can understand the first time they read or hear it. Written material is plain if your audience can find what they need, understand what they find, and use what they find to meet their needs."[5] The Federal government defines plain writing as "writing that is clear, concise, well-organized, and follows other best practices appropriate to the subject or field and intended audience."[6]

While this definition is clear, one of the problems with the plain language movement is that it lacks a consensus definition. Others see plain language as "reader-friendly language—designed to increase the individual's understanding of the text. It serves as a portal through which consumers can access and understand . . . information."[7] The differing views between Kimble and others refer to the usability of the information. Kimble advocates a usability of the language while others such as Stableford and Mettger advocate understanding. Understanding of the language is important especially when it is the law one seeks to understand. Understanding comes first, but once an individual understands the law they may choose to use with the law. Using the law may mean compliance, or it may mean access to government services. It is important to note that using the law becomes a two-step process—first individuals must learn the law, and only then can they use the law.

The idea of linguistic or legislative usability is important to note given the context in which this analysis takes place. Language may be coercive or permissive depending on the intent. Legislators have long used legal language to change the intent of a law as demonstrated in chapter 2 on complexity. The idea that language may be constraining might mean that legislators chose to make the language unusable in order to constrain potential challengers. The usability of the law means that the law ought to be less complex in order that citizens and other end users pay fewer learning and compliance costs when using the law. Laws that are more complex by contrast would have higher learning and compliance costs. The US government in passing a Plain Language law advocates less complexity in statutes, rules, and regulations for end users. The Plain Language government website is dedicated to helping bureaucrats within the US government make documents more usable.

Measuring Language

Plain language scholars seek to test documents to see how readable, comprehensible, and usable documents are. One of the main measures of plain language today is readability and its companion, grade level scores. Readability is generally the ease with which an individual can read a document. If a document is readable, it can be read and understood by an average citizen. An average citizen is generally taken to mean a 6th- to 8th-grade reading level. Because readability is fairly subjective, most plain language scholars use measures that are more specific. Some readability scores are subject to measurement validity issues where scholars are not sure what they are measuring is what they intend to measure, and users are not quite sure of the meaning of some readability scores.

To circumvent the measurement issue, readability scores are translated into grade reading level scores. Grade reading level scores measure the grade level on which an individual would have to read in order to understand the document. The question for the field is which readability/grade score to use. There are over forty different formulas for testing the readability or grade level of a document.[8] These formulas are mostly based or have grown from one of the original works of scholarship advocating for testing readability in documents. The original work compiled by Rudolf Flesch serves as a basic measure of readability scores.

Rudolf Flesch's[9] work on readability is one of the first to look at readability formulas. Flesch's readability formula used a very simple measure of average sentence length in number of words, number of affixes,[10] and number of references to people (i.e., mortgage guarantor, leasee, candidate etc.) to test the readability of a document. According to Flesch, this first formula tended to have an overreliance on sentence length, and failed to capture conversational writing.[11] The number of affixes was hard for researchers to determine and the references to people were unclear and not understood. Flesch created a new formula to overcome this problem. He used a very simple measure of average sentence length in words, average word length in syllables, number of references to "personal words" (words with natural gender, pronouns except neutral, and the words "people" and "folks"). Flesch finds that his new formula is a more usable measure of readability in that it is easier to interpret with a scoring system of 0–100. The Flesch Reading Ease is an indirect test of word complexity via number of syllables per word and sentence complexity via number of words per sentence.

As readability formulas developed, other scholars kept trying to tie language complexity to school grade levels. Fry's 1968 article updated his own 1948 readability formula for books, used mostly by international scholars. Fry's grade level formula is not applicable for US standards and grade levels because the grade levels do not correspond with US grade levels.[12] This presents a different validity issue for grade reading levels where the formula does not correspond to grade levels that may vary across time and areas. As Fry puts it, "[a readability measure] is complicated by trying to determine grade level when grade level won't stand still and when subjective judgments are about as good a standard as can be found." Grade reading levels change over time as new teaching methods develop and children learn to read at different rates dependent on time and place. To create a grade level measure, Fry randomly selects three one-hundred-word passages from a book or an article. The researcher plots the average number of syllables and average number of words per sentence on a graph to determine the area of readability level. A researcher could choose more passages per book if they find a large amount of variability in the passages.[13] Fry's contribution here is based, not only on the fact that he uses a formula and compares books, but also that he is trying to work out the inherent problem of grade level. He compares the various readability formulas available in the 1960s to his own and uses this information to create a graph of readability.

Another important contributor to the developing readability scholarship was Harry McLaughlin[14] who created the SMOG Grading score.[15] This score computes the grade level necessary to comprehend a particular piece of writing. This reading score eliminates some of the steps of the Flesch and Fry formulas by creating a multiplicative term in the formula. McLaughlin multiplies word and sentence length together therefore a researcher does not have to add up word length (counting syllables) and sentence length (counting words) if one just counts out a number of sentences and then counts the number of syllables in those sentences. McLaughlin was able to simplify the process of calculating readability for scholars. This figure is widely used in the health care field[16] which we will see below is one of the biggest proponents of plain language.

Today computer programs do much of this readability testing. This in itself creates another problem as scholars contend that there is much variability in computer-generated readability scores and little agreement on what the "grade level" scores mean.[17] In an effort to standardize the meaning of grade levels Root and Stableford[18] generally consider items that are 4th–6th grade "easy-to-read"; 7th–8th grade "average reading"; and 9th grade or higher they consider "difficult-to-read" items. Originally, these scores measured children's books, which caused some scholars to contend that using grade levels targets reading abilities at schoolchildren instead of end-users.[19] In creating such scales, it also means that materials and people are categorized into grade level scales. While the grade levels may seem constricting, it is important to remember that the point of plain language initiatives is to make the materials available and usable for average citizens. Average citizens must be able to access and use campaign finance materials in order to run for office. If the materials are inaccessible due to language constraints—that is, complexity—more individuals will have to pay higher learning and compliance costs in order to use the materials such as campaign finance regulations. This was found indirectly in the qualitative interviews completed. Several of the respondents discussed the need to seek help with their campaigns in order to register to run and to handle campaign donations correctly.

Limiting the flexibility into just three broad grade-level categories seems to limit the usefulness of these types of scales. Additionally, the readability ratings are discredited due to the wide range of ways readability can be calculated.[20] Readability scores also only test those factors in writing that can be counted, that is, sentences, words, and syllables. Readability fails to test on what level a reader would have to be in order to understand the language. Many of these measures have inherent issues; however most scholars use the grade reading level scores. The grade reading levels when not indexed into two or three groupings, serve as a more intuitive and useful measure of language. In the chapters on analyzing the campaign finance statutes, the grade level scores are used to analyze the campaign finance legislation. After collecting all the states campaign finance statutes, factor analysis of thirteen different plain language measures indicated that each measure was measuring the same underlying factor. Using grade reading levels is not much different from using readability scores or SMOG levels for instance. In order to use the most widely accepted measure of plain language, using the grade reading levels is most acceptable.

The readability measures, grade reading level measures, or usability measures are all intended to test documents to determine how difficult or easy to read they are and how or if users will be able to comprehend the documents. Grade reading level results allow us to say for example that a document is on a 9th grade level. From that measure, we understand that anyone who has completed the 9th grade should easily be able to understand this document. Documents on a grade reading level of 15 indicate a college student should be able to read and use this document. Readabilty scores on the other hand can range from 0–100. If one scholar uses a readability score and their document rates a 45 it is not clear what this means. It becomes especially unclear if another scholar uses a different readability score and comes up with a 67. Grade levels result in more easily understood and applicable results than readability scores. Keeping in mind the factor analysis done on these scores, it becomes clear that using grade reading levels are more intuitive measures while not losing any leverage that a readability score might provide.

While not the same as using a usability test, using grade level scores are more intuitive for most users than understanding readability scores.[21] Usability measures are the recommended way to measure comprehension and use of documents. In these tests, users read material while researchers document the effort.[22] This is a more qualitative measure of readability, and one that requires human intervention to measure. Usability allows users to be able to access materials and prevents constraints on users.

The experimental study presented in the next chapter gave users or respondents both a comprehension measure and a usability test. Respondents were given North Carolina's campaign contribution statute and were asked questions not only about comprehension but also about *how* they read the statute. For example, respondents were asked how many times they referred back to the reading, or how clear they thought it was. Referring back to the statute in order to answer comprehension questions allows us to understand how much effort was involved in understanding the statute. If respondents referred back to the statute numerous times, it is likely that they failed to understand the statute and had to refer back in order to completely understand it. Respondents also rated how clear they thought the statute was, allowing us to gauge the respondents' impression of the statute. Asking usability questions allows this part of this study to measure not only grade level, but also how difficult or easy it was to understand the campaign finance statute.

The Advantages/Disadvantages of Plain Language Use

Advocates and opponents of plain language continue debating many aspects of plain language including the measurement issue. Another issue debated is the rationale of plain language. Some scholars are advocates of its use, while others are against using plain language. The debate highlights the tension between precision or specificity plus the need for flexibility in language. Generally, those against the use of plain language point to a lack of specifics in plain language that may cause confusion in documents. Opponents also cite the cost of transitioning from legalese to plain language, and more generally, some people feel that using plain language is a dumbing down of linguistics for little apparent benefit.

One reason for not using plain language is the cost issue. Converting to plain language may be an added expense for businesses, law firms, or legislatures. Frooman[23] argues that legalese is used because it is convenient and cheaper to use than converting to plain language. Converting contracts to plain language would require lawyers to change their current computer forms and purchase new ones. The old ones are set in the legalese language and to buy new ones would cost more money. By changing the wording, lawyers would be taking a risk that the new contracts would be contested in court. Therefore, there is no incentive to change to new plain language forms and formats. Frooman also argues that using legalese is useful to lawyers because it keeps them in business, as they are the only ones who understand legalese. Frooman is not alone, Crow[24] points out corporations also—even those who want to use plain language—find themselves thwarted by the cost savings of official form letters that have been prewritten and used for years to good effect. Why spend the money rewriting these letters when doing so may create a "backlog of correspondence" and/or an increase in the number of customer service calls?[25] These cost arguments opposing plain language bolster support for the theory that language of statutes, like contracts, may be so difficult to read that it requires more time and effort to learn and comply with the statutes. Individuals may need lawyers or professional help to learn and comply with the statutes.

Plain language also may not be as effective as the advocates assert. The general argument here is that laws are laws despite the language in which they are written and the laws will be enforced based on their understanding to the court system, not based on how well users can understand the law. Scheibal[26] contends that plain language (or Plain English Laws, PELs, as he calls them) are useful but bring up several issues including how the Plain English within the law is interpreted. Scheibal contends that PELs are applicable in much the same way any other law is applicable. If it is ambiguous, whoever drafts the law must either rewrite it or explain the law. This would not change in the case of using plain language. The application of the law does not change; it is perhaps only the "affected" parties' understanding of the laws that changes. Extending this point, Assy argues that making the law comprehensible to those affected by it is an impossible task because no law could possibly take into account the diversity of individuals subject to the law.[27] In other words, so many different types of people are affected by laws so how can legislatures write the laws so that every potential person affected by it can use it without needing a lawyer to interpret the law. She further argues that there is a difference between linguistic and legal clarity necessary to the law.[28] Linguistic clarity is the ability to understand the language you are consuming. The difference between this and legal clarity is tense because legal language must be so precise that reduces the opportunity to create a litigious situation. Assy believes that plain language might give rise to more litigation because of its lack of precision. Assy does not discount the use of plain language altogether and sees it as a means of helping foster a better relationship between citizens and their lawyers.[29]

As demonstrated below, a lack of empirical evidence that plain language is effective also creates opposition to its use. In particular, the structure of the legislation framework may be so different as to have uncertain outcomes.[30] The legislative structure is the way in which plain language legislation is passed by (in this case) state legislatures. Some state legislatures are very generic and open about passing plain language statutes, while other states are very specific. Leete cites as an example the plain language legislation passed in New York and New Jersey. New York used an "open format" statute simply stating that contracts and regulations should be written in a "clear and coherent manner." New Jersey's plain language statutes were more structured and less flexible. New Jersey specified, for example, that consumer contracts be readable according to a specific readability test and not be longer than a certain number of words (depending on contract type). Leete points out that an open format might be preferable except that it is subjective to different interpretations of what is clear and coherent. He notes New Jersey's statute creates the question of whether or not there is any assurance that a contract will conform to the law until it is tested in court. Leete concludes that instead of passing statutes on plain language it would probably be better to allow the market to determine if plain language will ultimately be feasible or not. He points out that companies that use plain language are seeing improved business and perhaps this trend will continue.[31] For the plain language advocates, this debate is dying out as the federal government is involved and created a website to advocate and help federal agencies and any others to convert to plain language usage. The US federal government is pushing forward advocacy and use of plain language to make documents more easily accessible both to users but also between agencies.

Plain language is often seen as the "dumbing down" of language. Language is diverse and functional and reducing it to simple language loses some of the nuances and meaning of language. Seen this way some scholars see the plain language movement as an impediment to writing proper legislation. These scholars conclude that the "language of our legislation cannot be reduced to baby talk for consumption."[32] Hunt argues that language does matter; especially in legislation which needs to be very precise, clear, and technical so that those who must implement it can understand its meanings and interpretations. It cannot be reduced to common language.[33] He recommends that legislation be passed using legal language, but the regulations and/or administrative rules should be written in plain language. Taking this course would help alleviate much concern on both sides. While retaining the complexity and specificity necessary for legislation to articulate its meaning, users would benefit from access and understanding.

Not everyone is skeptical about plain language use. The medical, financial, and legal fields are working to simplify language in their respective areas. The medical field is working to simplify both technical terms and instructions to patients in order to clarify meaning and ensure care to citizens who are illiterate or have low literacy proficiency. As we see below these fields have taken the lead on using plain language for readability and comprehension.

Some lawyers favor using plain language in legal writing in order to make legal statutes or legislation more accessible to everyday people. By doing this people will be more aware of legal proceedings and understand their rights. Richard Wydick[34] points out that the legal profession is incorporating plain language into their teaching curriculum. This is especially the case for jury instructions (as discussed later) and general legal writing. Sullivan[35] points out that legal language targets a very specific audience. She does not advocate writing statutes so that everyone can read them, she advocates writing the statutes for the most affected person that is going to use that statute. For example, if a statute involving jury instructions is most likely going to be read by a judge, then it should be written in legal language. If the jury foreman is going to read the statute, plain language should be the format.

Arguing in the same legal genre, Assy[36] argues that even though some legislation and statutes have no need for translation into plain language, in other cases using plain language provides three benefits. These include the ability of individuals to engage in their own legal affairs and to reduce its costs. Assy argues that even though individuals might still need lawyers, allowing the law to be written more clearly provides an avenue on which both lawyers and their clients can better understand the law. If they can understand it better, litigation will be less expensive because there will be fewer errors in decision making, clients will be more empowered, and better protected from abuse. "The true value of plain English lies in its potential to enable clients to maximize the benefits of legal service."[37] The third benefit is reducing the "incidence of litigation" because users understand the law better and are better able to uphold the law.[38]

The financial industry in some ways is also incorporating the use of plain language into their documents. The Financial Modernization Act of 1999[39] requires financial firms to provide the privacy notices to consumers. While providing these documents to consumers is a good step, reading and using them is a completely different undertaking.

The debate over plain language is unlikely to subside any time soon as different users have diverse needs for language. The main issue for this book is the complexity of the language that may make a statute more difficult to comprehend and use in some cases. If language is more complex it may make it less accessible to users, in this case, candidates, who need to understand the law in order to comply with the law. Reducing the time necessary to comprehend the law may increase compliance with the law and reduce costs to candidates of hiring more lawyers or staff and may make it easier for candidates to decide to run for office. That is the end goal for campaign finance reform—to have more individuals participate in the electoral system. Whether or not that goal is the same for incumbents remains an open question. More testing of plain language gives leverage to its usage in statutes and legislation. There are few empirical studies of how plain language affects comprehension and usability. These are detailed below.

Plain Language Empirical Studies

Testing plain language empirically is not easy. Studies have ranged from a test of readability/grade level to tests of comprehension. The readability tests while valid lack the ability to show that increased readability improved comprehension or outcomes by the end users. Comprehension studies are moving in this direction. Both types of studies are included below because it is necessary to see where we have been and where the research needs to go.

The health care field in particular seems inclined to use readability measures in order to ensure that patients understand their treatment options, understand public health issues, and are clear on medically complicated information. Decision aids have been used to help patients decide on the best medical options, and communication guides help patients understand and remember orders from doctors. For example, Rudd et al.[40] studied the impact of public health communications to the average adult in the United Kingdom and Canada using the National Adult Literacy Survey conducted in the United States in 1992. They found considerable differences in what the average adult could read and understand and the type of language found in public health communications. The authors conducted a case study using new water resource authority regulations that were in the process of being rewritten. They subjected both the new and old regulations to a literacy test to determine how easy or difficult the regulations were to read and understand. The original text scored a readability of 14 and the subsequent revised text scored 8.5—a significant improvement as readability scores improve as they drop to lower grade level reading abilities. After further revision, they reduced the communication to a 6.7.[41] The goal is for this reduction in readability scores to help users understand the information given to them.

One of the most interesting uses of plain language is found in a study done of medical Decision Aids (DAs) given to men facing prostate cancer. The study did a formative evaluation of a decision aid given to these men. The researchers used a focus and then gave a survey to a sample of men recently diagnosed with prostate cancer. The authors gave the group a booklet regarding treatment options revised with plain language guidelines. They compared these focus groups to historical data based on factors such as knowledge of treatment options and knowledge of side effects. The researchers found that the respondents found the revised DAs useful but the effects were not that different from the historical data on knowledge of treatment options and knowledge of side effects. The researchers found gains in the "potential to improve on earlier gains in patient knowledge."[42] They suggest that using plain language is "central to quality [of care], cost containment, safety, and patients' involvement in decisions. They suggest that without attention to literacy, the move toward increased patient participation in health care decisions will exacerbate disparities in access and outcomes.[43]

Both of these examples—water regulations and health care decision aids do well to test the efficacy of the plain language formats. However, the water regulation study uses the readability score that is difficult to understand. At first glance, it is not clear that moving to an 8.5 from a 14 is an improvement.

The measure itself is counterintuitive. Further, the number means little and it is not clear how much of an improvement moving 5.5 points on the scale is, nor is the number itself an intuitive measure of how easy it is to read a document. The health decision aid study failed to find much difference between the treatment and control groups leading to a lack of conclusive evidence that the decision aid helped the patients. These are among the few medical plain language empirical studies available.

In 2010, the Affordable Care Act created the Patient-Centered Outcomes Research Institute (PCORI) to help provide decision aids and communications materials so that patients have easy access to the information they need on their health care decisions. PCORI helps with research on the decision aids to determine if the information provided makes patient choices easier. Hollada et al. study the plain language requirement that PCORI required for all research submitted. According to Hollada et al. PCORI required researchers to submit research on a 6th grade reading level to ensure that individuals would be able to understand and use the information. The study authors found that the PCORI materials were on a 15.97 grade reading level and of the 780 abstracts submitted, none was on the 6th grade reading level.[44] Clearly, the use of plain language has a long way to go if it is to reduce readings to a 6th grade level. A more helpful measure would be to study how users used this material. For example, were more users signing up for programs? Measuring outcome variables might make more sense than just measuring outputs if we want to help patients receive appropriate medical care. Even a special edition of the journal *Medical Writing*[45] was dedicated to plans and ways that the medical field can make language more readable for users. Unfortunately, none of the articles empirically tests whether or not the methods of making medical language more user-friendly work.

The plain language movement has much support and discussion about the movement, but the empirical evidence that plain language documents actually improve use and understanding is scanty. Scholars need to know if plain language increases the readability of documents and other media. We also need to understand if readability has an effect on outcomes—legal, medical, or otherwise. Masson and Waldron[46] test the question of whether or not contracts created in legal language and then converted to plain language increase the comprehension for the average reader and what changes in the document are most effective for comprehension. Masson and Waldron's study used legal documents that were most likely to be read by the general public. These included a mortgage agreement, an agreement for property sale, a bank loan document and a lease renewal document. The authors then drafted each of these documents into three different versions that were tested against the original.

1. The first revision removed archaic terms such as hereinafter and heretofore.
2. In the second version [The plain language version] "extremely long sentences were broken up into shorter sentences and difficult words were replaced with simpler terms. References to contracting parties (i.e., mortgagee and mortgagor) were replaced with personal pronouns "you" and "I"
3. The third revision replaced legalese terms (mortgagor/mortgagee) with simple words or they defined these terms in the text.[47]

Masson and Waldron tested the effects of plain language two ways (1) the speed of reading and (2) comprehension. The reading time results indicated that the respondents were able to increase their reading speeds on the legal-terms-defined document. This change was statistically significant. The authors conclude that because the legal terms were removed or defined, the document was easier to read thus resulting in the faster times.[48]

On the comprehension tasks, the subjects were tested in two different ways. They were asked to paraphrase the document and to answer questions about the document. On the paraphrase task, the use of plain language [versions 2 and 3] resulted in a significant increase in the ability of the subjects to paraphrase the documents. In addition, when the respondents paraphrased the first version (archaic terms removed) of the document the responses were more complete than when the respondents paraphrased the original version of the document.[49]

The "question answering" task was also used to test comprehension. The author's analysis concludes, "The use of plain language improved the accuracy of decisions [on the questions]." Looking at the cases "in which a response was made, the percentage of correct responses . . . across the original and archaic terms removed versions was 69 percent correct; across the plain language and legal-terms-defined version it was 84 percent."[50]

It is clear from Masson and Waldron's assessment that plain language improves the reading comprehension of the documents. Their study is also generalizable because it uses documents that average people would be likely to encounter.[51] It is also notable that the authors do not use readability or grade level assessments of the documents. Unlike other studies, they did not simply measure the "readability" but tested empirically for comprehension. While readability and grade level ratings have their uses, at the end of the day, we want to ensure that people are able to comprehend what they read.

Masson and Waldron's use of a legal-terms-defined version (version 3) is interesting because legalese is an important target of plain language. It is also very important in jury instructions. These instructions to juries—if not clear—could endanger a defendant's freedom. Severence et al.[52] look at jury instructions for clarification. This study tests standard versus revised jury instructions to see if jurors understand them. For a sample, they use previous jurors and current citizens on jury duty. The subjects are shown a mock trial produced to simulate reality as closely as possible. Once the "trial" is over, subjects were given a version of the jury instructions. One version was the normal pattern jury instructions and the second version was the revised jury instructions. After getting the instructions, each of the two groups divided and randomly assigned into one of two groups—a deliberate group and a non-deliberate group. The deliberate group was allowed to begin deliberations for up to thirty minutes. After deliberating, this group received a questionnaire regarding the instructions to test for comprehension. The second, non-deliberation group, was given the questionnaire immediately after viewing the trial. In addition to the questionnaire, the authors asked all jurors to give their definitions for terms such as "reasonable doubt" and "intent."[53]

Concerning the comprehension of the jury instructions, "jurors who heard the revised instructions tended to make fewer errors [on the questionnaire] than jurors who heard pattern instructions," with the difference in means statistically significant at the .05 level.[54] The jurors who deliberated who received revised instructions were found to have fewer errors on the questionnaire than those jurors who received the pattern instructions. Therefore, the authors find that when accompanied by an opportunity to deliberate, the revised instructions did improve comprehension on average.

The authors also asked the subjects to rate the instructions on a 1–5 scale where one is "not at all effective" and five is "effective." They found that the ex-jurors were less likely to benefit from the revised instructions versus the pattern instructions. The current jurors reported that the revised instructions more effective than the pattern instructions. As the authors point out, this could be indicative of the higher level of education among ex-jurors (14.6 years) versus current jurors (13.8); or it could be indicative of self-selection among the ex-jurors.[55]

As a final test, the subjects were asked to paraphrase the meaning of the legal terms "reasonable doubt," "intent" and "prior convictions." The authors found a higher number of correct paraphrases on the revised instructions than incorrect, especially for those groups who were allowed to deliberate.[56] Using questionnaires and paraphrase testing in both of the above cases seems to show that revising the language of documents/media helps to improve the comprehension of the respondents.

Government reports also show the effects of plain language. The Senate Report on the Plain Writing Act of 2009 gives some details of the effects of the law. The US Department of Veterans Affairs rewrote selected form letters in plain writing and tracked the effects. One unit sent out the standard letter and another unit sent out a letter in plain language. More people responded to the plain language letter than the standard letter (45 percent vs. 29 percent). They also found that all of the responses to the plain language letter were complete, while 18 percent of responses to the standard letter were not. The report also found reduced customer service phone calls (1,100 reduced to 200) regarding the letter.[57]

Many of the plain language empirical studies simply test the outputs of implementing plain language, such as an increase in veterans' responses. An empirical test on the readability of insurance contracts and subsequent legal action was researched by a team from the Netherlands. They conducted an experiment very similar in scope and nature to the one explained in the next chapter of this book.[58] The authors used a "difficult" and an "easy" version of an insurance contract to demonstrate that the easy contract was more clearly understood by consumers. The subsequent test of the consumers' willingness to engage in legal action because of a contract dispute, the authors conclude is evidence of confidence and trust in the insurance company resulting from consumers' understanding of the contract itself. The consumers reading the difficult contract scored 47.61 on a Dutch version of the Flesch-Kincaid reading ease scale using a scale of 0–120 with lower scores indicating more difficult to read or "illegible" and higher scores indicating easier to read. The consumer reading the easy version scored 61.18. Further discussion of this study's results is in the next chapter. On whole, the consumers in this study who read the easier version of the contract had different outcomes than those who read the harder version. This study, similar to the next chapter's, indicates that when plain language is used outcomes are improved. Users are better able to understand and then use the knowledge gained to make different choices in their lives.

CONCLUSION

From this look at the plain language research, it is clear there is desirability for using plain language at least in particular situations. The research clearly shows that readability is improved with the use of plain language. Indeed the next chapter of this book uses a plain language experiment to demonstrate this further. What the plain language literature lacks is a wide body of empirical research showing the effectiveness of using plain language to make learning or compliance less costly in terms of time and effort. Other than the studies reviewed here, there is very little research showing that the use of plain language is useful in increasing effectiveness of documents. The studies above by Severence et al.,[59] Masson and Waldron,[60] and Van Boom et al., all show positive signs of effectiveness when using plain language. However, a few studies are not enough to show effects on policy outcomes when using plain language. The study of plain language needs to move in this direction in order to maintain momentum.

The US government has adopted plain language policies with little to no evidence of their effectiveness on citizen outcomes. The following chapter moves in this direction. An experiment using campaign finance contribution statutes translated into plain language tests how much respondents comprehend the statute, but also tests how they use the statute to answer the questions. Based upon the results of this experiment and the studies noted above, chapters 7–9 of the book use the readability scores and word counts to measure participation rates of candidates in elections. This research adds to the plain language research by scoring each state's campaign finance statutes on readability and word count measures.

NOTES

1. John Gibbons, *Language and the Law*, ed. John Gibbons (Harlow, Essex, UK: Longman Group UK Limited, 1994).
2. Ibid., 7.
3. Ibid.
4. www.plainlanguage.gov, "Improving Communication from the Federal Government to the Public," accessed from https://www.plainlanguage.gov.
5. Ibid.
6. US Senate, "Plain Writing Act of 2010," in *124 STAT. 2862* (Washington, DC, 2010).
7. S. Stableford and W. Mettger, "Plain Language: A Strategic Response to the Health Literacy Challenge," *Journal of Public Health Policy* 28, no. 1 (2007): 79.
8. Jan Root and Sue Stableford, "Easy to Read Consumer Communications: A Missing Link in Medicaid Managed Care," *Journal of Health Politics, Policy and Law* 4, no. 1 (1999).
9. Rudolph Flesch, "A New Readability Yardstick," *Journal of Applied Psychology* 32, no. 3 (1948).
10. By affixes, the authors refer to suffixes, prefixes attached to the root of the word.
11. Flesch, "A New Readability Yardstick."
12. Edward Fry, "A Readability Formula That Saves Time," *Journal of Reading* 11, no. 7 (1968).
13. Ibid.
14. G. Harry McLaughlin, "Smog Grading—a New Readability Formula," ibid.12, no. 8 (1969).
15. SMOG is sometimes called the Simple Measure of Gobbledygook, but McLaughlin himself credited the name to a reference to an earlier FOG index (1969).
16. Philip Ley and Tony Florio, "The Use of Readability Formulas in Health Care.," *Psychology, Health & Medicine* 1, no. 1 (1996).
17. Root and Stableford, "Easy to Read Consumer Communications: A Missing Link in Medicaid Managed Care."
18. Ibid.
19. Janice (Ginny) Redish, "Readability Formulas Have Even More Limitations Than Klare Dicusses," *ACM Journal of Computer Documentation* 24, no. 3 (2000).
20. Roslyn Petelin, "Considering Plain Language: Issues and Iniatives," *Corporate Communications: An International Journal* 15, no. 2 (2010).
21. The use of readability versus grade level scores is an empirical question that is not adequately addressed in the plain language literature. The use of either is not tested in this book. However, both measures were evaluated using factor analysis. See chapter 6 for details.
22. Redish, "Readability Formulas Have Even More Limitations Than Klare Dicusses."
23. Hilary Frooman, "Lawyers and Readability," *Journal of Business Communication* 18, no. 4 (1981).
24. Peter Crow, "Plain English: What Counts Besides Readability?," ibid. 25, no. 1 (1988).

25. Ibid.
26. William J. Scheibal, "The Effectiveness of Plain English Laws: A Legal Perspective," ibid. 23, no. 3 (1986).
27. Rabeea Assy, "Can the Law Speak Directly to Its Subjects? The Limitations of Plain Language," *Journal of Law and Society* 38 (2011).
28. Ibid.
29. Ibid.
30. Burt A. Leete, "Plain Language Legislation: A Comparison of Approaches," *American Business Law Journal* 18 (1981).
31. Ibid.
32. Brian Hunt, "Plain Language in Legislative Drafting: Is It Really the Answer?" *Statute Law Review* 23, no. 1 (2002): 44.
33. Ibid.
34. Richard Wydick, "Plain English for Lawyers," *California Law Review* 66, no. 4 (1978).
35. Ruth Sullivan, "The Promise of Plain Language Drafting," *McGill Law Review* 47 (2001).
36. Assy, "Can the Law Speak Directly to Its Subjects? The Limitations of Plain Language."
37. Ibid.
38. Ibid.
39. Congress of the United States, "Gramm–Leach–Bliley Act (Glba)," in *Financial Services Modernization Act of 1999* (Washington, DC: US Congress, 1999).
40. R Rudd et al., "Rewriting Public Health Information in Plain Language," *Journal of Health Communications* 9, no. 3 (2004).
41. Ibid.
42. Margaret Holmes-Rovner et al., "Evidence-Based Patient Choice: A Prostate Cancer Decision Aid in Plain Language," *BMC Medical Informatics and Decision Making* 5, no. 16 (2005): 10.
43. Ibid.
44. Jacqueline L. Hollada et al., "Readability Assessment of Patient-Centered Outcomes Research Institute Public Abstracts in Relation to Accessibility," *Epidemiology* July (2017).
45. Medical Writing, "Medical Writing," *Medical Writing* 24, no. 1 (2015).
46. M.J. Masson and M Waldron, "Comprehension of Legal Contracts by Non-Experts: Effectiveness of Plain Language Redrafting," *Applied Cognitive Psychology* 8, no. 1 (1994).
47. Ibid., 71.
48. Ibid.
49. Ibid.
50. Ibid., 76–77.
51. The study used clerical staff from the University of Victoria and city residents taking courses through a university extension program. Whether or not these people are "average" is debatable.
52. L Severence, E Greene, and E Loftus, "Toward Criminal Jury Instructions That Jurors Can Understand," *The Journal of Criminal Law & Criminology* 75, no. 1 (1984).
53. Ibid.
54. Ibid., 218.
55. Ibid.
56. Ibid.
57. US Senate, "Plain Writing Act of 2009," (2009).
58. Willem H. Van Boom, Pieter Desmet, and Mark Van Dam, "'If It's Easy to Read, It's Easy to Claim'—The Effect of the Readability of Insurance Contracts on Consumer Expectations and Conflict Behaviour," *Journal of Consumer Policy* 39 (2016).
59. Severence, Greene, and Loftus, "Toward Criminal Jury Instructions That Jurors Can Understand."
60. Masson and Waldron, "Comprehension of Legal Contracts by Non-Experts: Effectiveness of Plain Language Redrafting."

Chapter Five

Plain Language Experiment

Allowing more citizens to participate in the electoral system through running for office or contributing to campaigns is an important democratizing goal of campaign finance reform laws. In the past, the campaign finance system allowed candidates to collect large donations from a small number of contributors. Democratization reduces the amount of contributions in an effort to push candidates to collect smaller donations from a larger base of support. This democratization effort also aimed to reduce the perception of corruption and payoffs where big donors allegedly gave money to candidates in return for votes. These anticorruption efforts focus on engendering the trust of citizens in the system. As more people become involved in the political arena, the hope of a democratic system would have a ready pool of citizens wanting to participate by running for office.

We want this pool of candidates to be diverse. Right now, we know that most candidates come from a pool of small business owners, career professionals, lawyers, or educators.[1] These people flowing into the political arena might already be familiar with regulations or have the resources to be able to hire political consultants and campaign managers to manage the rules and regulations of running for office. This leaves a significant portion of the American citizenry who are outside of the political arena at a disadvantage if they should want to run for office. The outsiders would have to learn the ropes so to speak. They would have to figure out all the rules, regulations, and processes involved in running a political campaign. Understanding if the campaign regulations are hard to comprehend and use is a central part of this study. First, there must be a way to measure the complexity of the rules and regulations. Measuring the difficulty of comprehension and compliance with rules and regulations is a difficult task. One way, tested here, uses the plain language of the rules and regulations. Theoretically, the "difficulty of understanding" and "compliance costs" are wrapped up in the concept of complexity. The rules and regulations add a learning and compliance burden which together create complex statutes.

The research on learning costs particularly in public administration research is robust. Candidates must gather all the required information to fill out a myriad of forms, figure out the candidacy requirements such as petitions and financial affidavit forms. Potential candidates must hire staffers or find qualified volunteers to fill staffing roles. In particular, the treasurer position is important to ensure that only qualified contributions are accepted, deposited correctly, and spent in accordance with campaign finance rules. These are just a few of the tasks facing a novice or potential candidate. As Moynihan el al. find, these rules and regulations are a fog of information[2] that potential candidates must wade through in order to get on the ballot. The campaign finance regulations may be so complex and embroiled in legalese that they are actually a deterrent to those wishing to run for public office. If the statutes are difficult to learn and comprehend, the statutes may fail to uphold the democratization goal of Campaign Finance Reform. The complexity of the law imposes a learning cost on candidates running for office.

In particular, novice candidates without campaign organizations may find the complexity costs add to the start-up costs of beginning a campaign. Having to hire staffers in order to comply with complex regulations is expensive and may be beyond the means of everyday citizens. In contrast, an incumbent or repeat candidate already has staff or staff volunteers ready to work; they have already been through this learning and compliance curve at least once. The rules and regulations may serve as a barrier to entry to everyday citizens contemplating a run for office.

Facing this environment is daunting enough if you are a successful lawyer, business professional, or educator—the professions from which most candidates come.[3] However, if you are a novice candidate the complexity of the system may add a psychological cost to the aversion to risk you already experience.

The learning, compliance, and psychological costs inherent in the administrative burden of the campaign finance system create systematic complexity. To study this burden or complexity, I use the written language of the statute. Complexity of written documents using language is tested using medical decision aids, jury instructions, and insurance contracts. Van Boom et al.'s experiment is especially revealing considering the similarity between their work and this experiment presented below. First, they use the whole contract to ensure external validity of the experiment. They contend that if only the relevant portion of the contract were used in their experiment it would not mimic real-life scenarios.[4] The entire campaign finance contribution statute is used in the below experiment because it was important to mimic the situation in which a novice candidate might find themselves. A good place to start learning the campaign finance contribution rules and regulations is to look to the statutes.

The Plain Language Experiment

The Plain Language movement advocates creating documents that are easy to read and comprehend, yet as pointed out in the previous chapter, few scholars have systematically studied such a contention. Understanding if the statutes are complex and if that complexity is deterring everyday citizens from running for office is important. This study asks if readers are better able to understand and use the North Carolina general statute on campaign contributions if written in plain language versus the original statute.

Using the plain language protocols introduced in the previous chapter to rewrite the NC campaign finance statute creates a more readable version of the law. The protocols for rewriting documents in plain language include changing legal terms such as "notwithstanding" to "with the exception of" to make it easier for everyday people to understand. It also recommends exchanging multisyllabic words with shorter ones, shortening sentences to ten words or fewer and changing legal names such as "mortgagee" with personal pronouns "you" and "he/she."[5] After rewriting the statute, it was sent to a plain language listserve of plain language experts. Their comments and feedback were incorporated into the rewritten NC statute ensuring that the plain language statute complied with plain language protocols.

Tests using readability or grade reading levels are common today utilizing the number of syllables per word, the number of words per sentence, and the number of sentences.[6] While plain language scholars debate if such tests of readability are valid, a simple readability test lacks the ability to show an actual connection between readability of the statute and comprehension level of the reader/user. To avoid this validity problem as discussed in the previous chapter, this study used a comprehension test and a usability test using both versions of the statutes. The reworded statute and the original statute were assigned randomly to individuals. It was expected that those who read the plain language statutes would have a higher score on a test of their knowledge of the law than those who read the original statute.

Usability is important to the study of plain language because while comprehending is important, being able to use what you read is even more important. This study also added usability tests to see how respondents used the statute. By asking respondents to rate the clarity of the statute, we get a sense of how hard/easy it was for the student to understand the statute. Respondents also were asked how many times they needed to refer to the statute and how closely they read the statute. Referring back to the statute more often would indicate a need to clarify the information. It also goes back to the premise of the study that more time and effort is necessary if the statutes are more complex. Respondents were asked how closely they read the statutes. A close reading would take more time and effort than a cursory scan of the material. If respondents refer back to the original statutes more often and/or respondents rate the original statutes as unclear this would support the hypothesis that the statutes are complex. Respondents as proxies for everyday citizens would have to spend more time and effort to learn the statutes in order to comply with the statutes.

The Statutes

The statutes chosen for this study were the North Carolina general statutes on election contributions.[7] Choosing the contribution limits section of the election statutes was important because this section is pertinent to anyone ever wanting to run for office. If you run for office, you have to know this information, or have a close advisor who knows it for you. The contribution limits were chosen because this legislation is one of the major reform tools used to meet the goals of campaign finance reform. The reform rationale is that if contribution size were limited, politicians would need to seek out a larger volume of smaller contributions in order to make up the monetary difference for their campaign coffers. By seeking out more contributions, they would contact more potential contributors and thus more people would be contributing to campaigns. The idea is that more people contributing spreads out the democratic effect of the reform.[8] In addition, contribution limits are intended to reduce overall spending by candidates by making fundraising more difficult.[9] When campaign finance statutes are more restrictive they favor challengers and not incumbents.[10] However, Hogan's analysis does not include the start-up costs of running for the first time or as a novice—including a knowledge buildup, hiring campaign staffers and aides.

Limiting contributions is one of the main tools of campaign finance reform because the public's perception is that there is too much money in campaigns. Thompson and Moncrief's[11] analysis of contribution limits shows that the reasons for this perception vary from just the vast amount of money being collected, to the idea among the public that this money must be contributed in hopes of a quid pro quo situation. Enactment of contribution limits is an attempt to try to reduce the amount of money in campaigns with the thought that if there are fewer contributions, there will be less corruption or the appearance thereof. The other potential advantage of campaign finance is to reduce the appearance of impropriety on the part of politicians accepting "big" donations from a small group of donors.[12] If they can no longer contribute the "big" donations, then there is less appearance of impropriety and the system is more open, the people trust the system more and therefore it is more democratic.

If the goal is to increase the number of contributors and as a result increase the net contributions, a candidate must know the law on how much he/she may accept and how much a person may contribute to a campaign. In order to find campaign finance information a candidate in North Carolina would first need to look at the statutes to find this information. If you were a lawyer running for office, or a seasoned politician, this may not be difficult. However, if you are new to politics and are an average citizen, then it could be difficult to find and understand this information. The present study seeks to test if an average citizen would be able to comprehend the original statute (when he or she located it) or if they would be better able to understand a plain language statute.

Study Design

To test this hypothesis the study randomly assigned respondents to read one of the two versions of the contribution statutes. One version is the original statute and the second version is the same statute rewritten in plain language. I rewrote the original statute into plain language using plain language protocols. I eliminated multisyllabic words into smaller words, substituted confusing terms for personal pronouns, and eliminated excessive wording. The rewritten/plain language version was submitted to a plain language listserve by Dr. Deborah Bosley, at the time of this writing, a retired member of the English Department of UNC–Charlotte. She is a plain language expert. Comments on the rewritten version were solicited from the listserve and incorporated into the plain language version of the statute. Following this procedure ensured that the rewritten statute was indeed a plain language version of the statute. The original statute has a Flesch Reading ease score of 28.71, while the plain language version reading ease is 42.99. Keeping in mind that the higher the score the easier the document is to read, the plain language version was clearly easier based on this score. On the grade reading level, rewriting the statute decreased the score from a school grade of 14.95 to 11.17 or from 15th grade (college) to 11th grade (high school). These grade levels are appropriate given that candidates must be at least eighteen years old in most states to run for the state legislature.

After reading the statutes, the study respondents answered a questionnaire pertaining to knowledge and understanding of Campaign Finance contribution statutes in North Carolina. If rewriting North Carolina's general statutes on Campaign Contributions in Plain Language increases the comprehension level of the reader this should be an indicator that the statutes themselves may be complex and may impose learning, compliance, psychological costs on potential candidates. Those costs may deter candidates from participating in the electoral system. The first hypothesis tests this idea. *H1: Respondents who read the plain language statute should have higher grade percentages than those respondents who read the original statute.*

An experimental design tests this research question. The experiment consisted of a questionnaire (see appendix A) given to respondents after reading the statutes. The questions pertained to knowledge and understanding of Campaign Finance statutes in North Carolina. The test should ascertain the level of understanding of the statutes after exposure. While a pre/post-test design was considered in order to test the level of comprehension before and after the reading; a post-test only design is most useful in this case because using a pre-test/post-test design may create a situation where the respondent "learns" by reading questions prior to reading the selection. If they read the questions, the respondents may get clues as to what information is most important prior to reading the selection. Further, little benefit is gained by giving a pretest. The questionnaire was not a test and to replicate conditions in reality, the full statute is presented, and respondents could look back at the material as many times as needed. Referring back to the statute is one of the independent variables measuring how respondents reacted to the material. Having a treatment and a control group allowed analysis of the different comprehension levels rather than just evaluating "learning." Using random assignment of subjects assigns those who may have some exposure to the law evenly between the treatment and control groups. This establishes internal validity for the idea that the simpler statutes lead to higher comprehension levels even if the level of respondent comprehension before the test is unknown. This study uses a post-test only design to avoid the learning problem.

Respondents were given one of two versions of the statutes (see appendix B). The first version is the statute in its original form and the second is the statute rewritten in plain language. Subjects were assigned randomly one of the statute versions to create control and treatment groups. Once the respondents read one of the statutes, they answered the same statute questionnaire. The comprehension questions are specific to the statute on Contribution Limits. The usability questions were described above. The contribution information queried is not general knowledge information, but is information typically only known either by candidates or by campaign staff.

A convenience sample of university undergraduates was chosen for the fall 2011 survey.[13] Studying actual candidates might add to the external validity of the study, but the point of the study is to test those everyday citizens who may run for office. If we sampled state legislators, for example, they would have already successfully completed at least one campaign and we assume would have "learned" at least some part of the campaign finance statutes. A sample of individuals without previous campaign experience to ensure objectivity to the material is ideal. University undergraduates would not be expected to know this information. Even undergraduates who may have worked on campaigns would not be expected to have previous access to this information, since we assume that these respondents' work on campaigns is generally limited to phone banking and get out the vote efforts. Any respondents working on campaigns would have little access to technical campaign information. The respondents chosen for the experiment were undergraduate students in the introductory political science, criminal justice, or economics courses at UNC–Charlotte in the fall 2011 semester. To ensure internal validity, even though respondents were assigned randomly, control questions were included such as items related to campaign experience or knowledge. The total enrollment in all of the surveyed classes was 1,600 which given our responses of 633 gives a response rate of 39 percent. However, it is clear that not every student was in attendance on the survey date so if we estimate that 80 percent of the 1,600 respondents were in class on the survey dates, this would give us a sample population of 1,280 and a response rate of 49 percent. However, not all students answered the comprehension questions. Of the 633 respondents, 49 students did not answer, did not use a #2 pencil lead, or otherwise failed to complete either the comprehension or demographic questions. This leaves a question response rate of 45 percent or 584 respondents.

Collection of data for the testing of the hypothesis came from the survey instrument using examination scantrons normally utilized on exams in these introductory classes. Because respondents in introductory classes should be familiar with the scantrons, this should alleviate any testing confusion for the survey. The comprehension grade variable ranged from 0–100 and is based on the answers to the survey questions found in appendix A (see questions 1–8). The scantrons were run through the university's optical scanner, which is a proven technique for accurate grading. Using the optical scanner should reduce human error in tabulating the grades. The comprehension grade scores are the dependent variable and are interval in nature because they are percentages of those questions correctly answered. There were twenty-three questions on the questionnaire but only eight of them were comprehension questions. The rest were control variable questions.

The main independent variable—the statutes—is expected to explain the differences in the comprehension grade scores. The statute variable is dichotomous with the original statute coded as 0, and the plain language statute coded as 1. Other independent variables in the model are designed to take into account the usability of the statutes. These variables include a self-report of how closely the respondents read the statute, whether or not the respondents thought the statute was clear when they read it, and how many times they had to refer back to the statute to answer the questions (see appendix A for the wording of these questions). Knowing how familiar the respondents were with campaign finance law was important for the study, so the analysis controls for factors that measure familiarity as well. These variables examine if the respondents have ever considered running for office, worked on a campaign, if anyone in their family had ever run for office, or if anyone in their family was a lawyer. Control variables were included for gender, race, ethnicity, age, class standing (freshmen, sophomore, junior, and senior), married, and level of family education.

Because of the percentage nature of the dependent variable Generalized Linear Model (GLM) regression was used to test the hypothesis. The students' percentages are bounded by 0 and 100 and thus GLM is the most appropriate regression tool. The expected results of this experiment and regression are that there will be a statistically significant relationship between the students' comprehension scores and which version of the statute read. If a statistically significant relationship is found, it should show that the less complex statutes are easier to understand and comprehend than the more complex statutes.

Study Results

In the experiment, 338 respondents read the original statute and 294 read the plain language version. There were 49 cases with missing data excluded from the analysis. Analysis of missing data found no patterns or concerns. It appears that respondents randomly forgot to answer or they randomly skipped questions. These responses were eliminated from the analysis.

The first section of this analysis shows how students used the statutes to answer the comprehension questions. Showing the usability of the statutes is important because understanding the statute is one part of the problem, but actually engaging with the statute in order to understand it is just as important. If the language is so complicated that users do not care to read the entire statute, they miss valuable information. In the Van Boom et al. study, they found that when users read that statute that was easier to read, they were more likely to take action afterward. The respondents of that study took action to secure benefits for themselves. In a similar fashion, this study hopes to show that respondents who read the plain language (easier) version, were more likely to score well on the comprehension questions. If respondents score better on those questions, they are more likely to have an easier time running a campaign correctly.

In figure 5.1, we see that for the different versions of the statute it is clear that when respondents read the plain language statute more respondents reported reading it very closely than those who read the original statute. More respondents reported reading the original statute somewhat or not very closely (302) (combining those two categories) than those in the same categories who read the plain language statute (251). Looking at the categories where respondents reported not reading the statute, the differences in the original statute (14) and plain language statute (6) are more evident. From the descriptive statistics here, it is clear that respondents presented with the original statute chose not to read it at all or not very closely when compared to the plain language statute. It seems evident that respondents either chose not to read, or not to read the more complex original statute as closely as the plain language version. Importantly this reminds us of the learning costs in rules and regulations. It takes time and effort to read and understand these statutes. Clearly, the difficulty of the language deterred students from reading the statute.

Respondents were also asked to rate the clarity of the readings. Respondents who read the Plain Language version of the statute reported more Very Clear responses (71) than those respondents who read the original statute (47). Those who read the original statute reported more Somewhat Unclear and Very Unclear responses (111) than those reading the Plain Language statute (62). These descriptive graphs again indicate that respondents reading the Plain Language statute reported more clarity than those respondents who read the original version.

Table 5.1 presents the results of the GLM regression analysis for the Plain Language experiment. Respondents who read the plain language version of the contribution statutes had a 3.5 percent change in the log odds on the questionnaire on average than those respondents who read the original statute. Or when respondents read the plain language version of the statute, they increased the odds that they would score well by 3.5 percent. Respondents clearly scored better when they read the plain language version of the statute as depicted in figure 5.4, indicating that when they read the plain language version, they understood the information contained in it and then successfully answered questions on the statute.

On the "closely read statute" variable (coded from less closely to more closely read), respondents who indicated reading the plain language statute more closely had a 28 percent change in the log odds on the comprehension

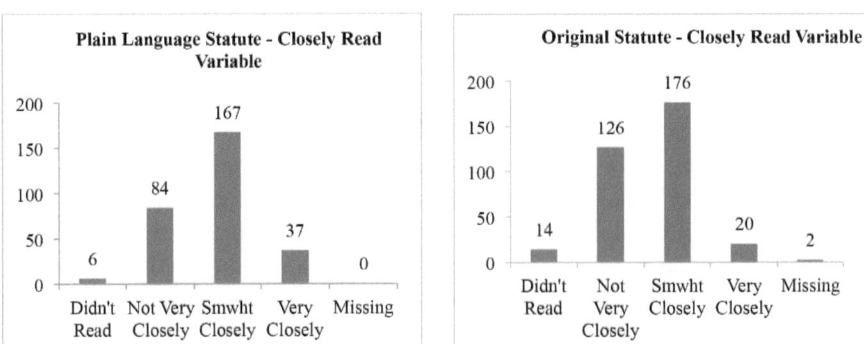

Figure 5.1. How closely do you feel you read the reading?

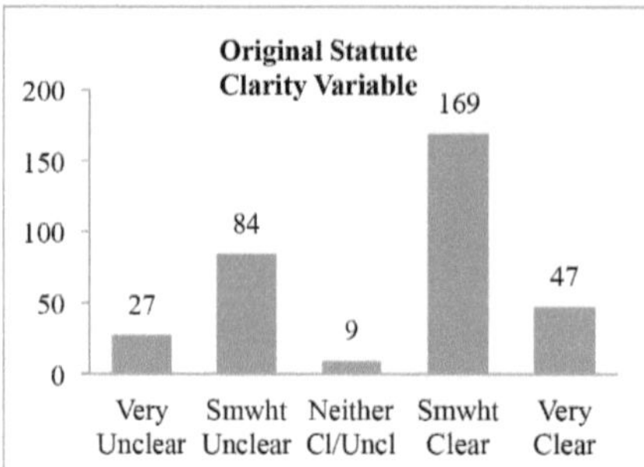

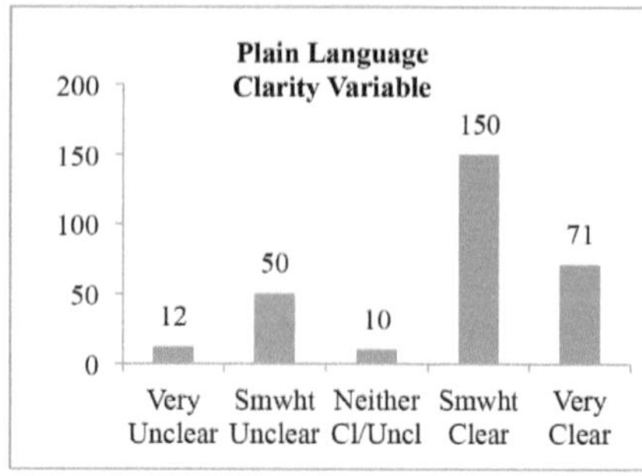

Figure 5.2. How clear did you think the readings were?

questionnaire on average than those respondents who read the plain language statute less closely. This relationship is statistically significant at the .01 level. This indicates that respondents who read the statute more closely increased the odds of scoring higher on the survey. The crux of this book is that candidates would have to spend more time learning the campaign finance legislation if it is complex and thus might be deterred from running for office. This current analysis seems to indicate that respondents took extra time to be able to do better. Respondents had read the statute more closely which translates into more time spent reading the statute in order to score better. This significance allows us to reject the null hypothesis with 99 percent confidence that respondents had to read the statute more closely to score better.

As a control for perceived clarity, respondents were asked to rate the statute for clarity (from "very unclear" to "very clear"). As the rating increased, respondents had a 14 percent change in the log odds on average. This relationship makes intuitive sense and is statistically significant at the .01 level. It is also an indicator of the effort required to comprehend the statute. As the statute was rated with higher clarity, respondents did better on the questions. From the previous figure 5.2, respondents rated the plain language statute as more clear than the original statute.

Another relationship that is interesting is the number of times a student reported referring back to the reading. Respondents reading either statute reported referring back to the statute similarly in the first two categories (less than 1 and 1–3 times). As the number of times respondents referred back to the reading increased to greater than six, the initial reporting shifts dramatically. When reporting from the last three categories is summed (7–9, >9 times) 53 respondents who read the plain language statute reported needing to refer back to the statute compared to 91 of those who read the original statute. Based on the GLM model results in table 5.1, as respondents reported

Table 5.1. Campaign Finance Statutes and Plain Language

Generalized linear models			Robust Standard Errors
Students Grade Percentage	Which statute read (1 = plain language; 0 = original)	0.035	(0.030)
	How closely did you read the statute?	0.287	(0.052)**
	How clear did you think the reading was?	0.142	(0.040)**
	Have you ever considered running for office?	0.162	(0.083)
	Have you ever worked on a campaign?	-0.044	(0.109)
	Has anyone in your family ever run for office?	-0.072	(0.129)
	Is anyone in your family a lawyer?	0.055	(0.115)
	About how many times did you refer back to the reading?	0.160	(0.035)**
	What is your age?	-0.043	(0.045)
	What is your class standing?	-0.034	(0.039)
	What is your gender?	-0.140	(0.070)*
	Do you consider yourself Hispanic or Latino?	-0.174	(0.070)*
	What race or ethnicity do you consider yourself?	-0.056	(0.031)
	What is your marital status?	-0.100	(0.075)
	What is the highest level of education in your immediate family?	0.040	(0.075)
	Constant	-0.593	(0.519)
N		584	

referencing the statute more often they had a 16 percent increase in the log odds of doing well on the questionnaire on average. In order to score higher, respondents had to refer back to the statute more often. Respondents had to make the effort to go back and check the statute to ensure they got the answer correct. While this relationship is statistically significant at the .01 level, it indicates effort on the part of the respondents to ensure they understood the statute. Going back to reread the statute indicates that it was unclear or hard to comprehend the first time the respondents read it.

Respondents were asked other control questions such as had they ever worked on a campaign (yes = 1, no = 2) and had anyone in their family ever run for office (yes = 1, no = 2). For both of these questions the relationship indicates that when they had worked on a campaign or considered running they scored worse on the questionnaire. Experience was clearly not a factor in this analysis. Respondents who had no experience did worse on the questionnaire as was expected, but not by a statistically significant amount.

Respondents were also asked if they ever considered running for office (yes = 1, no = 2). This analysis indicates that when respondents reported that they had considered running, they increased the odds by 16 percent of doing better on the questions. This brings up an interesting issue as to whether or not the consideration of running for office was affected by which statute the respondents read. This analysis will be done at a later time as it is beyond the scope of this current book.

While most of the relationships found in this analysis are not statistically significant, the data substantively indicate that when respondents read the plain language statute they found it clearer and had to refer back to it less often in order to score better. The above score distributions also indicate that those respondents who read the plain language statutes understood them better than those respondents who read the original statute. The trend line indicates an increasing slope for the respondents who read the plain language statute versus those who read the original statute.

CONCLUSION

This study of the comprehension of North Carolina campaign finance statutes shows that individuals who read the plain language version of the statute

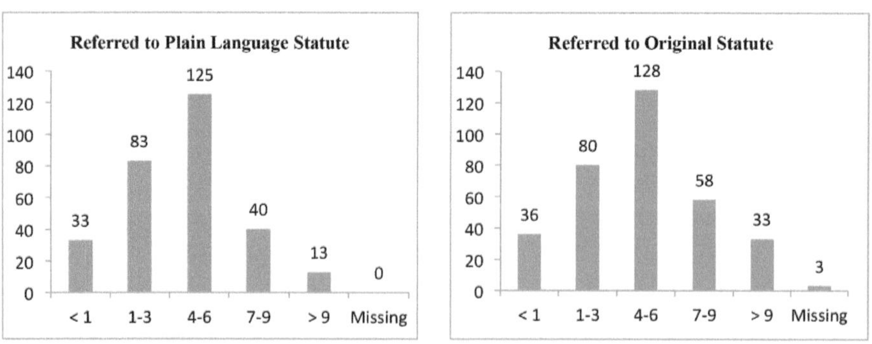

Figure 5.3. While answering this questionnaire, about how many times did you refer back to the reading?

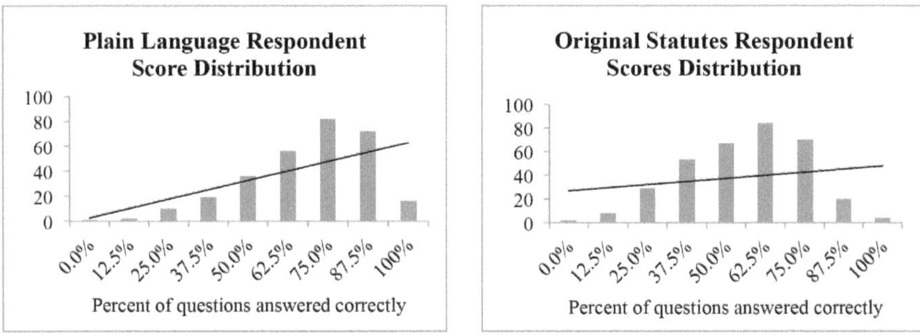

Figure 5.4. Distribution of respondent scores for plain language and original statute reading.

scored higher on a reading comprehension test than those who read the current North Carolina law. While this effect on comprehension levels does not appear large nor it is statistically significant, it is important to note that the control variables measuring statute clarity, referrals back to the reading, and how closely the respondents read the statute, are substantively important as an indicator of how challenging it is to run for office, especially for novices.

Respondents who read the plain language statute more often reported the statute as clear and were more likely to closely read the statute indicating a higher level of engagement with the statute. When responding to the questionnaire, those who read the plain language statute referred back to it on fewer occasions than to the original statute. Finally, those who read the plain language statute, scored better on the comprehension test than those reading the original statute. All of these factors indicate that the plain language statute was more easily accessible and usable than the original statute. Because respondents referred back to the plain language statutes on fewer occasions, it should have taken them less time and effort to use the statute to answer the questions. These findings uphold the contention of this study that the plain language version of the statute decreases the administrative burden or complexity of the campaign finance statute.

However, this study also makes an important contribution because it is the first one that I am aware of that compares the comprehension of plain language to legal text in a current law that users need to use every year running for office. While plain language scholars have long contended that plain language is easier to read, this is one of the first studies to test the contention on an issue of such importance as elections. The most important issue here is that the wording of the statutes could pose complications and problems for individuals running for office, especially for the first time.

Campaign finance statutes are an important regulator of elections in the United States and campaign finance reform efforts have targeted increasing participation as one of its main goals. Therefore, if the statutes are difficult to comprehend, the cost of learning and complying may limit the ability of everyday citizens to participate in the electoral system. If a candidate cannot comprehend the statutes that govern his ability to run for office, he may decide not to run at all or may have difficulty with compliance. In order to look at this question this study rewrote campaign contribution statutes using plain language. Based on the above results, it is clear that when the respondents read the original contribution limits statute they scored worse on the comprehension questionnaire than the plain language version.

NOTES

1. Richard L. Fox and Jennifer L. Lawless, "To Run or Not to Run for Office: Explaining Nascent Political Ambition," *American Journal of Political Science* 49, no. 3 (2005).
2. Moynihan, Herd, and Harvey, "Adminsitrative Burden: Learning, Psychological, and Compilance Costs in Citizen-State Interactions."
3. Fox and Lawless, "To Run or Not to Run for Office: Explaining Nascent Political Ambition."
4. Van Boom, Desmet, and Van Dam, "'If It's Easy to Read, It's Easy to Claim'—the Effect of the Readability of Insurance Contracts on Consumer Expectations and Conflict Behaviour."
5. Masson and Waldron, "Comprehension of Legal Contracts by Non-Experts: Effectiveness of Plain Language Redrafting."; Rudd et al., "Rewriting Public Health Information in Plain Language."
6. Root and Stableford, "Easy to Read Consumer Communications: A Missing Link in Medicaid Managed Care."; Flesch, "A New Readability Yardstick."; McLaughlin, "Smog Grading—A New Readability Formula."
7. "North Carolina General Statutes Ch. 22, § 163 278.13."
8. Gross and Goidel, *The States of Campaign Finance Reform*.
9. Eom and Gross, "Democratization Effects of Campaign Contribution Limits in Gubernatorial Elections."
10. Robert E. Hogan, "Challenger Emergence, Incumbent Success and Electoral Accoutability in State Legislative Elections," *The Journal of Politics* 66, no. 4 (2004).
11. "Exploring the "Lost World" of Campaign Finance."
12. Gross and Goidel, *The States of Campaign Finance Reform*.
13. A pilot survey was given to a section of the Introduction to American Government courses in the spring 2011. This test was expected to ascertain any technical or logistical problems with the survey and to determine the general response level in the classroom. A technical problem was found with the collection of the materials after the respondents had taken the survey. The original statute was printed on white paper and the plain language statute was printed on yellow paper in order to ensure that the surveys and responses were collected correctly. Taking this precaution helped some but not enough and there was potential for a mix-up especially doing this with a larger sample size. In the fall 2011 survey, an item was added in order to differentiate between the original and plain language versions to ensure that the correct survey was being tabulated. The pilot study indicated no other changes in the design.

Chapter Six

Candidate Decisions

In their well-regarded book, *Who Runs for the Legislature*, Moncrief, Squire, and Jewell note, "State legislative elections today do not attract enough candidates. . . . Potential challengers are scared off by the difficulties of a campaign against a better known, more politically experienced, well-funded incumbent."[1] Why would an individual give up a normal, private life and subject themselves to grueling campaign schedules, endless fund-raising, and reputational risk in order to run for office? The traditional literature points us to the utility equation[2] where the benefits and potential utility of holding office are greater than the costs. But what about those costs? Many scholars have looked at the costs of running for office and tallied up totals. Still we find that individuals see the benefits outweighing the costs. This book takes on a new look at costs and adds regulatory complexity to the list of costs borne by individuals seeking office. As noted in chapter 2 on complexity, there are learning and psychological costs, which are intangible and harder to measure, and tangible or compliance costs such as forms, fees, or petitions. These tangible costs are more easily measured using indices or adding up the fees. Intangible costs of learning and the potential psychological costs of the regulatory system are difficult to measure, but may be measured using the language of the statutes. The regulatory environment differs from state to state. "Because of the wide variety of campaign finance laws in different states, fundraising is harder in some states than others."[3] These regulations and costs of the regulations may create an additive effect of reducing the number of people willing to run for office.

Many factors affect candidates' decisions to run for office. Regulatory complexity is one factor not found extensively in the candidate emergence literature. It is important to note some of the limitations in candidate emergence literature. First, some scholars study US congressional elections and some look at state legislative elections. This study looks at state legislative elections. The factors reviewed here affect both state legislative and US congressional elections similarly unless noted. Second, scholars use different categories for the various factors affecting candidate emergence. Some scholars focus on district and candidate factors while others focus on strategic, political, institutional, personal, and contextual factors affecting candidate decisions. Grouping these factors into strategic, political/institutional, and personal categories is useful because it conforms to much of the candidate emergence literature.

Finally, when dealing with candidate emergence we are just beginning to understand what Fox and Lawless[4] call "nascent" candidate ambition. Most studies look at more developed or "progressive" ambition by looking at how challengers react to incumbents in various races.[5] While Fox and Lawless are on the right path for the future, the literature bears scrutiny on both nascent and progressive candidates because it gives us an overview of the various factors that could affect any stage of the candidate's decision, whether it is nascent or somewhat developed. These limitations contribute to the various and sometimes confusing or conflicting factors affecting candidate decisions.

Because there is little research compiled on the administrative burden or complexity of campaign finance statutes, it is important to understand what it is scholars know about how candidates make their decisions. While no study can test all of the factors at one time, this book collectively compiles several of them by taking a whole systems analysis at the campaign finance regimes in place in each state.

Strategic Factors

Strategic factors are those factors such as a candidate's chances of winning an election, contribution limits, and incumbent's quality and strength based on which a candidate may make a decision regarding running for office. One of the biggest strategic factors is the probability that a challenger will win an election.[6] The rationale here is that candidates are strategic and make rational decisions[7] based on whether or not there is a chance for them to win an election. Maisel and Stone found that when an incumbent held a seat, a challenger was more likely to account for this in their decision to run for office. Hogan[8] found the similar results. An incumbent's level of support in the previous election was a deterrent for challengers seeking that office. Most scholars in this area seem to be asking the same question that Kazee[9] asks whether the chances of winning are high enough to justify the effort required. Can the challenger win against an incumbent when we know the advantages that incumbents have to stay in office? These advantages can be many. Incumbents have access to media coverage in their home district or state, at the US Congress level they have free mailing privileges and may get support from the party. Challengers have almost none of these advantages, thus giving the incumbents strength against challengers. Kazee questioned potential challengers if the incumbent announced they were not running for office, would that influence the challenger's decision to run for office. Kazee found that just the perception of incumbent strength was enough to deter challengers from seeking office.[10]

While the argument of incumbent deterrence is logical, it is not quite as simple as we may think. There are other factors playing into this deterrence effect. One contributing factor is the strength or weakness of the incumbent. Another factor is which election cycle scholars are studying. Are scholars looking at the general election or the primary? Lazarus[11] looks at both of these types of elections and finds generally that when the incumbent does poorly in the previous primary and/or general election there will be more challengers both from the incumbent party and the out-party. Interestingly he also finds that when the out-party does not have an experienced challenger running for office, this party will have more amateur candidates challenging the incumbent.[12] Maisel and Stone[13] find also that a challenger's decision to run is more likely to be affected by their chance of winning their own party's nomination in the primary than by their chance of winning the general election. Therefore, the primary election is an important factor also.

What is it about the incumbent that is the biggest deterrent for challengers seeking a seat? As noted above Lazarus finds deterrence may depend on which election cycle we are looking. Another possibility is the so-called war chest of the incumbent. The war chest is the amount of money the incumbent has saved from previous elections or from campaign contributions while in office. Hogan[14] finds that the size of the war chest has a negative impact on the probability that a challenge will occur in both the primary and general election cycle. Contributing to the war chest deterrent is the possibility that states that have campaign finance laws that restrict contribution limits may also affect challenger emergence positively by leveling the playing field. If the campaign finance laws governing contributions restrict an incumbent, then this would level the playing field. By creating a level playing field there is less of a risk and more ability for challengers to compete with incumbents. This lowered risk plays directly into their calculus of whether or not it is worth the risk to run for office. The idea here is that if incumbents were unhindered by contribution limits it lowers the deterrent or risk to challengers. Maestas and Rugeley[15] find similarly when assessing the experience of incumbents over challengers. They find that the advantage depends on what type of incumbent one is. If you are a statewide officeholder or federal candidate, you may have an advantage in raising funds when compared to ambitious amateurs. This is an important point for the theory that complexity deters some candidates. Amateurs or novice candidates who want to run are encumbered by the rules and regulations that take up their time to learn.

While learning and complying with all the new (to them) rules and regulations, they are unable to use their time more effectively by soliciting campaign contributions.

Hogan[16] also finds that as the attractiveness of the state legislative seat diminishes, the effect of the war chest paradoxically increases. This means that the war chest has a bigger effect when there is a seat for which no one wants to run. This could be that the war chest is adding onto some other deterrent effect. Hogan does not discuss what makes a seat more or less attractive, so we are not sure. We do know that war chests are primarily effective as deterrents in state legislative seats and not US congressional seats.

Hogan notes that, generally, the American people understand that if a member of Congress does not vote in accordance with their constituents' wishes, they may lose their office. This theoretically should provide an opportunity for a challenger to attempt to take over the seat. Despite the conventional wisdom, however, this does not appear to be the case. Hogan[17] looked at the incumbent's responsiveness to policy demands. He found that when the incumbent's policy voting was in line with what his constituents wanted, he got a higher percentage of the votes than incumbents that did not vote in line with constituents. However, he does not find this helps or hurts a challenger. He only found that it affected the vote total for the incumbent. Whereas policy responsiveness matters, it apparently does not matter (or help) for challengers seeking that office. Challengers may put less emphasis on voting responsiveness when considering a run for office.

As noted by the quote at the beginning of this chapter, Moncrief, Squire, and Jewell[18] observe that the difficulties of running for office may scare off potential challengers. There is a lot of research on strategic candidates that scrutinizes the many difficulties that face challengers seeking to run for office. However, do we know all of those difficulties? Much of the literature infers that the difficulty will be with raising contributions to wage an effective race against a sitting incumbent. From war chests to contribution limits, the candidate emergence research rightly focuses on the money needed to wage an effective campaign. Money is not the only factor though. The complexity literature points to additional burdens faced by any challenger, but particularly a novice challenger.

A challenger faces an incumbent unconstrained by all the benefits of a sitting legislator. Challengers may be deterred because they face a learning curve that has the potential to exacerbate the advantages enjoyed by the incumbents. In a similar situation, welfare recipients often failed to receive all their benefits because of the learning costs involved in applying for social welfare programs.[19] In similar ways, novice challengers face a much steeper learning curve than sitting incumbents to learn the rules and regulations of a campaign finance system.

Political and Institutional Factors

Strategic factors have a direct impact on the political factors of a candidate's decision. When a candidate is looking at their prospects within their district strategically, they also must consider the political factors such as partisan balance in the district. If balanced in their favor they may have a higher probability of winning than otherwise. Hogan finds that when the district partisan balance factor favors the incumbent, that it is a deterrent to challenger emergence. When the partisanship is changing or has changed however, Hogan[20] finds that challengers will emerge at that point. Hogan also finds that the population within the district is also a factor. When the population is larger, it may make the campaign more expensive and acts as a deterrent to challengers. If candidates have to expend more campaign resources to reach a larger population, this would increase the cost of the campaign. These costs then become the deterrent to challenger emergence. Candidates implement their campaign policy or strategy based on the scope of their constituency. If they have a larger population to reach, that changes how they will implement their campaign. The scope of policy implementation increases the complexity of that policy.[21] As challengers face an increased population, that simply exacerbates the complexity of their implementation task. The challengers face a scale issue where the costs of campaigning are magnified by the population they need to reach.

Concerning the structure of the institution in which one desires office, the professionalism of the legislature is another factor that some scholars think plays into the challenger's decisions. Legislature professionalism refers generally to the time legislators spend in session, the amount they are paid, term limits, amenities or perks of office, level of political knowledge and political experience of the legislators. States that provide higher salaries, more amenities, and staff are considered to have a more professional legislature. States that do not provide these benefits for their legislators are considered less professional. Hogan looks at the professionalism of the legislature and finds that where states have a more professional legislature it is a strong influence on challenger emergence. He finds that there will be more challengers emerging with more legislative professionalism, but the strength of the challengers will decrease. Because the legislative seat becomes more enticing more challengers emerge but they are not necessarily the strongest candidates. Squire and Powell both argue that developing a higher quality potential candidate pool enables more challenger emergence. Simply having a larger pool of qualified candidates allows more of those candidates to challenge incumbents. Allowing a larger pool of candidates to grow, makes possible better representation in the long run as your pool of candidates are better able to grapple with running for office.[22]

Term limits increase the probability that state legislators will run for their state's US House seat whether they are the incumbent or the challenger. However, this effect is reduced for the challenger compared to the incumbent.[23] Term limits are a negative factor when considering legislative professionalism. The idea here is that states would want legislators to stay in office, gain experience, and thus become more professional. By limiting this ability, states may end up having a less professional legislature. We see from the above discussion that a more professional legislature encourages challenger emergence. We would expect that term limits would decrease professionalism and thus decrease challenger emergence. Powell,[24] however, finds the opposite that term limits "have a stimulating effect on the decision of state legislators to run for the House."[25] It is possible that the effect is based on leaving one seat (the State Legislature) to try for a higher seat (the US House), whereas other studies have looked at challenger emergence for the same level of seats.

Ballot access laws also affect candidacy decisions. Burden[26] finds that ballot regulations "affect the number of candidates on the ballot" in some states although he is primarily looking at senatorial and gubernatorial races. Stratman[27] finds similar results when testing ballot access restrictions on candidate entry in state house elections. He uses the filing fee, dollar amounts, and signature requirements and finds that "higher filing fees reduce" the number of candidates. Signatures requirements also reduce the number of candidates but that is mainly among the major party candidates. Either finding indicates that the institutional regulations put on candidates can reduce candidate entry.

A number of institutional or political factors affect candidate decisions. Adding to these factors is the concept of institutional rules and regulations. The campaign finance regulatory regime has numerous rules with which candidates must learn and with which they must comply. Moynihan, Herd, Harvey[28] break down the administrative burden into learning, compliance, and psychological costs. Rules and regulations may not always be burdensome; in some cases, rules are important and serve to provide boundaries and clarity to processes. Rules create norms of behavior, normal operating procedures, or an equal playing field. Much of the rules in campaign finance stem from the latter—creating an equal playing field—so that incumbent and challengers ostensibly face the same environment when deciding to run for office. However, we already know that incumbency has advantages (see more below). The question here is whether the campaign finance regulatory regime creates an unequal playing field by creating a burden to challengers, but not to incumbents who have already learned the rules.

At some point that is not clear to scholars, the rules and regulations become a burden rather than a benefit.[29] The point of this book is to determine if there is an effect on candidates of the rules and regulations put in place to make the campaign finance field more level and more democratic. Initially candidates face the rules and regulations for filing to run for office and secondly face the contribution regulations in order to ramp up their campaign. If you are a novice candidate, how do you learn the rules?

Novice or inexperienced challengers have to figure out what forms are necessary to fill out, what personnel do they need to hire, what training for themselves and campaign personnel is required. They have to determine how many signatures are required on a petition, what kind of signatures are acceptable. There is an extensive list of tasks candidates must complete. Facing this regime without any experience or help is daunting to challengers. Incumbents face very few of these challenges having already learned how to run. This leaves the challengers with a higher administrative burden than incumbents.

In addition to learning how to fill out forms and start up a campaign, candidates must also learn how to comply with numerous campaign finance regulations. Some of compliance is covered by the learning. Other compliance issues come from understanding the law. Candidates must know how large of a campaign contribution they are allowed to accept from an individual, a PAC, or other entity. The candidates have to be trained on how to comply with the reporting and disclosure requirements by their state. Candidates have to comply with proper campaign etiquette, and the norms of running for office. Failure to comply with campaign finance regulations and norms risks ruining their reputation as it gives ammunition to their opposition to use against them. Compliance failure also risks election loss. Even the suspicion of having incorrectly or inadequately filling out campaign disclosure forms may lead to opposition candidates using this information to sully your reputation in the hopes of damaging your election prospects.

The campaign finance regulatory institutions were put in place to increase participation in the democratic process and to alleviate any corruption or suspicion of corruption. These institutions may have grown beyond their usefulness to their goals. If candidates' decisions are affected by an administrative burden created by these complex institutions, we may conclude that they have gone beyond green tape and morphed into red tape.[30]

Personal Factors

Whereas political, institutional, and strategic factors are beyond the reach of the candidate's influence, personal factors are those that affect the candidate's person in his or her life or family. These include such factors as income, displacement, the length of sessions, ability to campaign, and candidate quality. I would add to these factors the psychological costs of running for office. All of these factors affect candidates in different ways.

The income factor can be especially difficult to overcome. This factor can affect candidate's decisions in two ways. The first is where the legislator salary is low. If the legislature is not professional and has relatively low salaries for the legislators then leaving or taking time off from a lucrative business or profession may put an undue cost of running and serving as a legislator. Candidates have to make this choice prior to deciding to run. On the other hand serving in the legislature may be a stepping stone to higher office or even the first step in a candidate's desire for a political career. They then may not care about the salary but see holding the office as a long-term benefit. The second effect of legislators' salaries results from higher legislator salaries indicating a more professional legislature. Increased legislator salaries are indicated by institutional rather than individual factors. The thinking on this factor is that higher salaries and more professionalism would serve as an incentive for more challengers to enter the race.[31] Regardless of high or low legislator salary, individuals must often pay for part of their campaigns as well as taking time off from their business in order to run for office.[32] Additionally the costs of hiring campaign staff to comply with campaign regulations may be burdensome. Added to the income effect is the displacement factor. The displacement factor is the necessity of maintaining two households while in the legislature. Legislators must have a residency in the district from which they are elected. Most legislators also need a place to stay or live while in session. For the state legislatures, this effect can vary by the amount of time spent in session. If states have a more professional legislature that meets every year, the displacement costs will be higher than in states where the legislature meets every other year or for only a few weeks at a time. Some of the displacement costs will be offset by per diems while in session. However, as most state employees know, per diems never cover the whole cost of expenses. While we would expect that the income and displacement effects would be high on the list of factors affecting candidate emergence, scholars have not found evidence for this. Maisel and Stone[33] examined these two factors and only found minimal evidence that they affected candidate emergence decisions. They found that the strategic factors were much stronger in decision making than these two personal factors.

One of the respondents in the qualitative interviews done for this book remarked on the difficulty of both maintaining employment and running for office. When he chose to run, his employer advised him not to run. The respondent felt his employer's reluctance was because of his fear of losing business if one of his employees was running for office. The respondent who is now a campaign consultant also remarked how easy it is to be on the campaign consultant side of the business. He no longer has to worry about the risks of losing his job, the difficulties of working for an employer and at the same time running for office. The respondent stated that he actually finds it hard to find people willing to run for office because of the risk of humiliation or the risk to their business.[34]

Other personal factors are also tied to the cost of running for office. These include the probability of negative advertising in a campaign. If you are running against a strong candidate, and the incumbent has a large war chest then they will be able to run negative ads against your campaign. This can cause increasing costs to your campaign because you must respond to these ads. Again, Maisel and Stone[35] find that these personal factors are minor when compared to the strategic factors.

Candidate quality is another important factor for candidate emergence. Candidate quality is lumped into one category. Generally, it means some combination of campaign experience, oratorical skills, organizational skills and physical or telegenic appeal. The problem with these types of factors is that it is not clear if the skills or qualities are a factor in candidate emergence or if candidates emerge, gain experience and then develop these skills and qualities. The expectation is that candidates with higher levels of qualities would be able to raise more money for their campaigns and thus be able to challenge incumbents more successfully. Squire studies these personal factors and finds that where we would expect to see higher qualified challengers against incumbents, we tend to see weaker challengers against incumbents and stronger challenger quality against open seats.[36] Even Squire notes that these factors are harder to understand and quantify than originally thought. Stone, Maisel, and Maestas[37] find similar effects of candidate quality. Incumbent candidate quality deters strong challengers and low quality incumbents stimulate other potential candidates to run.

Underlying some of the personal factors affecting candidates is risk aversion or the fear of public humiliation or failure. The public administration literature is instructive here. It tells us that citizens facing an application process for welfare benefits often decrease their participation rates[38] when they face a hurdle or obstacle to their application such as a long wait in line or forms to fill out. Conversely, some scholars found that when the administrative burden was removed or changes implemented, the participation rates increased as found in the Wisconsin case.[39] Just the perception that citizens felt regarding the outcome of their application for welfare benefits left them feeling burdened or unburdened by the rules and regulations.[40] If the clients felt positive about getting benefits, they saw the rules and regulations in a more positive light. We cannot know without testing this empirically but we can hypothesize that candidates who are more risk averse might view the rules and regulations of the campaign as more burdensome because they are facing an unknown outcome. Incumbents' outcome is more assured and they can therefore face the regulatory system with more confidence. Candidates that wait for the right opportunity would view the burden as lower, but that leaves the rest of the elections with fewer challengers.

Throughout the study of candidate emergence and looking at the factors there always seems to be some factor, some element missing in the analysis. Some more recent studies have noticed this factor and have looked for it to describe the desire to run for office. It is alternately called progressive ambition[41] or nascent ambition.[42] Maestas et al. describe progressive ambition as preceding any evaluation of a campaign or seat. Progressive ambition would come before evaluating any seat as a potential prospect. They evaluate progressive ambition by asking state legislators if they expect to run for the US House in the future. Maestas et al. look at the expected utility of winning an office, but they say that this expected utility model is flawed because it does not take into account the long-term costs and benefit of running for office. When you consider long-term benefits and long-term costs you get progressive ambition that the authors think must be present to run in the first place. Every candidate must have some form of progressive ambition; otherwise, the costs would be too high in the short term.[43]

This idea of measuring ambition is also considered by Fox and Lawless[44] who look not at state legislators but at a potential pool of candidates. They surveyed a sample of individuals selected from professions that historically have seen politicians emerge. These professions include law, business, education and political/community activism.[45] Fox and Lawless look at these actors prior to this emergence process to look at the nascent candidates' decisions. They wanted to see what factors affected the likelihood that potential candidates would ever enter a race. The authors surveyed these folks to gauge their nascent political ambition or the embryonic or potential interest in seeking office that precedes the actual decision to enter a specific political contest. This study used a survey of what Fox and Lawless describe as "successful individuals" who form part of a potential candidate pool. The authors use this sample as a way of broadening the base of potential officeholders—meaning that instead of looking at just potential candidates for state legislature or city council; they are looking at a broad spectrum of potential candidates from which most expressed candidates come.

Fox and Lawless find numerous factors contribute to nascent candidates such as "a general sense of efficacy . . . exerts the greatest relative impact on nascent ambition."[46] When individuals feel qualified to run they are more likely to decide to investigate the possibility of running for office. Another major factor is a politicized upbringing such as family members had previously run for office, politics had been a part of family life and discussions, or individuals had run for office in high school. This earlier exposure to politics contributed to their decisions to run for office in the future. Minority status tended to make the potential candidates less likely to run for office possibly because they "lack the key ingredients that foster ambition,"[47] they self-assess as "not at all qualified" or lacked "encouragement from their parents to enter politics." Fox and Lawless agree that more work needs to be done to "flesh out more thoroughly the role of nascent ambition in the candidate emergence process."[48] Part of this study does this. By qualitatively interviewing candidates, this book develops a better idea of what factors contribute to their decisions.

Qualitative Interviews

"Even with no incumbent running, many qualified people do not want to undertake the very arduous task of campaigning."[49] Moncrief et al.'s findings are backed up by the evidence of the qualitative interviews conducted. Candidates simply did not like the difficult work involved. The question is not only about if candidates liked the work, but if the work was more difficult because candidates were incumbents versus novices. The interviews also serve to help us understand if any extra work is a function of the regulatory system of campaign financing. Because the idea that campaign finance laws might deter candidates from running for office it is important to understand if this ever occurs to individuals who may or may not have run for office. Interviews of fourteen potential and actual candidates were conducted in 2014 and in 2016. The interviews aimed to ascertain factors affecting candidates' decisions to run for office and to investigate whether or not campaign finance laws entered the candidates' calculations. Of the fourteen individuals interviewed, ten were men and four women. All but three had previously run for office. The answers the individuals gave regarding reasons to run or not to run for office coincided with much of the literature on the subject. Answers given for why the individual ran for office ranged from the strategic to personal. When the respondents were asked if they would run those that said they would not gave reasons such as the system is too political, they did not want to risk losing their reputation or jobs, and they did not like asking for money. When asked about the logistics of running for office such as filing, and getting the information on how to run, respondents said they got information from previously experienced candidates, the state boards of elections/registrars, campaign consultants. This question often led into a discussion of the nuts-and-bolts of running for office. Two candidates commented on the difficulty of the process, one respondent going so far as to say, "Someone just off the streets would find it impossible [to run]. They will not be able to fill out the forms. They would need to be researchers to do this."[50] Another candidate stated that his profession as a lawyer gave him a "leg up" on other candidates and "I don't know the code off the top of my head, but the average person would need help."[51] It is clear from the interviews that campaign regulations are on the minds of individuals. It might not be the main issue, but the regulations weigh on their minds and the extra work created by the regulations certainly impact decisions. When it comes to deciding to run and giving up family time or time at your job the extra time spent campaigning to raise more money becomes a factor.

The qualitative interviews point to some institutional complexity as a factor affecting decisions and there is some scholarly work supporting this theory. Even though Zetterberg[52] fails to find evidence that gender quotas (institutions) have an effect on female candidates' decisions to run, he does find that the struggle for representation comes from within the parties. Zetterberg finds that the parties are the institutions that constrain female candidates, not the quota systems. The interviews support the idea that parties fail to support some candidates while favoring others. Novice candidates must seek outside the party help via mentors, candidate schools, or advocacy groups. The party as an institution was rarely mentioned as "backing" a candidate.

This review of the literature looks at numerous factors that affect candidate decisions. It is clear from this review that the question of what factors affect candidate decisions is far from settled. The decisions may be different for incumbents vs. challengers, the office for which the candidate is running, the costs involved in the decision making and so on. So many factors can come into play in making the decision to run for office. It is important to study these factors ongoing to ensure that the electoral system is open for participation.

CONCLUSION

Candidates make their decisions to run for office based on many factors. Most of these factors such as the structure of the electoral system, political factors, and personal factors such as salary have all been studied. What is new here is the idea that the complexity of the campaign finance regulatory system may impose an additional burden on candidates. That burden may then add to the other factors leading candidates to decide it is too costly to run.

The administrative burden of learning the rules and regulations of the campaign finance regime is daunting. This book does not pose this task as the leading cause of candidates deciding not to run for office. Rather, administrative burden or complexity may be an additional layer adding to other factors such as risk aversion, family life strains, and the incumbency advantage. Importantly, it is one factor not considered in the candidate decisions literature. Added together potential candidates may decide it is just not worth their effort to run for office. If you are a novice challenger, the costs are even higher than if you are an experienced candidate running for office. Novices especially may be turned off by the high cost of learning and complying with campaign rules and regulations. Everyday individuals are running other businesses, working for other entities, raising families, teaching school. They do not have time to spend learning the ropes of campaigning, while incumbents have already reordered their lives. Incumbents who we know tend to be lawyers, teachers, or retirees who may have an easier time incorporating campaigning into their schedules and lives. Everyday citizens have a lot to juggle and adding a complex campaign finance system to their plate may seem to be too much.

In the next chapter, the complex statutes are analyzed as to how they affect candidate decisions. It is important to understand every possible factor affecting candidates as it is generally agreed that having more political participation is better than less. More candidates increase the pool of knowledge, experience, and innovation in government.

NOTES

1. Gary F. Moncrief, Peverill Squire, and Malcom F. Jewell, *Who Runs for the Legislature* (Upper Saddle River, NJ: Prentice Hall, 2001).
2. Gordon S. Black, "A Theory of Political Ambition: Career Choices and the Role of Structural Incentives," *The American Political Science Review* 66, no. 1 (1972).
3. Moncrief, Squire, and Jewell, "Who Runs for the Legislature" 83.
4. Richard L. Fox and Jennifer L. Lawless, "To Run or Not to Run for Office: Explaining Nascent Political Ambition," *American Journal of Political Science* 49, no. 3 (2005).
5. Thomas A. Kazee, "The Deterrent Effect of Incumbency on Recruiting Challengers in Us House Elections," *Legislative Studies Quarterly* 8, no. 3 (1983).
6. L. Sandy Maisel and Walter J. Stone, "Determinants of Candidate Emergence in US House Elections: An Exploratory Study," ibid.22, no. 1 (1997).
7. Martin D. Levine and Mark S. Hyde, "Incumbency and the Theory of Political Ambition: A Rational-Choice Model," *The Journal of Politics* 39, no. 4 (1977); Black, "A Theory of Political Ambition: Career Choices and the Role of Structural Incentives."; Cherie D Maestas and Cynthia R. Rugeley, "'Assessing the "Experience Bonus' through Examping Strategic Entry, Candidate Quality and Campaign Receipts in US House Elections," *American Journal of Political Science* 52, no. 3 (2008). Walter J. Stone, L. Sandy Maisel, and Cherie D. Maestas, "Quality Counts: Extending the Strategic Politician Model of Incumbent Deterrence," ibid., 48 (2004).
8. Robert E. Hogan, "Challenger Emergence, Incumbent Success and Electoral Accoutability in State Legislative Elections," *The Journal of Politics* 66, no. 4 (2004).
9. Kazee, "The Deterrent Effect of Incumbency on Recruiting Challengers in US House Elections."
10. Ibid.
11. Jeffrey Lazarus, "Incumbent Vulnerabilty and Challenger Entry in Statewide Elections," *American Politics Research* 36, no. 1 (2008).
12. Ibid.
13. Maisel and Stone, "Determinants of Candidate Emergence in US House Elections: An Exploratory Study."
14. Robert E. Hogan, "Campaign War Chests and Challenger Emergence in State Legislative Elections," *Political Research Quarterly* 54 (2001).
15. Maestas and Rugeley, "Assessing the "Experience Bonus" through Examping Strategic Entry, Candidate Quality and Campaign Receipts in US House Elections."
16. Hogan, "Campaign War Chests and Challenger Emergence in State Legislative Elections."

17. Robert E. Hogan, "Challenger Emergence, Incumbent Success and Electoral Accoutability in State Legislative Elections."
18. Moncrief, Squire, and Jewell, "Who Runs for the Legislature."
19. Donald Moynihan, Pamela Herd, and Hope Harvey, "Administrative Burden: Learning, Psychological, and Compliance Costs in Citizen-State Interactions," *Journal of Public Administration Research and Theory* 25 (2014); James J. Heckman and Jeffrey A. Smith, "The Determinants of Participation in a Social Program: Evidence from a Prototypical Job Training Program," *Journal of Labor Economics* 22, no. 2 (2004).
20. Hogan, "Challenger Emergence, Incumbent Success and Electoral Accountability in State Legislative Elections."
21. Keith E. Hamm, "U.S. State Legislative Committee Decisions: Similar Results in Different Settings," *Legislative Studies Quarterly* 5, no. 1 (1980).
22. Hogan, "Challenger Emergence, Incumbent Success and Electoral Accoutability in State Legislative Elections," 1293. Peverill Squire, "Challengers in US Senate Elections," Legislative Studies Quarterly 14, no. 4 (1989). Richard T. Powell, "The Impact of Term Limits on the Candidacy Decisions of State Legislators in US House Elections," ibid., 25 (2000). Cherie D. Maestas et al., "When to Risk It? Institutions, Ambitions, and the Decision to Run for the US House," *American Political Science Review* 100, no. 2 (2006).
23. Powell, "The Impact of Term Limits on the Candidacy Decisions of State Legislators in US House Elections."
24. Ibid.
25. Ibid., 656.
26. Barry C. Burden, "Ballot Regulations and Multiparty Politics in the States," *www.apsanet.org* (2007).
27. Thomas Stratmann, "Ballot Access Restrictions and Candidate Entry in Elections," *European Journal of Political Economy* 21 (2005).
28. Moynihan, Herd, and Harvey, "Administrative Burden: Learning, Psychological, and Compliance Costs in Citizen-State Interactions."
29. Barry Bozeman, "A Theory of Government 'Red Tape,'" *Journal of Public Administration Research and Theory: J-PART* 3, no. 3 (1993).
30. Ibid.
31. Maisel and Stone, "Determinants of Candidate Emergence in US House Elections: An Exploratory Study."
32. Moncrief, Squire, and Jewell, "Who Runs for the Legislature."
33. Maisel and Stone, "Determinants of Candidate Emergence in US House Elections: An Exploratory Study."
34. QI11, ed. Mary Jo McGowan Shepherd (2014).
35. Maisel and Stone, "Determinants of Candidate Emergence in US House Elections: An Exploratory Study."
36. Peverill Squire, "Candidates, Money, and Voters. Assessing the State of Congressional Elections Research," *Political Science Quarterly* 48, no. 4 (1995).
37. Stone, Maisel, and Maestas, "Quality Counts: Extending the Strategic Politician Model of Incumbent Deterrence."
38. Donald Moynihan and Pamela Herd, "Red Tape and Democracy: How Rules Affect Citizens Rights," *The American Review of Public Administration* 40, no. 6 (2010).
39. Donald P. Moynihan, Pamela Herd, and Elizabeth Ribgy, "Policymaking by Other Means: Do States Use Adminsitrative Barriers to Limit Access to Medicaid?," *Administration & Society* 48, no. 4 (2016).
40. Wesley Kaufmann and Mary K. Feeney, "Effect of Outcome Favourability on Red Tape Perceptions," *Public Administration* 92, no. 1 (2014).
41. Maestas et al., "When to Risk It? Institutions, Ambitions, and the Decision to Run for the US House.."
42. Fox and Lawless, "To Run or Not to Run for Office: Explaining Nascent Political Ambition."
43. Maestas et al., "When to Risk It? Institutions, Ambitions, and the Decision to Run for the US House."

44. Fox and Lawless, "To Run or Not to Run for Office: Explaining Nascent Political Ambition." "Entering the Arena? Gender and the Decision to Run for Office," *American Journal of Political Science* 48, no. 2 (2004).
45. "To Run or Not to Run for Office: Explaining Nascent Political Ambition," 647.
46. Ibid., 652.
47. Ibid., 654.
48. Ibid., 654–55.
49. Moncrief, Squire, and Jewell, "Who Runs for the Legislature."
50. QI4, ed. Mary Jo McGowan Shepherd (2014).
51. QI13, ed. Mary Jo McGowan Shepherd (2014).
52. Par Zetterberg, "The Downside of Gender Quotas? Institutional Contraints on Women in Mexican State Legislatures," *Parliamentary Affairs* 61, no. 3 (2008).

Chapter Seven

Study Methods

The literature is clear on the many factors influencing candidates' decisions to run for office. What is unclear is whether the regulatory complexity of the campaign finance system has an impact on deterring candidates from running. Complexity may increase the time and effort to learn and comply with campaign finance rules and regulations. As noted, complexity is unlikely to be the main reason why a candidate would not run for office, but complexity adds to the burden or costs of the decision to run. This chapter lays out the methodology for studying the relationship between campaign finance regulations and candidate decisions in all fifty US states.

If complexity affects candidate decisions, fewer candidates should run for office in states that have more complex campaign finance laws, and more candidates should withdraw from running in those same states. To determine if there is any effect on candidates' decisions, this study analyzes two dependent variables created from candidate data. These two variables are the Candidate Participation Rate (CPR) and the Candidate Withdrawal Rate (CWR).

The unit of analysis is the subject about which we can generalize. Units of analysis may be different from the units of observation.[1] This study observes only the collective behavior of individual candidates. Generalization about individual behavior is not possible because there are no data on candidates' individual demographics, parties, and decision-making factors. Thus, the unit of analysis is state/year because this study will allow inferences about candidates in each state for a given year based on those candidates' exposure to candidates' respective state contribution limits, candidacy requirements, and the state's general statutes.

The following hypotheses test the theory that complex campaign finance law may exist in some states and this complexity is leading to fewer candidates running for office in those states. The first hypothesis is *H1: In states where the campaign finance legislation is more complex, the Candidate Participation Rate (CPR) will be lower than in states with less complex statutes.* This tests the rate at which candidates participate in those states with less complex statutes. The second hypothesis pertains to withdrawals. *H2: In states where the campaign finance legislation is more complex, the Candidate Withdrawal Rate (CWR) will be higher than in states with less complex statutes.* Withdrawals are those candidates who signed up to run for office but for unknown reasons withdrew from the race.

Dependent Variables: Candidate Participation Rate (CPR) and Candidate Withdrawal Rate (CWR)

As noted in previous chapters of this current work, there are numerous factors affecting candidates' decisions to run for office. A number of studies have looked at a wide variety of factors and yet there does not seem to be any agreement on exactly what factors affect candidates consistently. This study takes the approach that institutions and rules affect the behavior of candidates. Using the campaign finance rules and regulations is not a new measure as referenced by the use of campaign finance stringency indices.[2] What is new here is using the complexity of the whole statute measured by plain language, adding a new variable to the study of candidate decisions. Measuring the statute as a whole allows us to measure what candidates face when deciding to run for office. Candidates would need to understand at least the candidacy statutes and the contribution statutes from the beginning of their campaign.

There are two main dependent variables in this study in the format of candidate rate variables. The data for candidate dependent variables come from the National Institute on Money in State Politics.[3] The data stretches from 1998 through 2016. Using these data across eighteen years and ten election cycles allows a look at the effect of the law on the rates of candidates over time. The National Institute on Money in State Politics serves as a repository for state level electoral data collected from each of the US states. During the data collection for the quantity of candidates for each state, candidate withdrawals were also found and collected. Candidate withdrawals are candidates who signed up to run for office, but then withdrew for reasons other than disqualification or death. The candidate counts and withdrawal count data form the two candidate rate variables. As noted, state legislative elections form the basis for this analysis, because the quantity of candidates and variation across states allows measurement of the effect of campaign finance laws over a wider swath of the election process. Data collected from both state House and Senate elections aggregate to form both the Candidate Participation Rate and the Candidate Withdrawal Rate.

The first dependent variable is the Candidate Participation Rate (CPR). These data in their original form were count data. For each state and year, the total number (count) of candidates running in each state legislative election per year were collected. Using these data as a count is not intuitive because counts may vary by state and legislature size. Participation rates are created from the data to create a more intuitive measure of participation across the states.

The National Institute on Money in State Politics collects candidate data from campaign finance reports filed through the states. These reports update throughout an election cycle. The last year of this study is 2016 ensuring that any reporting would be complete. The data consist of candidates from both the primary and general elections. However, the goal for this analysis is to study the effects of the law as candidates begin their election process. To do this, primary candidacies are included.

Two additional rates are created from the total candidate count data. The first variable—the CPRs—is the total number of candidates per the total number of seats up for election in the current state/year. The second variable for the CPR for the number of permanent seats in the chamber in that state/year. This is the CPRp. The permanent seats in the chamber is the number of seats legislated to exist by chamber. The number of permanent seats in the chamber gives a more stable analysis over time because the number of permanent seats does not change from year to year, whereas the number of seats up for election does at least for House seats. However, the CPRs for the number of seats up for election may be more intuitive because it seems more likely the measure candidates would look at strategically when deciding whether to run for office. These two variables allow comparison of any effective differences between the seats that are actually available for election, and the number of permanent seats in the chamber.

A second dependent variable is the Candidate Withdrawal Rate (CWR) for each state legislative election from 1998–2016. This rate measures candidates who filed for office and then at some point prior to the primary withdrew. The data were collected from the National Institute on Money in State Politics under the candidates section for each state/year. The website gives the aggregate information on candidates' status. The CWR should indicate an interest, willingness, and ambition to run for office because the candidate actually signed up, paid any registration fee or completed a petition, and was a viable candidate. The candidate for some reason then withdrew from the race. There is no data on why a candidate would withdraw from the race. We only know that the candidates did withdraw.[4] The data are clear that the candidates did not withdraw due to death or disqualification. Those two scenarios are coded differently in the data than withdrawals. In considering withdrawals, the logic here is that the possibility exists that candidates withdrew because they found the process too cumbersome to run. The CWR is also a rate of candidates and creates three new variables: the CWRt, which is the rate of withdrawals out of total candidates, the CWRs or the rate of withdrawals of total seats up for election and the CWRp or the rate of withdrawals per permanent chamber seats.

Qualitative Component of Dependent Variable

In order to build the theory on candidate decisions and to investigate other possible factors affecting candidates' decisions to run or not to run for office, investigative interviews were compiled. The interviews questioned individuals from various states regarding their motivations to run for political office. Including qualitative interviews adds to the internal validity of this study by substantively asking individuals who may be considering running for office or have run for office about their experiences.[5] This approach allows the investigator to understand if potential candidates have ever considered the logistics or costs of running for office. It is important to understand if the theory applies in real life. Does complexity of the campaign finance system deter potential candidates from running? Have potential candidates ever considered this? Knowing if they have or have not adds depth to this study by allowing the researcher to understand the realistic situation facing potential candidates. It also allows researchers to determine if all controls have been included into the model.

Individuals were contacted from states with different types of legislatures such as professional, citizen or hybrid legislatures. The methodology for contacting individuals is via e-mail to set up a telephone interview. Individuals were found to do the survey by initiating contact with various political actors via Facebook or e-mails. The purposive sample will include potential and actual candidates from states with both complex and not-complex campaign finance statutes. States must also have a variety of legislature types, that is, professional, citizen, or hybrid. The sampling method involves contacting potential candidates in these states and asking them qualitative questions on why they chose to or chose not to run for office. They were also asked about their political background and upbringing, the logistics of running for office and any factors that influenced their decision to run either negatively or positively. The interviews were free flowing and to allow the individuals to bring up any issues or concerns regarding running for office. The point of the interviews being mainly to assess whether individuals had ever considered the legislation or regulations in their contemplation of running for office.

Independent Variable: Complexity of Campaign Finance Reform Statutes

The literature on campaign finance reform efforts examines many campaign factors to see how campaign finance reform affects elections, contributions, and voter turnout among others. However, one variable has not been addressed adequately by the literature so far. That variable revolves around how the complexity or administrative burden of campaign finance legislation affects a candidate's decision to run for office. It is important to understand if the rules and regulations create a barrier to entry to candidates thinking of running for office. The time and effort to learn and comply with the regulatory regime in place may be cumbersome enough to create additional drag on candidates who otherwise would run for office.

There are generally two schools of thought on campaign finance related to how contribution limits affect candidates,[6] although both involve low contribution limits. On one hand, low contribution limits might make it easy for the incumbent to raise money since they have experience doing so making it harder for the challenger to compete. This comports with the theory for this book that restrictions (in general) may inhibit candidate participation. In particular, novice candidates might be deterred because they have to spend the extra time to learn how to campaign and how to comply with campaign laws. Incumbents do not have to face this learning curve the second attempt at running for office. I do not explicitly test for this effect in this book but future research should differentiate any effect on different candidate types.

Another main school of thought on contribution limits, says low contribution limits puts both challengers and incumbents on an equal playing field and makes it more likely that challengers will emerge. Hogan[7] finds for the second effect that if campaign finance laws are strong, it should be an incentive for challengers to run because the incumbent is hampered or prevented by contribution laws from gaining the upper hand. However, Hogan's study analyzes twenty-five states over four years and three election cycles. Hogan's work also looks at how likely it is for a challenger to run against an incumbent using a dichotomous variable for the primary and general elections. Hogan's independent variable is an additive index from 1-5 indicating the number of restrictions on contributions. For example, if a state restricts only labor unions from contributing, then that state has a score of one on the scale. This study takes a different and much wider approach to the question of how campaign finance laws affect candidate decisions. Using the approach advocated by complexity theorists Teisman and Klijn,[8] this study uses a whole systems approach and looks at all fifty states over eighteen years and ten election cycles and measures the institutional factor of complexity in the law. It is not just the restrictions on who may contribute to one's campaign that may constrain an individual's choice to run for office.

Learning, compliance, and psychological costs inherent in understanding the policy may also deter a candidate from running. By measuring the overall complexity of the law, this study incorporates many factors such as transaction costs, contribution limits, and candidacy requirements to measure the full effect of what a candidate faces when making the decision to run for office. Using complexity theory to study an entire political system makes sense so that we can understand the effect of a system or policy on other variables or outcomes. We want to understand the collective effect of the campaign finance system on individual's choices to run for office. As discussed in the chapter on campaign finance, there are many factors involved in the campaign finance system. As campaign factors accumulate, they increase the burden on individuals seeking to run for public office. It is important to understand the measurement and the effect on citizens of this burden.

The electoral costs of complying with the laws stems first from an understanding of the law. I do not calculate directly the real cost of running for a state legislative office but rather look at the transaction cost embodied in the complexity of the law. In states where campaign laws are more complex, we should see a lower CPR. The time cost involved in learning and understanding and ultimately complying with the law is reflected in complexity. If individuals have difficulty understanding the legislation because it is complex, this may lead to a situation in which fewer candidates run for office. Understanding if the complexity of the law has an effect on candidates' decisions to run for office is imperative. It allows us to measure each state's statutes in a consistent manner.

Understanding where, when, and how citizens make decisions affected by campaign finance reform is important. We know citizens who run for state legislature often run businesses or are employed elsewhere. Adding on the task of understanding and complying with campaign finance regulations can add to a potential candidate's burden. Campaign finance may be so complex that ordinary citizens wanting to participate may not do so because they do not understand all the regulations. If they want to join in the system, they must incur the cost involved with hiring professionals to help them run their campaign according to the regulations. This extra cost can be a deterrent to non-wealthy citizens wanting to run for office. Complexity could lead to fewer candidates running for office and those candidates that do run being the incumbents who have the resources and knowledge with which to navigate the campaign finance regulations. This issue has not yet been studied, but it is vital that this research is done. If citizens cannot understand the laws meant to regulate this situation the democratization goals of campaign finance reform are in peril.

Campaign finance reform statutes in this study refer to at any state legislation pertaining to pre-bank candidate contributions. Any regulation that affects a candidate prior to them depositing the contribution in the bank is considered for the study. Other post-bank legislation concerning treasurer qualifications, committee organization, reporting requirements, and disposal of leftover funds are not considered. Considering only the pre-bank regulations measures a candidate's situation just as they are deciding whether to become a candidate. Once they move to organization, and reporting, the candidate has already made a more firm decision to run for office. By measuring only pre-bank regulations, this study captures the first type of information a candidate would need to know.[9] It is the first hurdle the candidate needs to clear. I collected campaign finance regulations for all fifty states. This collection indicates that pre-bank legislation is also found in almost every state except those that have no limitations on donations. Yet even in those states without limitations, there are still regulations on how any money collected must be handled. However, because some states have no limitations on contributions this presents a potential validity issue. If only states with contribution limits are studied, bias is introduced where only states with some potential complexity are studied. This would exclude states that have no complexity or no contribution limits. Including only those states with contribution limits would measure only those states with some complexity. To circumvent the problem in which some states have no contribution limits, contribution definitions were also collected from each state. These definitions should be written in the same form and style as the contribution statutes and therefore can serve as a validity check for the study. The candidacy requirement statutes in figure 7.2 and campaign finance definitions in figure 7.3 as measured by the Flesch-Kincaid Grade Reading Level and word counts are included in graphs in Appendix C. The Contribution statutes measured with both the Flesch-Kincaid grade reading level and word count is demonstrated in figure 7.1.

The pre-bank contribution limits are the current limits set by each state legislature. In most states, this legislation does not change very often allowing testing of the effects over several years. The static nature of the legislation is ensured by comparing across databases. The contribution statutes were collected using each state's statute repository. Each state differently stores their statutes so a comprehensive search was done to gather all the contribution legislation for each state. This first wave of data collection included everything pre and post-bank related to contributions. In order to ensure that the same information was collected from each state, a Microsoft Excel spreadsheet was created to record each statute section for each part of the contribution statutes. For example, I recorded the chapter and section for each state pertaining to contribution limits, loans, anonymous contributions, corporate and labor union contributions, treasurers, reporting and disclosure requirements, and definitions. Only those sections corresponding with the pre-bank contributions were used in this analysis. As noted above only the pre-bank contribution data (hereafter "contribution legislation") is collected because this is the main part of the law that will touch all candidates when deciding to run for office. The contribution data from each state's statutes is compared to summary files from the National Conference on State Legislatures, containing all the contribution statutes and numbers for the past nine years. The statutes are compared to the NCSL database to ensure that no major changes to the legislation occurred during the 1998–2016 period. I found no major changes in legislation.

This study also looks at legislation pertaining to requirements for candidacy such as age, residency, filing procedures, and filing to run for office. Looking at this legislation gives a well-rounded vision of what a candidate faces when deciding to run for office including all the requirements, filing paperwork, fees, and obligations. Advisory opinions or rules, or rulings by ethics boards are not part of the complexity measure of the legislation. These should be considered in future research if states issue them. They are omitted here for convenience but also because some states may be like North Carolina, which does not issue advisory opinions or rules but rather work closely with legislators to write the laws obviating the need for advisory opinions.[10]

The contribution definitions collected are those definitions pertinent to the campaign finance sections in each state's statutes. For example, states have definitions of polling places, ballots, and so forth, which are not pertinent to candidate decisions. States have separate definition sections just pertaining to campaign finance. These definitions include terms such as candidate, contribution, loans, and filing petitions that are pertinent definitions a candidate would need to understand before running for office. These definitions are also included in this study because some states do not have contribution requirements as noted above. A lack of a contribution statute presents a validity issue where only those states with contribution statutes, and hence some complexity, are studied.

Contribution statutes, candidacy requirements, and contribution definitions from all 50 states are used to test for complexity. Using the contribution statutes from all fifty states allows for variability of the data. Using the statute from only one state would not allow for any variability because most statutes do not vary much over time. Using all fifty states' statutes allows study of the effects of the legislation on candidate decisions in a variety of settings. Each state has different treatments of candidates and various types of legislation. Data were collected from 1998–2016 because these were the available years and collecting from these years ensures we have at minimum ten election cycles over the eighteen years.

Each state's contribution, definitions, and candidacy requirement statutes were run through a plain language online utility to measure complexity. Complexity is measured based on language components. These components include the Flesch-Kincaid Grade Reading level that gives us a measure of what US grade level should be able to comprehend the legislation.[11] The utility also gives a Flesch Reading Ease score, word count, and syllable-per-word count. The readability measures are all continuous variables; the other variables are count variables. The process for measuring complexity involves copying and pasting the contribution legislation, definitions, and candidacy requirements into the online utility. The online utility calculates all the complexity or plain language factors.

The online utility gives thirteen complexity or plain language factors such as those described above. This presents a possible issue of multicollinearity where each variable is measuring the same underlying factor. To determine if this is the case or not, factor analysis of the plain language variables is included in this study. Factor analysis is appropriate here because this study tests the assumption that there is an underlying concept of complexity inherent in the language of the campaign finance statutes. After running the factor analysis, it was clear that the thirteen plain language indices were measuring the same underlying concept. The factor analysis retained three factors with an eigenvalue > 0. These three factors have highly loaded factor scores indicating that they are measuring the same thing that the variables are measuring.[12]

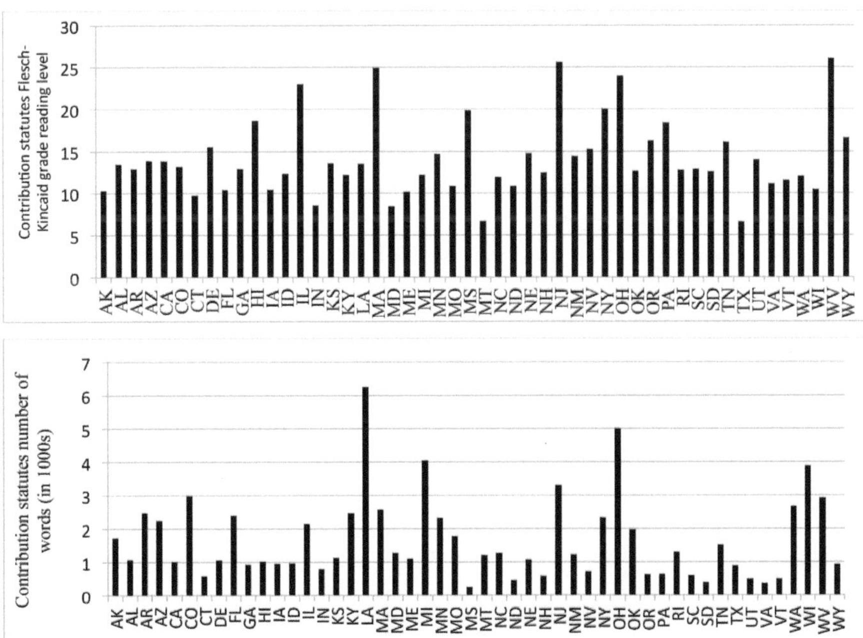

Figure 7.1. Contribution statutes measured by Flesch-Kincaid grade reading level and number of words.

As a robustness check a regression and Variance Inflation Factor were run. This indicated a very high level of multicollinearity between the plain language measures. To ensure that this multicollinearity does not provide unreliable estimates, this study includes only two of the plain language measures. These two measures are the Flesch-Kincaid Grade Reading Level measuring US grade level needed to understand the legislation, and the word count. Both of these indices are used in plain language studies and studies of constraining legislation. They were chosen for the study because of their broad theoretical impact in previous studies.

Control Variables

Control variables include most political variables contained in similar studies of candidate decisions. The political control variables include a dummy variable for chamber type. The chamber type dummy is included in the model to restructure the data for only one year per state. The chamber dummy is coded so that House = 1 and Senate = 0.

Other factors might affect candidates' decisions to run for office including such political factors as the professionalism of the legislature. The professionalism measure included here is legislator salary. Professionalism of the legislature is thought to be a strong determinant of whether or not an individual decides to seek office.[13] Salary data were collected from the NCSL website for each year. The salary data is the base salary data not including per diems, or voucher and unvouchered expenses.

Institutional or strategic factors also play a role in candidates' decisions to run. Strategic factors are those factors based on which a candidate may make a decision regarding running for office. The rationale here is that candidates are strategic and make rational decisions[14] based on whether or not there is a chance for them to win an election. Maisel and Stone[15] found that when an incumbent held a seat, a challenger was more likely to account for this in their decision to run for office. Hogan[16] found the similar results. Kazee found that just the perception of incumbent strength was enough to deter challengers from seeking office.[17] There are many strategic and institutional reasons why a candidate might decide to run for office. Incumbent data[18] were collected from the National Institute on Money in State Politics[19] for all fifty states from 1998–2016.

Methods

This study uses percentages of candidates and candidate withdrawals to create rates with which to measure participation in elections. The CPR is the participation rate in elections. It is a percentage of the number of candidates per total seats up for election and permanent chamber seats. The CWR is the number of withdrawals as a percentage of the total number of candidates, as a percentage of the total number of seats up for election and as a percentage of the permanent seats in the chamber. Because theoretically these percentages could be unbounded on the upper level, a Tobit regression model is used. Although it is unlikely that there would be an infinite number of candidates running for a seat, there is no true limit to that number. Since it could be greater than 100 percent using the Tobit model allows for an uncensored regression model[20] that ensures that the data are not censored on the upper level.

This model includes data from 1998–2016. This indicates the possibility of serial autocorrelation. If this were the case, finding errors in one time-period correlated with errors in another time-period would be expected. To correct for this a fixed effects model for time is appropriate. It is not appropriate to use a fixed effects model for the state in this analysis because the main independent variable for complexity was only measured one time for each state. As a robustness check, the analysis was run twice using clustered standard errors for both the state and the year. While the regression results were similar, the standard errors when clustered for the state were higher. Therefore, the clustered standard errors for the year were used for the analysis.

NOTES

1. M. S. Lewis-Beck, Bryman, A., & Liao, T. F., *The Sage Encyclopedia of Social Science Research Methods.*(Thousand Oaks, CA: Sage, 2004).
2. Christopher Witko, "Measuring the Stringency of State Campaign Finance Regulation," *State Politics and Policy Quarterly* 5, no. 3 (2005). Christopher Kulesza, Christopher Witko, and Eric Waltenburg, "Reform Interrupted? State Innovation, Court Decisions, and the Past and Future of Campaign Finance Reform in the States," *Election Law Journal* 2 (2016).
3. Institute on Money in State Politics, "Followthemoney," in *Institute on Money in State Politics.*
4. At the author's request, North Carolina's Board of Elections searched for the hard copies of the withdrawals to see if some reason for the withdrawals could be gleaned. Unfortunately, North Carolina does not keep any data on the withdrawals.
5. Jerome Kirk and Marc L. Miller, *Reliability and Validity in Qualitative Research* (Newbury Park, CA: Sage Publications, 1986).
6. Robert E. Hogan, "Challenger Emergence, Incumbent Success and Electoral Accoutability in State Legislative Elections," *The Journal of Politics* 66, no. 4 (2004).
7. Ibid.
8. Geert R. Teisman and Eric-Hans Klijn, "Complexity Theory and Public Management," *Public Management Review* 10, no. 3 (2008).
9. L. Sandy Maisel and Walter J. Stone, "Determinants of Candidate Emergence in US House Elections: An Exploratory Study," *Legislative Studies Quarterly* 22, no. 1 (1997).
10. Kim Strach, "NC Board of Elections Campaign Finance Division," ed. Mary Jo Shepherd (2012).
11. "Online-Utility.Org," in *Online-Utility.org.*
12. Leandre R. Fabrigar and Duane T. Wegener, *Exploratory Factor Analysis* (New York: Oxford, 2012); "Stata Statistical Software: Release 14," (College Station, TX: Stata Corp LP, 2015).

13. Hogan, "Challenger Emergence, Incumbent Success and Electoral Accoutability in State Legislative Elections."

14. Martin D. Levine and Mark S. Hyde, "Incumbency and the Theory of Political Ambition: A Rational-Choice Model," ibid., 39 (1977). Gordon S. Black, "A Theory of Political Ambition: Career Choices and the Role of Structural Incentives," *The American Political Science Review* 66, no. 1 (1972).

15. Maisel and Stone, "Determinants of Candidate Emergence in US House Elections: An Exploratory Study."

16. Hogan, "Challenger Emergence, Incumbent Success and Electoral Accoutability in State Legislative Elections."

17. Thomas A. Kazee, "The Deterrent Effect of Incumbency on Recruiting Challengers in US House Elections," *Legislative Studies Quarterly* 8, no. 3 (1983).

18. Originally, data on challengers, incumbents, and open seats were included in the analysis. However, challengers would be included in the total number of candidates and so was not used as a separate variable. Open seats would also be included in the creation of the CPR and CWR based on seats in the legislatures for each state. Because of these factors, only the incumbent data are included in the book analysis.

19. "Followthemoney."

20. J. Scott Long and Jeremy Freese, *Regression Models for Categorical Dependent Variables Using Stata* (College Station, TX: Stata Press, 2006).

Chapter Eight

Data Analysis

The models presented here measure the hypotheses that as the complexity of legislation increases, the percentage of candidates will decrease and the percentage of withdrawals will increase. Complexity or the administrative burden of legislation measures use the plain language variables described in chapter 5.

A Tobit Model for limited dependent variables is the appropriate statistical method to use for percentage or proportional dependent variables that may be uncensored on the upper level.[1] The analysis is divided into two models. The first model tests the percentage of candidates, or the CPR, both using candidates as a percentage of the total seats up for election and candidates as a percentage of the permanent chamber seats. Each percentage is regressed by the two plain language measures—the Flesch-Kincaid grade level and the word count measure. In the second model, the percentage of withdrawals or the Candidate Withdrawal Rate (CWR) is regressed using the same methods except using in the number of withdrawals as a percentage of total candidates. Each model analyzes three different types of legislation: the campaign finance contribution statutes, the campaign finance definition statutes, and the candidacy requirement statutes.

MODEL 1

Complexity and the Candidate Participation Rate

The Candidate Participation Rate (CPR) is a rate of the total number of candidates running in a race. Because it is important to analyze this correctly, the total number of candidates' variable was transformed into two rates. The first variable is the total number of candidates divided by the total number of seats up for election or the CPRs. This percentage measures the rate of candidates as it increases or decreases depending on the number of seats that are up for grabs in that specific election. The second rate is the total number of candidates running divided by the permanent seats in the chamber or the CPRp. The permanent seats in the chamber are the number of seats legislated to exist in each chamber and state.

Plain Language Complexity Effects on Candidate Participation Rate (CPR) and Candidate Withdrawal Rate (CWR)[2]

Total number of candidates (CPR) was hypothesized to decrease in states with more complex legislation. When the contribution statutes were more complex across the fifty states, there was a modest decrease in the participation rates on average regardless of whether the contribution statutes were measured by word count or by the Flesch-Kincaid grade level. As the word count increased, there was a rate decrease of eight candidates per 1,000 or .008 for the total seats up for election and the permanent seats in the chamber. Although this relationship is in the hypothesized direction, it is not statistically significant. When the contribution statutes were measured using the Flesch-Kincaid grade reading level the rate decrease in the CPR for both total seats and permanent chamber seats was .044 on average. They were not statistically significant. All four of the contribution statute variables saw decreases in the CPR indicating that a more robust relationship might exist between the complexity of contribution statutes and the number of candidates running for office. This relationship ought to be investigated further. As theoretically discussed in chapter 4 on plain language theory, the Flesch-Kincaid model is more likely the best measure of complexity since it is measuring what individuals read rather than just the number of words. Even though this relationship is not statistically significant, it does indicate that, the statutes' complexity is a drag on candidate participation rates. Even a small decrease indicates that some candidates chose not to run for office in those states having statutes that are more complex. This is important given the goals of campaign finance regulation is to increase participation in electoral systems.

The CPR was hypothesized to decrease also when the candidacy requirements were more complex. Logically as candidates navigated the statutes to determine what they needed to do when running for office, the learning required might deter some candidates from running. On average, when measured by word count the average participation rate increased .190 for the total seats in the chamber and the permanent chamber seats, respectively. This increase in the number of candidates instead of a decrease was opposite of the hypothesized direction and was statistically significant at the .01 level. The results for the Flesch-Kincaid grade reading level were statistically significant at the .05 level of the CPRs and CPRp. This indicates that as the candidacy requirements were on a higher grade reading level, 88 more candidates out of 1,000 signed up to run for office. This relationship is opposite the hypothesized direction. It is not clear why this relationship is opposite to the hypothesized direction but clearly more study is warranted. It is possible that candidates are not required to understand the law but just required to fill out forms provided by secretaries of state or registrars offices. This is discussed further below. It is also possible that candidates see the candidacy phase as very different from the contribution/campaigning phase of running for office. This is borne out in some of the candidate interviews where respondents talked about the initial decision to run in optimistic and happier tones, but when asked about fund-raising, they were less enthusiastic. Candidates described filing to run and the actual decision in terms of fulfilling a duty and making a difference. When the same candidates described campaigning and soliciting contributions, they were grimmer and lacking in enthusiasm, which points to a possible explanation of a two-stage mentality governing the process of running for election. Candidates visualize the candidacy filing stage as a different endeavor than the actual campaign activities such as collecting contributions and filling out reporting forms.

Campaign finance definition statutes were included in the model as a validity check but were hypothesized to have similar effects to either the contribution statutes or candidacy requirements on the CPR. It is hypothesized that the CPR would decrease if the definition statutes were complex. All four models allow rejection of the null hypothesis with 99 percent confidence. For the word count model the candidate rate decreased .074 for both the CPRs and CPRp. While in the Flesch-Kincaid grade reading level model, the candidate rate decreased .311. This supports the hypothesis that when the statute is more complex, fewer candidates will run for office. At issue here, however, is that the definitions were originally included only as a check on validity. It seemed unlikely that candidates actually look at the definitions to determine if or how to run a campaign. Perhaps this contention is incorrect and candidates do look at the definitions. Definitions provide introductory information defining terms such as contributions and contributors. Definition statutes have a higher Flesch-Kincaid grade reading level and word count mean making them a longer and more difficult part of the statute to comprehend. Assuming candidates use this part of the statute, this supports this book's contention that the more complex the statute, the more likely it is that candidates will not run for office. Future research must study if candidates use this portion of the statute to account for this finding.

Table 8.1. Complexity and Candidate Decisions

	Candidate Participation Rates		Candidate Withdrawal Rates		
Tobit Model	CPRs	CPRp	CWR	CWRs	CWRp
Contribution Limits					
Word Count	-0.008	-0.008	-0.003	-0.005	-0.006
	(0.024)	(0.024)	(0.003)	(0.007)	(0.007)
Flesch-Kincaid Grade Reading Level	-0.044	-0.044	**0.022**	**0.046**	**0.043**
	(0.050)	(0.050)	(0.008)**	(0.018)**	(0.015)**
Candidacy Requirements					
Word Count	*0.190*	*0.190*	**0.010**	**0.025**	**0.023**
	(0.030)**	(0.030)**	(0.003)**	(0.006)**	(0.005)**
Flesch-Kincaid Grade Reading Level	*0.088*	*0.088*	*-0.019*	*-0.039*	*-0.038*
	(0.039)*	(0.039)*	(0.006)**	(0.013)**	(0.012)**
Definitions					
Word Count	**-0.074**	**-0.074**	*-0.012*	*-0.025*	*-0.021*
	(0.015)**	(0.015)**	(0.005)*	(0.011)*	(0.010)*
Flesch-Kincaid Grade Reading Level	**-0.311**	**-0.311**	-0.010	-0.021	-0.019
	(0.042)**	(0.042)**	(0.006)	(0.012)	(0.010)
Legislator salary	0.000	0.000	-0.000	-0.000	-0.000

		(0.000)**	(0.000)**	(0.000)	(0.000)	(0.000)
State population by seat		-0.000	-0.000	-0.000	-0.000	-0.000
		(0.000)**	(0.000)**	(0.000)	(0.000)*	(0.000)**
Number of incumbents		-0.001	-0.001	-0.000	0.000	0.000
		(0.001)*	(0.001)*	(0.000)	(0.000)	(0.000)
Chamber type		-0.557	-0.557	-0.007	-0.017	-0.021
House=1, Senate = 0		(0.041)**	(0.041)**	(0.004)*	(0.007)*	(0.006)**
Term Limit Dummy		0.191	0.191	0.025	0.058	0.052
		(0.036)**	(0.036)**	(0.002)**	(0.006)**	(0.005)**
	Constant	2.148	2.148	0.024	0.008	0.007
		(0.239)**	(0.239)**	(0.053)	(0.117)	(0.098)
sigma	Constant	0.518	0.518	0.039	0.087	0.078
		(0.014)**	(0.014)**	(0.002)**	(0.004)**	(0.004)**
N		903	903	903	903	903

*p < 0.05; **p < 0.01 Robust Standard Errors Clustered by Year

Political Effects on CPR

Legislator salary is a proxy for professionalism of the legislature. The hypothesized result would indicate that a more professional legislature would attract more candidates to run for office. A statistically significant relationship is found in legislators' salary. As the average salary (or professionalism) increased, the CPR for both total seats and permanent chamber seats increased and this relationship was statistically significant at the .01 level. This relationship coincides with Hogan[3] who also finds similarly that legislative professionalism increases the probability of challengers emerging.

The literature varies on the effects that various types of candidates such as incumbents or challengers have on the CPR.[4] In general, the models presented here found that when the number of incumbents increased, the CPR decreased on average .001 for the total seats up for election and permanent chamber seats.[5] Both of these relationships were statistically significant at the .05 level indicating that incumbents are an important variable deterring candidates from running for office. This finding is important; as one issue with the complexity of campaign finance statutes is that there may be a different effect on different types of candidates. Challengers would face higher costs than incumbents who have already learned how to campaign and run for office. This finding supports this contention because the candidate participation rate overall decreases in a statistically significant relationship when incumbents are in the model.

The chamber type variable is a dummy variable where the House = 1 and the Senate = 0. These data seem to indicate that when the chamber type is the House there is a .557 reduction in the CPR on average for the total seats up for election and for permanent seats in the chamber. Both of these findings are statistically significant at the .01 level. This allows rejection of the null with 99 percent certainty for this relationship.

The term limits variable is a dummy indicating if term limits are in place (1) or no term limits (0). When we look at the CPR, it is .191 higher for total seats up for election and permanent chamber seats respectively than when term limits are not in place. Both of these relationships are statistically significant at the .01 level allowing us to reject the null with 99 percent confidence. This relationship is also intuitive, when term limits are in place the chance for more candidates to participate presents itself as evidenced here.

MODEL 2

Complexity and Candidate Withdrawals

The hypothesized relationship in this second model posits that in the fifty United States where the legislation is more complex, more candidates withdraw their candidacy for office. Candidate withdrawals were an unexpected find when collecting candidate rates in each state. Withdrawals have different coding for candidacies than disqualifications or deaths of candidates. As noted earlier, there is little information on who or why withdrawals occur. Candidates file to run for office and then for unknown reasons, withdraw their candidacy. When the number of words increases or the Flesch-Kincaid grade level increases the expectation is that more candidates would withdraw from their races. The legislation is measured three ways using the contribution statutes, the campaign finance definitions, and the candidacy requirement statutes. Each type of legislation is then measured using the two plain language measurements—either the Flesch-Kincaid grade level or the word count.

Table 8.1 shows mixed results for the different independent variables. Looking at the complexity of contribution statutes measured by the Flesch-Kincaid grade reading level, we see that as the grade level increased the CWR for all three models on average increased from 22 to 46 candidates per 1,000. We can reject the null hypothesis at the 99 percent level for this relationship. Here the data indicate that as the number of words in the statute increase, there is a decrease in the CWR. However, none of the three models is statistically significant. As discussed earlier, the word count measure is a less intuitive measure of complexity because it only counts the number of words in the statute whereas the Flesch-Kincaid is a more robust measure of what candidates would be able to understand.

Candidacy requirements measured by the Flesch-Kincaid indicate a relationship opposite to the hypothesized direction. As hypothesized, when the grade reading level increases, an increase in the CWR is expected as candidates withdraw from the race. In this analysis, as the grade reading level increases, the CWR decreased on average .019 to .039. The relationships for all three measures are statistically significant at the .01 level. Interestingly, this relationship is opposite the expected hypothesized direction. As discussed above with the participation rates, it is possible that candidates view campaigning as two separate processes—one, the candidacy portion, and two, the campaigning portion. This is discussed further below and potentially bolstered by interviews with candidates.

When the number of words for the candidacy requirements was measured, the results were quite different. The CWR for all three relationships increased on average .010 to .025. These relationships were significant at the .01 level allowing rejection of the null with 99 percent confidence. Taking the opposing results for Flesch-Kincaid grade level and the word count analysis together with the previous analysis that word count may not be the most potent measure of complexity, these findings should be taken with utmost caution. It is unclear why the two measures of candidacy requirements would have opposite effects and this will have to be studied in more depth most especially because candidacy requirements are something that every candidate will need to know. There is the possibility of multicollinearity given the opposite findings. However, robust standard errors (clustered by year) were used and the models were run separately with similar findings.

The campaign finance definitions as measured by the Flesch-Kincaid grade-reading level indicate that as the grade level increased the number of withdrawals decreased on average from .010 to .019. This relationship is not statistically significant. The campaign finance definitions as measured by word count are statistically significant at the .05 level but opposite the hypothesized direction. This indicates that as the statute definitions had more words, on average the number of withdrawals decreased. Even though this is statistically significant, as noted above the definitions were only included as a validity check and as less important part of the statute it is unlikely that candidates will read them.

Control Variables

The political variables included in the model represent professionalism of the legislature and are expected to have an effect on candidate decisions. Salary is a proxy for professionalism of the legislature. As legislative salaries increase candidate withdrawals decrease is not statistically insignificant for any of the models.

When candidates face incumbents, there is an expectation that the number of withdrawals would increase. This result is found when looking at the total candidate CWR. If the number of incumbents increased, the CWR is expected to decrease by .000 on average. For the withdrawal rates for the total number of seats up in the election and total number of permanent seats, as the number of incumbents increased there was an average increase of .000. It may be that candidates when seeing a large number of candidates many of whom are incumbents chose to withdraw. None of these relationships are statistically significant.

Whether or not the candidate was running for the House or Senate appears to have some effect on candidate withdrawals. The Chamber Type variable is a dummy variable where the House is coded as 1, and the Senate as 0. In this analysis, when the Chamber type is the House (1), it appears that candidate withdrawals are expected to be lower (–.007 to –.021) on average. All three CWR variables are statistically significant with the CWRt and CWRs at the .05 level and the CWRp at the .01 level. There is the possibility that this indicates the House is an easier seat for which to run. If we see fewer candidates withdrawing in House races than Senate, it would indicate that potential candidates see these races as easier. The Senate districts in the states are larger so the costs are higher to run for those seats versus the House districts. Logically the costs would be amplified by the larger sized districts.

The term limit variable is coded for 1 if term limits are in place and 0 if no term limits are in place. This variable is statistically significant at the .01 level indicating that when term limits are in place more candidates are expected to withdraw from races on average than when there are no term limits in place. This makes sense, as we would expect to see more candidates withdrawing when they see the barrier of term limits. We would assume however, that most candidates would realize this barrier is in place before contemplating a run for office.

Qualitative Analysis

In order to add to the internal validity of the study,[6] and to build the theory that complexity might deter people from running qualitative interviews were completed on fourteen former or potential candidates from around the country.[7] Respondents were asked about their political background, and general interest in politics. Respondents were also asked if and why they would run for office or if they would run again. No respondent considered running again with enthusiasm. Most of the negative responses contained some element of hesitancy such as the dislike of asking people for contributions, the dirty nature of politics. Time commitment was a problem with some of the respondents but with variation. Some respondents said time away from their job would cause an income loss, while others said time away from family was more of an issue. Another respondent who is now a campaign consultant talked about the difficulty of finding people to run for office because of the fear of losing their reputation. He spoke in particular of business owners who would be unwilling to run for fear of losing business. Even somewhat successful candidates remarked on the negative aspects of running for office.

Respondents were asked to describe the process of running for office. This question was left purposely vague in order to allow respondents to answer how they chose. Respondents spoke of getting on the ballot and raising money as the top issues. Most respondents had help from either their state/local party or an experienced politician within their party. One respondent had help from a candidate school; another had help from campaign consultants. One respondent spoke of being groomed within the party with the eventual expectation that he would run for office.

Regarding the logistics of running, none of the respondents explicitly said that the complexity of the campaign finance system was a deterrent to running. However, three of the respondents referred indirectly to this idea. One respondent stated that running for office in his state would require people to be researchers and someone off the street would not be able to do it.[8] This respondent was discussing the process of filing for office that requires petitions. Another respondent said that being a lawyer gave him the "sense that he had a leg up" in running for office, and "while he didn't know the [election/campaign] code off the top of his head, he would be able to find it and use it if needed. The average person would need help."[9] These responses indicate some candidates had difficulty figuring out the process of running for office.

There seems to be a disconnect between the candidacy requirements and the contribution statutes. There are different sentiments among respondents who were enthusiastic and engaged when discussing how they made decisions to run for office and the filing process versus the more negative and discouraging tones when discussing gathering contributions and the difficulty of the process. When asked about their decision to run for office, the respondents were optimistic and enthusiastic about the opportunity to serve in elected office, change public policies with which they disagreed, and to change the political discourse. When the subjects discussed collecting contributions, they sounded more discouraged and unenthusiastic. It was generally at this point that candidates voiced concerns or complaints about the campaign process and how difficult it was to run for office. This disconnect is a possible explanation for the different results in the regression analysis. When facing candidacy regulations, candidates were more likely to file to run for office and participate in the process. However, when faced with contribution regulations, the candidate participation rates were negative.

CONCLUSIONS

Table 8.2 summarizes the study findings in a format that highlights each legislation type for easier review. The results in the hypothesized direction are marked with bold while those opposite the hypothesized direction are indicated with italics.

Looking first at the Candidate Participation Rate (CPR) in the left columns, results consistent with the hypothesis are found using the Flesch-Kincaid measure and word counts for both contribution limits and definitions. The definitions relationships are statistically significant in the hypothesized direction, while contribution requirements are in the hypothesized direction but statistically insignificant. Even without the statistical significance, the models show that there is a decline in the participation rates of candidates in those states with more complex statutes. Clearly, statutes are affecting some candidate decisions. While the impact may be statistically insignificant, even a small number of individuals choosing not to run for office is problematic when the goal is to increase participation rates. However, much caution is warranted given the novelty of these measures and the lack of statistical significance in the models. These findings are somewhat consistent with what the qualitative interviews found. Candidates were hesitant to run for office for a variety of reasons, but collecting money was one of

Table 8.2. Summary of Findings

Candidacy Participation Rates (CPR)			Candidacy Withdrawal Rates (CWR)		
Contribution Limits			**Contribution Limits**		
	Flesch-Kincaid	Word Count		Flesch-Kincaid	Word Count
			Total Candidates	**pos**	neg
Total Seats Up	neg	neg	Total Seats Up	**pos**	neg
Permanent Chamber Seats	neg	neg	Permanent Chamber Seats	**pos**	neg
Candidacy Requirements			**Candidacy Requirements**		
	Flesch-Kincaid	Word Count		Flesch-Kincaid	Word Count
			Total Candidates	*neg*	**pos**
Total Seats Up	*pos*	*pos*	Total Seats Up	*neg*	**pos**
Permanent Chamber Seats	*pos*	*pos*	Permanent Chamber Seats	*neg*	**pos**
Definitions			**Definitions**		
	Flesch-Kincaid	Word Count		Flesch-Kincaid	Word Count
			Total Candidates	neg	*neg*
Total Seats Up	**neg**	**neg**	Total Seats Up	neg	*neg*
Permanent Chamber Seats	**neg**	**neg**	Permanent Chamber Seats	neg	*neg*

the main reasons. It is not the contention of this study that candidates equate asking people for money with complexity of contribution statutes. When faced with contribution requirements, candidates may want to comply but might have difficulty understanding the statutes if they are complex. The difficulty understanding and complying with the statute may increase the fear of reputational risk for everyday candidates. Incumbents may have overcome this risk, but an average business owner or educator wishing to run for office may be unlikely to face the risk incumbents do. The Flesch-Kincaid contribution findings indicate that when the statutes are more difficult, fewer candidates are expected to run for office on average. Furthermore, potential candidates when interviewed stated that because they were experienced they would have an easier time understanding how to run for office.[10] Average citizens running for office for the first time may have more difficulty in understanding the statutes and complying with them.

The same results are not found for candidacy requirements. These coefficients are positive indicating that as the candidacy requirements were more complex, more candidates ran for office. This is contrary to the hypothesis that fewer candidates would run. This relationship is unclear. Based on the candidate interviews, when the respondents spoke about the logistics of running they seemed to indicate that it was difficult, they were hesitant to run, or unwilling to put themselves through the process. It was only if the opportunity arose or life circumstances made it possible that candidates voiced a desire to run again. There was no sense that the candidates were eager to run again. This lack of enthusiasm pointed at the process. This process gives a hint of possibly why candidacy requirements were opposite the hypothesized direction. During the interviews, the candidates seemed to equate the campaign process more with the fund-raising and campaigning, than with candidacy filing. Perhaps they see candidacy in general as a two-stage endeavor. Candidate filing is the first stage that individuals may find easier, whereas the second stage of collecting contributions and campaigning was more difficult.

Table 8.2 summarizes the results from Model 2 in the right-hand columns. The Candidate Withdrawal Rate (CWR) anticipated increases in the percentage of withdrawals with corresponding increases in the Flesch-Kincaid Grade Reading level of the legislation and the statute word count. The contribution limits results were in the hypothesized direction (an increase) and all were statistically significant. These results show with an increase in the Flesch-Kincaid grade reading level or an increase in the word counts, an average increase in the CWR appear for the contribution statutes. This is important because one of the main contentions of this study is that contribution statutes may be constraining or difficult to understand for candidates. Combined with supported findings for the CPR in the first model, the contribution limits may be a factor both in reducing the number of candidates running for office and increasing the number of withdrawals.

Candidacy requirements measured by word count are all statistically significant and in the correct direction, whereas the Flesch-Kincaid results are also statistically significant but in the opposite direction. Candidates would need to understand the basic requirements to run for office because misunderstanding these may cause candidate disqualification or reputational harm. It is not clear why these two relationships are in the opposite directions. Further research and testing are necessary to tease out these differences especially between the plain language complexity measures. It is unclear whether this is an issue with the Flesch-Kincaid/Word Count measurement tools or the candidate decisions. Because studying regulations using these methods are so novel, conclusions are made cautiously. The campaign finance definition statutes, measured with either the Flesch-Kincaid or the word count, are contrary to hypothesized expectations.

Both of these models add a novel way with which to measure candidate decisions to run for office. By using complexity measured via grade reading level and word count, this study is able to add to the literature on campaign finance and candidate decisions.

Even though the results are not straightforward, there is some support for this study's contention that complexity—as measured by grade reading level and word count—do contribute to candidate decisions. With more research, this picture will become clearer. Clarity on this issue is very important to uphold the goals of campaign finance reform and to democracy in general. One of the goals of campaign finance is to increase participation in the electoral system. Clearly, if the statutes are constraining and difficult to understand this goal might be in jeopardy. It is important that campaign finance statutes remain accessible to those candidates they are intended to help.

NOTES

1. J. Scott Long and Jeremy Freese, *Regression Models for Categorical Dependent Variables Using Stata* (College Station, TX: Strata Press, 2006).
2. In chapter 8 tables, the bold coefficients indicate statistically significant relationships in the hypothesized direction. Italics signify relationships opposite the hypothesized direction. The year dummy variables are presented in the full table in the appendix.
3. Robert E. Hogan, "Challenger Emergence, Incumbent Success and Electoral Accoutability in State Legislative Elections," *The Journal of Politics* 66, no. 4 (2004).
4. Ibid.; Thomas A. Kazee, "The Deterrent Effect of Incumbency on Recruiting Challengers in US House Elections," *Legislative Studies Quarterly* 8, no. 3 (1983); L. Sandy Maisel and Walter J. Stone, "Determinants of Candidate Emergence in US House Elections: An Exploratory Study," ibid. 22, no. 1 (1997).
5. Some literature indicates an effect on candidate decisions by the presence of challengers and open seats. These two variables were omitted in this analysis. Challengers were omitted because challengers would be included in the total candidate rate. Open seats were omitted because these seats would be included as part of the total seats or permanent chamber seats. Regardless, a model was run with open seats included. Unless noted in the text, there were no significant differences.
6. Jerome Kirk and Marc L. Miller, *Reliability and Validity in Qualitative Research* (Newbury Park, CA: Sage Publications, 1986).
7. Respondents were from California, Connecticut, Kentucky, Kansas, Missouri, North Carolina, New Jersey, Pennsylvania, and Virginia.
8. QI4, ed. Mary Jo McGowan Shepherd (2014).
9. QI13, ed. Mary Jo McGowan Shepherd (2014).
10. QI12, ed. Mary Jo McGowan Shepherd (2014); QI13; QI4.

Conclusion

When a citizen of one of the US states considers becoming a candidate for office, many factors go into making that decision. Potential candidates may consider their families, work situations, reputational risk, and costs. Costs must also include the time and effort required to learn and comply with campaign finance regulations. Scholars study candidate decision factors and study how campaign finance reforms affect candidate campaigns. As a regulatory system, the statutes governing campaigns are complex. The statutes require time and effort to comply adding onto the burden candidates already face. Additionally, if new to running for office, candidates face a steep learning curve on how to run for office. Even though campaign finance is well studied, one factor not yet considered is how the campaign finance regulatory system, created to democratize campaigns, may affect candidate decisions. This study finds that the campaign finance regulatory system deters candidates from running for office in those states with statutes that are more complex.

Rules are Complex Institutions

This book treats rules and regulations as institutions that constrain behavior. Institutional treatments in previous research look at rules and regulations created by one institution with effects on a different institution. For example, constraint happens when legislatures constrain bureaucrats or judges. This study treats those rules and regulations covering campaign finance as institutions that affect individuals. Understanding how rules are institutions and how to measure complexity of institutions is a central feature of this work.

Regulatory systems guide behavior and influence policy outcomes by setting up rules that signal agencies or bureaucrats regarding desired actions or behavior. Rules help to ensure that agencies or individuals comply with the legislative intent for policy implementation. Sometimes legislatures define rules narrowly to specify exactly how they intend agents to act and other times direction is ambiguous. By setting standards or guidelines, rules intend to create situations where bureaucrats or agencies treat other actors equally or fairly. Regardless of intent, as part of government, are inherently coercive institutions. Rules are coercive institutions with formal and informal features that translate the values or goals of a principal actor into actions. Post implementation, rules become stable and normalized, and as time goes on rules produce additional regulations and rules. The layers of rules and regulations build up, become intertwined, and may have intended and unintended consequences. Public administration scholars call this administrative burden. As consequences occur, rules create a burden for administrators and those to whom the rules apply. Individuals or administrators must take the time to learn new rules and to determine how to implement the rules. This burden creates additional transaction costs such as learning, compliance or psychological costs for the implementers. The rule situation becomes one of increasing costs, scope, and burden as rule followers try to comply with the rules. This burden and the costs of compliance create a complex regulatory regime—or complexity.

Complexity is the time and effort required to comply with a regulatory system. It is a potential situation facing an individual agent or agency complying with legislative statutes. Agents or agencies could also face a non-complex system. This could be construed as a simple system, but the laws passed by legislatures are rarely simple. A non-complex or simple statute would require less time, effort, scope, and costs to comply with the statute. However, most statutes deal with complicated policy issues with a wide implementation scope. When issues are legislated, there may be little review of past rules or regulations, or legislatures may want to pass a cumbersome implementation policy to create a drag on implementation. Whatever the reason, some statutes become complex when they create a burden for compliance in terms of the time and effort required to comply. Campaign finance is a regulatory system with many rules and regulations governing candidate behavior. Candidates comply with formal rules such as those governing how and when to file for office, or what types of contributions are allowed. Informally, there is a compliance expectation because candidates fear the risk to reputations if they do not fully and correctly comply.

Campaign finance as a regulatory policy may have different effects when applied to either legislators or citizens. As an institution, campaign finance has direct effects on individuals and their manner and ability to run for office. From contribution limits to disclosure reports, individuals must comply with this institution. Because individuals have incentives to comply with the rules, often, potential candidates must incur additional costs to hire attorneys or campaign consultants in order to run for office. Candidates hire these professionals to protect their reputation in the event of inadvertently (or purposefully) violating campaign finance rules. If you are an incumbent, this cost (time and effort) is less than for novice candidates who must climb a steep learning curve. This increased complexity deters some candidates from running for office.

Different states have different treatments of how to regulate campaign finance. Some states have particularly simple statutes in terms of language—that are easy to understand. Other states' statutes are more complex in their language measured by the grade reading levels and word counts. How can language serve as a proxy for complexity? The language of the statutes is the embodiment of all the rules and regulations required for compliance. The statutes contain every part of the campaign finance regulatory system. We know that legislatures have long used ambiguous or vague language to constrain bureaucrats. In the particular case of campaign finance, legislatures have the unique ability to influence the costs of running for office by making campaign finance legislation more complex. While the ability of legislators to create more or less complex campaign finance regulation is not tested here, the complexity of the statutes is measured using language.

Measuring the complexity of campaign finance statutes using language allows testing of the constraining effect of the statutory language. More or less precise language allows legislators to control bureaucrats ex post or ex ante depending on the legislator's wishes. Legislators are using the language of institutions to constrain other institutions. Using the studies of how institutions constrain presents a useful tool to measure the complexity of statutes and then test that complexity on outcomes. Political institutionalism literature indicates that institutions not only can be constrained, they often are.

This relationship between legislators and agencies is construed in the principal/agent context. Legislatively politicians set up principal/agent type controls to ensure legislators maintain control over bureaucrats. As this theory develops, however, the agents are able to provide feedback and negotiate with the principals. In campaign finance regulations, if we consider the agents being controlled as the candidates, the feedback mechanisms can be missing because the candidates/challengers have no way to give feedback or complain to their principals—the bureaucracy/legislators. The candidate—especially a novice candidate—has little recourse to challenge the regulation or they face the possibility of losing elections. The candidates also face a higher compliance cost than legislators. Legislators have already successfully run for office and gone through the learning curve, new candidates have yet to pay this learning price. The possibility exists for legislators to make rules more difficult for potential challengers.

Campaign Finance Complexity Constrains Candidate Decisions

Campaign finance as a regulatory institution is a system of rules and regulations in some states. In those states with complex rules and regulations, even if applied equally to every candidate they are still complex rules and regulations. Regulatory systems require time and effort to learn and comply with the rules. Complexity, defined for this book, is the time and effort required to learn and comply with the regulatory system. When a regulatory system has more rules and regulations, it is more costly in terms of complexity because it requires more time and effort to comply with additional rules. In the case of campaign finance, the regulations also may apply different costs to different types of candidates. Incumbents and novice challengers have different learning and compliance times that affect each candidate's ability to campaign.

Complexity theory uses the concept of a whole systems approach, feedback mechanisms, and self-organizing networks to use complexity as a means to measure the regulatory structure of campaign finance. Looking at the entire system structure captures the situation faced by candidates when deciding to run for office. Candidates must confront an entire network of rules and regulations governing a system of contributions, reporting, and spending. A whole systems approach, utilized in this book, analyzes whole parts of the campaign finance system and the effect of those parts on candidate decisions. The book uses the entire statute for each state on contribution limits and candidacy requirements to assess if they affect the candidate participation rate in each state. By looking at the collective regulations contained within the statute, we get a picture of what candidates are facing when deciding to run for office. While it is very important to look at discrete factors such as union contributions, or how much a candidate can donate to their own campaign, it is also important to understand the cumulative effect of all the rules and regulations written over time. Indices tally up the effect of multiple factors, but indices are proxies for a count of factors affecting decisions. Using the statute as a whole allows study of what candidates actually face when deciding to run for office. This also gives a more robust idea of complexity.

As complexity theory applications in policy studies advance, a question of how to measure complexity is necessary. In the past few decades, political science scholars have begun to incrementally advance on a definition and measure of complexity using language. This book adds to this idea by measuring complexity using the statutory language to capture the whole campaign finance system facing candidates. The language of campaign finance constitutes not only the rules and regulations but also the learning and compliance burdens within the statute language. Political science has defined complexity in terms of content, the technical considerations of legislation, and the language of legislation. The content of legislation is a more ambiguous definition sometimes measured using vignettes. Use of vignettes provides one way to measure complexity but it is a cumbersome method mostly used on a small number of respondents. Other scholars use word counts. Scholars consider longer legislation as more complex than most legislation because of the need for extensive information, rules, and provisions within a bill. However, length alone is insufficiently robust to determine complexity. Using the technical nature of a piece of legislation or the number of technical issues in a statute intuitively works better than using word counts, but ultimately this becomes a subjective measure as what is technical to some people might not be technical to others. Ultimately, for the book I settle on the language of the statute measured using both word counts and Flesch-Kincaid grade reading levels.

The use of word counts and grade reading levels are more often accepted use in political science, especially measuring constraint. Using the length and readability of language to measure constraints on judicial or administrative offices, scholars are inherently using a measure of language to gauge the constraining effect of complexity. Constraint on judges and administrators consists of how their behavior is coerced depending on the quantity and content of restrictions in the law. The quantity and content add length to a statute that may increase its complexity. The quantity and content also add a comprehension or learning component to the statute that makes it easier or more difficult to understand. The length and readability of a law therefore increase its complexity.

Political science uses language measures to understand policy decision aids such as information on the Affordable Care Act or jury instructions. Many of these studies that look into using plain language to affect policy understanding, measure the readability of the policies or the materials that customers use. The studies need to advance toward measuring specific outcomes such as take up rates for government programs. Creating comprehensible materials is a step in the right direction, but having users use the materials in a meaningful way means improved understanding with potentially better policy outcomes.

Plain language measurement takes numerous forms. From readability scores, to grade reading levels, to word counts, there are many ways to measure how complex or how easy text is to read and comprehend. The research shows that political science is and other empirical studies are moving to use grade-reading levels because they are an intuitive measure that makes sense to scientists and the general public. It is not easy to understand what a hypothetical score of 52 is on a readability score. Understanding that a grade reading level of 11 is the equivalent of a high school junior or a grade reading level of a six is 6th grade is more user friendly and intuitive. This study uses the Flesch-Kincaid grade reading level to measure the complexity of language within the campaign finance statutes. I also use the word count measure to look at the effectiveness of this measure compared to the Flesh-Kincaid measure.

Other empirical studies use similar measures to test the effectiveness of plain language protocols. In particular, the Dutch study by Van Boom, Desmet, and Van Dam finds that consumers reading the "easy" version of contracts were more likely to take legal action—or in other words—engage with and use the contract information than those consumers given the "hard" version of the contracts. Other studies show positive signs of effectiveness when using plain language. This study adds to the plain language research of how plain language can be used as a tool to increase optimal outcomes in policy goals. Using the experiment in chapter 5 tests if individuals misunderstand the campaign finance statutes. Everyday individuals' misunderstanding of the statute adds to the face validity of this study. Everyday citizens, who otherwise might choose to run for office, face a complex campaign finance system for which they have to pay extra costs to learn and comply. The experimental results indicate not only the difficulty of comprehending a campaign finance statute, but also the extra time and effort required to understand it. The implications of this experiment are clear. If it is more difficult for the average citizen to understand the campaign finance contribution statutes as written today, the statutes themselves may be a deterrent to average citizens running for office. Extra costs in terms of time, effort, and learning are an added burden of running and campaigning that average citizens may find too difficult to pay. If this is the case, one of the original goals of campaign finance reform—the increased participation of more people in the system—is in jeopardy

As definitions and measurements for complexity advance, other factors are also necessary to consider. Including different aspects such as the costs of compliance and learning are necessary to understanding complexity. Studying complexity borrows the idea of administrative burden from public administration research. Administrative burden demonstrates the costs of learning, compliance, and psychological costs on candidates running for office. Economists call these the transaction costs imposed by institutions. Complexity reminds us of Supreme Court Justice Potter Stewart's famous definition of obscenity "I know it when I see it." The same squishiness applies to complexity.

The cost of learning the rules is a central focus of this book. Candidates, who previously ran for office, have the experience of climbing the learning curve and they know the rules and regulations surrounding campaign finance. New or potential candidates do not have this knowledge yet and will have to spend time learning the ropes instead of campaigning. This creates a lag on their campaign where the newer candidates are playing catch up with the incumbents. Learning costs accrue when candidates must gather the information necessary to run for office. Candidates face two main tasks when deciding to run for office. Candidates must determine how and when to file using candidacy requirements, and they have to figure out how much money they need to raise and can raise for their campaign according to their state's rules. These two things occur prior to collecting any money or giving a speech. Contribution statutes tell candidates not only how much money they can raise, but also how to raise the funds, from whom they can and cannot get contributions, if and how they can get loans for their campaign, and the initial requirements on how to report any contributions. Candidacy requirements contain information on filing forms, fees, petition requirements (if required), affidavits, financial disclosure forms among others. Candidates are required to know all of the requirements before they make decisions to run for office. Some states make this information easily obtainable and compliance easy. In other states, it is more cumbersome and difficult to figure out. Looking at the whole statute for contributions and candidacy requirements allows a look at what candidates in each state face.

After learning how to run and how to fill out forms, gather signatures, and form committees, candidates have to comply with the law and complete those tasks. The compliance costs in the context of elections apply to the study of ballot access restrictions. Ballot access restrictions are the petition and other requirements necessary to get on the ballot in some states. Compliance costs accrue as candidates spend man-hours getting these tasks completed. Most studies of campaign finance assume that these regulations are not red tape but the proper rules and regulations necessary to fulfill campaign finance goals of more participation and less corruption. At some point, however, the rules and regulations of any bureaucracy can morph into red tape. The red tape costs further break down into direct and opportunity costs of compliance. Directly, candidates have to use man-hours to learn how to gather signatures or fill out forms. Indirectly, candidates pay an opportunity cost of using time they could spend campaigning against an opponent to comply with rules and regulations.

Managing to learn a new regulatory system can wear on individuals especially those individuals who may be running a business or working full-time in addition to running a campaign. In public administration literature, the psychological costs of rules include the idea that citizens might not participate in social or political programs because the rules and regulations are so complex they make citizens feel inferior and unworthy of benefits. For example, if the college financial aid form is so cumbersome a less educated citizen might feel the costs outweigh the benefits of finishing the form. Much of the psychological effects are studied with respect to social welfare programs. Citizens that suffer longer wait times to meet with administrators, the difference between means tested and universal access policies, and various other administrative burdens create a negative connotation to prospective clients. These burdens generally indicate that as the burdens are increased, the social-welfare policy take-up rates decrease; whereas if the burdens decrease participation increases. Moynihan and Herd's look at Wisconsin's Medicaid policies and find additionally that political party affects the burden put in place. It is therefore reasonable to speculate that if democrats and republicans use administrative tools to increase or decrease participation in social policies, legislators in general might use the same type of tool to decrease participation or competition in elections. An important caveat here is to determine if those campaign regulations are actually complex and do they create an administrative burden for candidates. To accomplish the correct measurement, understanding how statutes or legislation can be complex is important. The content of legislation is an obvious factor in affecting whether or not legislation is complex.

Candidates must learn the different rules and regulations if they want to run an effective campaign. If candidates have issues with the campaign finance regime, candidates have little recourse to get the rules changed. In most institutional settings bureaucrats and citizens are able to tell legislators what they like and dislike about a particular policy. Through the feedback loop, citizens and bureaucrats give legislators vital information about what is and is not working with a particular policy. If citizens have issues with the DMV or their child's school, or potholes in the roads, citizens can tell their legislators there is a problem that needs fixed. In campaign finance, those feedback loops are broken as the citizens most likely to complain about burdensome campaign finance regulations are potential challengers. Legislators have a motivation (assumed here) to keep the campaign finance regulatory system burdensome as a barrier to entry to challengers. Citizens as potential challengers are unlikely to give feedback or have any feedback accepted willingly by legislators. Part of the reason for the lack of feedback is that challengers or citizens interested in running for office fail to form self-organizing networks able to create enough momentum or salience to get the regulatory system changed. It is unlikely that multiple challengers, who potentially will run against one another in primaries, would form an advocacy coalition to lobby legislators for less complex rules and regulations on campaigns.

Using language as a measure of complexity conforms to the ongoing research using language as a measure of constraint. If language can constrain judges and bureaucrats, it can also constrain individual citizens. While this is a novel use of the idea of linguistic constraint, it is a valid way to measure complexity. When judges and bureaucrats are constrained by rules and regulations that are ambiguous or even specific, there is no reason individuals cannot also be constrained this way. This study finds that those states with more complex campaign finance regulations have lower candidate participation rates than in states with less complex regulations.

Campaign finance regulations are different in different states. This allows us to compare across states to determine what happens in states with more or less complex statutes. Statutes that are less complex have fewer words and are on a lower grade-reading level than complex statutes. Less complexity means that candidates should spend less time learning how to run for office and less time complying with statutes. They should be able to spend more time campaigning rather than complying. Candidates should spend fewer resources on campaign consultants, lawyers or other campaign professionals in states with less complex regulations. The lack of complexity should free candidates to use their time on policies and issues rather than filling out compliance forms.

Campaign finance statutes with less complexity are easier to understand and use. The plain language experiment in chapter 5 asked respondents how they used the campaign finance statute. In particular, candidates were asked how many times they had to refer back to the statute in order to answer the comprehension questions. Respondents were asked to rate the statute in terms of how clear they thought it was and how closely they read the statutes. The test scores of respondents who read the plain language statute indicate that the plain language was easier to understand and use based on how many times they referred back to the statute, their rating of how clear it was, and how closely they read the statute.

This ease of understanding and higher comprehension of a plain language statute is an indicator that the original statute may indeed be difficult to understand. This difficulty of understanding is central to this study's research. Assumed here is that potential candidates will want to obey the law in a boundedly rational way. They want to comply but may not fully understand the law's requirements if it is complex. This potential misunderstanding is problematic in two ways. One, the desire to comply with the law presents an opportunity for incumbents to constrain challengers. Two, candidates may have to incur higher transaction costs in order to comply.

The implications of this experiment and the study results are clear. Statutes that are more complex create more time and effort costs for citizens. Extra costs in terms of time, effort, and learning are an added burden of running and campaigning that average citizens may find too difficult to pay. In those states with more complex statutes, that is, higher time and effort costs, fewer candidates participate in elections. If this is the case, one of the original goals of campaign finance reform—the increased participation of more people in the system—is in jeopardy.

Policy Implications

Complexity in rules and regulations matter primarily because complexity appears to impair the effectiveness of campaign finance laws to reach policy goals. Campaign finance laws intend to make the campaign finance system more transparent and democratic. Campaign laws require disclosure of contributors, tracking of donations, reports, and financial affidavits among other requirements. A highly regulated system allows tracking of contributors and contributions to ensure that there is no quid pro quo between contributors and politicians. Additionally, requiring smaller donations would democratize the system by leveling the playing field giving equal status to less affluent donors. The result is a campaign finance system layered with numerous rules and regulations. Potential candidates navigate this system fearing a corrupt construction of their reputation for any failure to report contributions correctly. If reputational risk were the only pitfall of the campaign finance system, changes to reporting systems could help alleviate this risk to candidates. The reporting systems are only one aspect of the campaign finance system. Other aspects such as the filing requirements, the petition requirements (in some states), the difficulty of determining who and how much an individual can contribute, creates a regulatory system that imposes transactional and opportunity costs on candidates.

Transaction costs consist of the time and effort required to learn and comply with all the requirements of a cumbersome campaign finance system. Currently candidates must spend time filling out numerous forms, going to training classes for treasurers, collecting petitions (where required), and learning contribution statutes. All of these tasks, while fulfilling a valid policy goal, create a situation where candidates spend an inordinate amount of time learning how to run for office instead of spending time on citizen needs, policy issues, and policy solutions. Instead of campaigning, candidates are complying with a regulatory system that takes them away from the job they set out to do.

Additionally, different candidate types—incumbents versus novices—have different transaction costs. Incumbents have already learned and set up a campaign system and process leaving novices at a disadvantage. That disadvantage adds onto the opportunity cost novices must pay. They must take time away from actual campaigning against an opponent to spend on learning the campaign finance system. Future research might look at how many novice candidates run a "test" campaign in one year to set up the processes and networks necessary to run a successful campaign in a subsequent election year. Looking at these "test" campaigns would indicate how difficult it is to set up campaign structure and it would help us understand the transaction and opportunity costs involved in setting up a campaign.

The additional costs imposed by a complex campaign finance system contribute to a deterrent effect on candidate decisions. It is not too large of a stretch to say that if we have fewer candidates running for office, we have a less diverse pool of candidates, fewer policy innovations, and less competition for policy choices. Making it simpler for candidates to run for office should be a consideration when creating or revising campaign finance regulations. Much of the research on candidate decisions tells us there are many factors involved in a candidate's decision-making process. Complexity is not the *only* factor contributing to candidate decisions. Complexity of the campaign finance system is one of many factors for consideration. Running a factor analysis of all decision inputs would be ideal but it is unrealistic to include everything in such an analysis. Regardless, complexity is an input into candidates' decisions as determined by this study. Complexity may not be an explicit or major input, but navigating the learning curve and the time and effort put into campaigning is present when candidates decide whether to run. Complex campaign regulatory systems contribute to extra costs for candidates. Those costs might mean more time away from home or business, it might mean less time campaigning. If the benefits of winning office are offset by too many costs, citizens may determine that running is not worth the effort.

Democratically it is beneficial that every individual wishing to run for political office has an opportunity to run. Ensuring the availability of that opportunity for individuals is important of course. The policy question regarding the method of securing those opportunities remains. Some will argue that the only way to ensure that everyone has an equal opportunity to run for office is to create a completely public finance system of elections. However, having a more centralized system does not guarantee that the regulatory system will be less complex. Public finance systems also create numerous rules and regulations to which candidates must comply. The rules and regulations for public finance systems focus on what is or is not a contribution and the qualifications for public elections assistance. For example, Hawaii has a public finance option for state legislators but also has one of the higher Flesch-Kincaid grade reading levels for campaign definitions. Definition statutes had a statistically significant negative impact on candidate decisions on average. Even though the goal of the statute was to simplify the campaign system, the statutes were still very complex in terms of regulatory language that candidates would have to learn. Creating a less complex policy structure may seem like the answer but caution is necessary. It is not only the system structure that is important. The rules and regulations governing any structure must also construct a system with lower transaction and compliance costs.

A different option would entail using plain language when citizens—as potential candidates—come into contact with the campaign finance system. Keeping the rules and regulations on a lower grade reading level indicates that users can both comprehend and comply more easily with the statutes. Legislatures may still write complex rules, but when everyday citizens encounter those rules they should be constructed using plain language protocols to minimize confusion and costs associated with learning and complying with the rules. Additionally, many interviewed candidates discussed using mentors or campaign consultants. Using campaign schools or training camps may increase the ability of everyday citizens to access the necessary information, tools, and contacts to run a campaign. Many campaign schools are nonprofits and charge little to nothing for this training. This training can serve less well-funded candidates and create a pipeline of candidates for public office. Both using plain language and candidate schools alleviate the complexity problem by making the system more accessible to everyday citizens.

Because of the move by the federal government to implement plain language protocols on many new regulations and statutes, the states are likely to follow. Some states have been leaders in this area and are already using plain language in many materials that citizens use. Language is not the only constraint though. Constraint via the need to learn and comply is intrinsically part of the hurdles candidates face. Reducing the learning and compliance time individuals face is also important. Making the process of becoming a candidate easier and more inviting is an important facet of any reform. Reducing the quantity of hurdles individuals have to overcome and making those hurdles easier to understand by writing them in plain language are important steps. Many of the survey respondents discussed how they sought help from sources outside of the party. Having political parties participate in candidate training could help both candidates and parties. Parties would gain candidates ready to run and individuals would get lower cost training and access to party officials eager for new talent.

Reducing the complexity of the campaign finance system would be beneficial to all candidates. Reducing the transaction and opportunity costs to candidates would require eliminating some regulations or streamlining the regulatory system. Regulatory systems generally require administrative oversight of rules to determine compliance. Future research might ask whether the benefits of the regulatory system such as reduced corruption outweigh the transaction and opportunity costs to candidates. How many citations for corruption or fraudulent campaign activities are issued in each state? How many candidates are affected? Do these numbers justify the regulations? The US Supreme Court answered the constitutional question regarding campaign regulations but the question of costs versus benefits of the regulations remains. Scholars might also ask if opposition and incumbent candidates use the regulations as a tool with which to cite their competitors for campaign violations. This unintended use of the system creates additional reputational risk for candidates. Candidates can be cited for violations of campaign finance regulations that can mean anything from forgetting to cite a contribution to quid pro quo situations. Because the policy debate is largely ideological, this area of policy is ripe with questions regarding the efficacy of campaign regulations meeting policy goals.

Campaign finance systems also purport to democratize the campaign finance system. The intent is to widen the base of contribution collection to include a larger number of smaller donations. Collecting more contributions on a smaller scale reduces the need to compete in elections against fat cat incumbents with large campaign war chests. The benefits of widening the base should include more individuals willing to run for office. This benefit is uncertain given the results of this study finding that fewer candidates run when the regulations are more complex. If the benefits of having more candidates are not realized by the reforms, we must ask if the costs of the reforms are too high. Studies of take up rates for social welfare policies indicate that when those policies have fewer complications, the take up rate increases. The same structural argument can be made for campaign finance regulatory systems. Decreasing the complexity of the systems, that is, decreasing the transaction and opportunity costs, should increase the numbers of individuals seeking to run for office.

On an individual level, having more complex rules that constrain candidate decisions means that some individuals who would like to participate in their country's electoral systems will not do so. Maybe that individual is unsuited for running if they cannot overcome a series of hurdles. In the pool of candidates who generally run for office consists of lawyers, businessmen, and educators. What if having the local small business owner or entrepreneur could make policy innovations the current legislature fails to consider. Having diversity in legislatures is a bonus. By constraining everyday individuals from running, we constrain that diversity.

I began this book looking at institutions and their ability to constrain behavior of other institutions and individuals. Campaign finance rules and regulations are institutions that affect individual's choices to run for office. To ensure that the electoral system remains open to all types of individuals, the regulatory burden on candidates should be carefully evaluated to ensure that the costs imposed on these individuals do not decrease the benefits to our democracy of having more and more individuals run for office.

Appendix A

Plain Language Experiment Questions

This study is being conducted to help determine the level of understanding of campaign finance laws. As a part of the research, we are seeking volunteers to participate in a brief survey on issues surrounding campaign finance laws. On average, completing this survey should only take 15–20 minutes of your time. You will be asked to read a portion of the law and then answer a few questions based on what you read. Your participation is completely voluntary but will help to further research in this important area.

Please answer the following questions on the scantron to the best of your ability.

As you answer these questions:

- Remember that this is NOT a test. You may refer back to the reading.
- Assume you are a candidate running for a state-level office in North Carolina.
- Keep in mind that state and federal campaign finance laws are separate.

1. How much money in campaign contributions can a candidate accept from one person, political committee or other entity?

    a. $4,500
    b. $2,000
    c. $4,000
    d. $5,000
    e. Don't know

2. You are a candidate running for office. You accept a contribution from an individual that you plan on paying back. How long do you have to pay it back?

    a. 45 days
    b. 15 days
    c. 4–5 days
    d. 7 days
    e. Don't know

3. If you are a candidate running for office, can you or your spouse make a loan to your campaign?

    a. Yes
    b. No
    c. Don't know

4. Which of the following family members are NOT allowed to make unlimited contributions to your campaign?

    a. Child
    b. Brother
    c. Spouse
    d. Uncle
    e. Don't know

5. If you are running for judge in North Carolina, do the same limitations apply to you as would apply to candidates for other office?

    a. Yes
    b. No
    c. Don't know

6. As a candidate, can you use your own money to contribute to your campaign?

    a. Yes, but with a $1,000 limit.
    b. No, you may not use your own money to contribute.
    c. Yes, candidates may make contributions to their own campaigns.
    d. No contributions are allowed, but you can make a loan to your campaign.
    e. Don't know

7. The North Carolina Voter-Owned Elections Act says that you (a candidate) may not accept contributions to your campaign for a period of ______ days prior to the election.

    a. 22
    b. 30
    c. 45
    d. 21
    e. Don't know

8. Not including the exceptions listed in this law, what is the maximum amount any person, political committee or other entity may contribute to your campaign?

    a. $4,500
    b. $2,000
    c. $4,000
    d. $5,000
    e. Don't know

9. How closely do you feel you read the reading?

    a. Very closely
    b. Somewhat closely
    c. Not very closely
    d. I didn't read the reading.

10. How clear did you think the readings were?[1]

    a. Very clear
    b. Somewhat clear
    c. Somewhat unclear
    d. Very unclear
    e. Neither clear nor unclear

Now I just have a few questions that will help me compare your responses to those of your fellow students.

1. Have you ever considered running for political office?

    a. Yes
    b. No
    c. Unsure

2. Have you ever worked on a candidate's political campaign?

    a. Yes
    b. No
    c. Don't know.

3. Has anyone in your current or former household ever run for public office?

    a. Yes
    b. No
    c. I don't know

4. Is anyone in your immediate family a lawyer?

    a. Yes
    b. No
    c. I don't know

5. While answering this questionnaire, about how many times did you refer back to the reading?

    a. Less than 1 time
    b. 1–3 times
    c. 4–6 times
    d. 7–9 times
    e. More than 9 times

6. What is your current age?

    a. 18–21
    b. 22–25
    c. 26–30
    d. 31–40
    e. Over 40

7. What is your current class standing?

    a. Freshman
    b. Sophomore
    c. Junior
    d. Senior
    e. Don't know

8. What is your gender?

    a. Female
    b. Male

9. Do you consider yourself to be Hispanic or Latino?

    a. No
    b. Yes
    c. Not applicable

10. What race or ethnicity do you consider yourself?

    a. White
    b. Black
    c. Asian/Pacific Islander
    d. Native American
    e. Other (Please provide) ________________________

11. What is your marital status?

    a. Married or living with someone.
    b. Single (never married)
    c. Divorced/Separated
    d. Widowed
    e. Other

12. What is the highest level of education anyone in your immediate family (parents and siblings) has completed?

    a. Some High School, High School Diploma, or GED
    b. Some College or two-year Associate Degree
    c. Four-year BA/BS undergraduate degree
    d. Master's or PhD degree
    e. Don't know

13. On the bottom of the reading it says "this is reading ____." Put the letter of the reading on the scantron.

    a. A[2]
    b. B

NOTES

1. This variable was recoded to Very Clear, Somewhat Clear, Neither, Somewhat unclear, Very unclear.
2. A refers to the original statute; B is the plain language version.

Appendix B

The NC Original and Plain Language Statutes

B.1 The Original Version of the Contribution Statute

163-278.13. Limitation on contributions.

(a) No individual, political committee, or other entity shall contribute to any candidate or other political committee any money or make any other contribution in any election in excess of four thousand dollars ($4,000) for that election.

(b) No candidate or political committee shall accept or solicit any contribution from any individual, other political committee, or other entity of any money or any other contribution in any election in excess of four thousand dollars ($4,000) for that election.

(c) Notwithstanding the provisions of subsections (a) and (b) of this section, it shall be lawful for a candidate or a candidate's spouse, parents, brothers and sisters to make a contribution to the candidate or to the candidate's treasurer of any amount of money or to make any other contribution in any election in excess of four thousand dollars ($4,000) for that election.

(d) For the purposes of this section, the term "an election" means any primary, second primary, or general election in which the candidate or political committee may be involved, without regard to whether the candidate is opposed or unopposed in the election, except that where a candidate is not on the ballot in a second primary, that second primary is not "an election" with respect to that candidate.

(d1) Notwithstanding subsections (a) and (b) of this section, a candidate or political committee may accept a contribution knowing that the contribution is to be reimbursed to the entity making the contribution and knowing the candidate or political committee has funds sufficient to reimburse the entity making the contribution if all of the following conditions are met:

(1) The entity submits sufficient information of the contribution to the candidate or political committee for reimbursement within 45 days of the contribution.
(2) The candidate or political committee makes a reimbursement to the entity making the contribution within seven days of submission of sufficient information.
(3) The candidate or political committee indicates on its report under G.S. 163-278.11 that the good, service, or other item resulting in the reimbursement is an expenditure of the candidate or political committee, and notes if the contribution was by credit card.
(4) The contribution does not exceed one thousand dollars ($1,000.00).

(d2) Any contribution, or portion thereof, made under subsection (d1) of this section that is not submitted for reimbursement in accordance with subsection (d1) of this section shall be treated as a contribution for purposes of this section. Any contribution, or portion thereof, made under subsection (d1) of this section that is not reimbursed in accordance with subsection (d1) of this section shall be treated as a contribution for purposes of this section.

(e) Except as provided in subsections (e2), (e3), and (e4) of this section, this section shall not apply to any national, State, district or county executive committee of any political party. For the purposes of this section only, the term "political party" means only those political parties officially recognized under G.S. 163-96.

(el) No referendum committee which received any contribution from a corporation, labor union, insurance company, business entity, or professional association may make any contribution to another referendum committee, to a candidate or to a political committee.

(e2) In order to make meaningful the provisions of Article 22D of this Chapter, the following provisions shall apply with respect to candidates for justice of the Supreme Court and judge of the Court of Appeals:

(1) No candidate shall accept, and no contributor shall make to that candidate, a contribution in any election exceeding one thousand dollars ($1,000) except as provided for elsewhere in this subsection.
(2) A candidate may accept, and a family contributor may make to that candidate, a contribution not exceeding two thousand dollars ($2,000) in an election if the contributor is that candidate's parent, child, brother, or sister.
(3) Repealed by Session Laws 2008-150, s. 7(a), effective August 2, 2008.

As used in this subsection, "candidate" is also a political committee authorized by the candidate for that candidate's election. Nothing in this subsection shall prohibit a candidate or the spouse of that candidate from making a contribution or loan secured entirely by that individual's assets to that candidate's own campaign.

(e3) Notwithstanding the provisions of subsections (a) and (b) of this section, no candidate for superior court judge or district court judge shall accept, and no contributor shall make to that candidate, a contribution in any election exceeding one thousand dollars ($1,000), except as provided in subsection (c) of this section. As used in this subsection, "candidate" is also a political committee authorized by the candidate for that candidate's election. Nothing in this subsection shall prohibit a candidate or the spouse of that candidate from making a contribution or loan secured entirely by that individual's assets to that candidate's own campaign.

(e4) In order to make meaningful the provisions of the North Carolina Voter-Owned Elections Act, as set forth in Article 22J of this Chapter, no candidate for an office subject to that Article shall accept, and no contributor shall make to that candidate, a contribution during the period beginning 21 days before the day of the general election and ending the day after the general election if that contribution causes the candidate to exceed the "trigger for matching funds" defined in G.S. 163-278.96(17). As used in this subsection, the term "candidate" also includes "candidate campaign committee" as defined in G.S. 163-278.38Z(3). Nothing in this subsection shall prohibit a candidate from making a contribution or loan secured entirely by that candidate's assets to that candidate's own campaign or to a political committee, the principal purpose of which is to support that candidate's campaign. This subsection applies with respect to a candidate only if both of the following statements are true regarding that candidate:

(1) That candidate is opposed in the general election by a certified candidate as defined in Article 22J of this Chapter.
(2) That certified candidate has not received the maximum matching funds available under G.S. 163-278.99B(c).

The recipient of a contribution that apparently violates this subsection has three days to return the contribution or file a detailed statement with the State Board of Elections explaining why the contribution does not violate this subsection.

(e5) The contribution limits of subsections (a) and (b) of this section do not apply to contributions made to an independent expenditure political committee. For purposes of this section, an "independent expenditure political committee" is a political committee whose treasurer makes and abides by a certification to the State Board of Elections that the political committee does not and will not make contributions, directly or indirectly, to candidates or to political committees that make contributions to candidates. The State Board of Elections shall provide forms for implementation of this subsection. This subsection shall not apply to a candidate or a political committee controlled by a candidate. The exception of this subsection is in addition to any other exception provided by law.

(f) Any individual, candidate, political committee, referendum committee, or other entity that violates the provisions of this section is guilty of a Class 2 misdemeanor.

B.2 The Plain Language Version of the Contribution Statute

163-278.13 Contribution Limits for Candidates

1. No one (any individual, any type of political committee, or any other entity) may contribute more than four thousand ($4000) dollars for your election campaign.
2. You may not accept more than four thousand dollars ($4000) from anyone (any individual, any type of political committee, or any other entity) for your election campaign.
3. Exceptions to (a) and (b):

You, your spouse, your parents, and your brothers and sisters may make and you may accept more than four thousand dollars ($4000) for your election campaign.

a. For the purposes of this section, "election" means any primary or second primary (sometimes called a runoff) or the general election where your name is on the ballot.
b. You may accept a contribution (from anyone) if you know that your campaign will be reimbursing the donor for the contribution and if you know that your campaign has the funds to do so. In order to do this you must follow these conditions:

    (1) Whomever gave the contribution has to inform you about the contribution (for the purpose of reimbursement) within 45 days of the contribution.
    (2) Once the contributor gives you this information, you have seven (7) days to reimburse the contributor.
    (3) You must put in your report (under G.S. 163-278.11) that the contribution for which you are reimbursing was for campaign spending. You must also note if this was a credit card transaction.
    (4) The contribution cannot be more than one thousand dollars ($1000).

(5) Any contribution under section (d1) that you do not submit for reimbursement or that you do not reimburse is treated like any other contribution.

1. This section does not apply (except where noted) to any national, state, district, or county executive committee of any political party. For the purposes here, "political party" means only those political parties recognized under G.S. 163-96.

(e) Referendum committees, which received any contributions from a corporation, labor union, insurance company, business entity, or professional association, may not contribute to another referendum committee, to a candidate, or to a political committee.

(e1) If you are a candidate for justice of the Supreme Court and judge of the Court of Appeals the following provisions apply to you:

(1) You may not accept and no one may contribute any contribution of more than one thousand dollars ($1,000). Exceptions to this are below.
(2) You may accept and a family contributor may contribute to you up to two thousand dollars ($2,000) in an election, if the contributor is your parent, child, brother, or sister.

"Candidate" in this subsection also means a political committee authorized by the candidate for your election. No part of this section prevents you or your spouse from making a loan or contribution to your campaign secured by your assets.

(e2) If you are a candidate for superior court judge or district court judge, you may not accept and no one may contribute more than one thousand dollars ($1000) to your election. The family exceptions in subsection part (c) also apply in this subsection. "Candidate" in this section also means a political committee authorized by you for your election. No part of this section prevents you or your spouse from making a loan or contribution to your campaign secured by your assets.

(e3) The North Carolina Voter-Owned Elections Act uses public funds to finance elections. If you are a candidate subject to this act, you may not accept and no one may contribute to your campaign for a period prior to the general election if that contribution causes you to exceed the "trigger for matching funds" as defined in G.S. 163-278.96 (17). This period begins 21 days before the general election day and ends the day after the general election.

"Candidate" also includes "candidate campaign committee" as defined in G.S. 163-278.96(17). No part of this section prevents you or your spouse from making a loan or contribution to your campaign secured by your assets.

This subsection applies to you only if both of the following statements are true:

(1) You are running in an election where you have a certified opponent. A certified opponent is defined in Article 22J of this Chapter.
(2) Your certified opponent has not received the maximum matching funds available under G.S. 163-278.99B(c).

If you violate this provision by receiving a contribution, you have three days to return the contribution or file a detailed statement with the State Board of Elections explaining why the contribution does not violate this subsection.

(e4) An "independent expenditure political committee" (IEPC) is a political committee that does not and will not contribute directly or indirectly to candidates or to political committees that contribute to candidates. The contribution limits in subsection (a) and (b) do not apply to contributions made to independent expenditure political committees. The State Board of Elections will give forms to IEPCcfs to implement this subsection. This section does not apply to candidates or a political committee controlled by a candidate.

(f) If you violate the provisions of this section, you are guilty of a Class 2 misdemeanor.

Appendix C

Additional Chapter 7 Charts

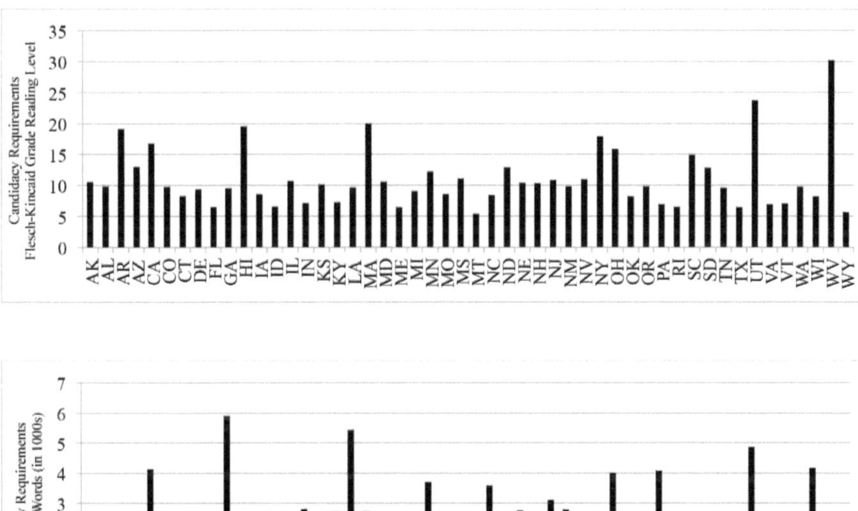

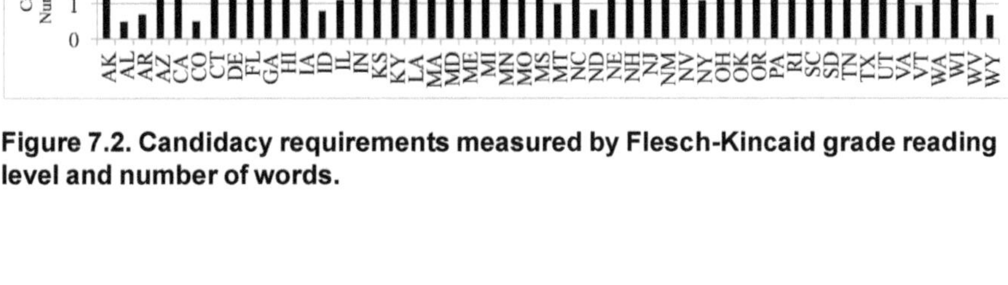

Figure 7.2. Candidacy requirements measured by Flesch-Kincaid grade reading level and number of words.

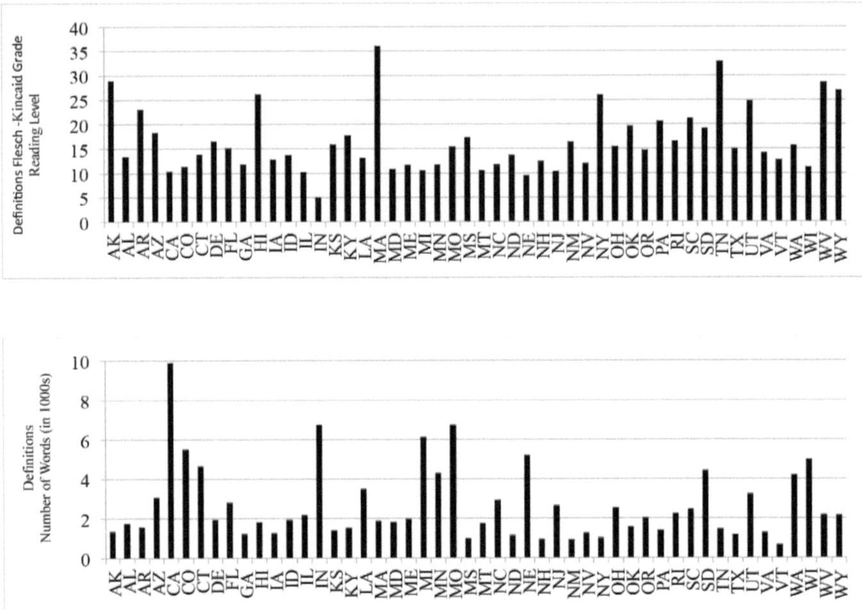

Figure 7.3. Campaign finance definitions measured by Flesch-Kincaid grade reading level and number of words.

Appendix D

Regression Charts, Variable Definitions, Descriptive Statistics

Table 8.1 [Full]. Complexity and Candidate Decisions—full table with year dummy variables

COMPLEXITY AND CANDIDATE DECISIONS						
		Candidate Participation Rates		Candidate Withdrawal Rates		
Tobit Model		CPRs	CPRp	CWR	CWRs	CWRp
Contribution Limits						
	Word Count	-0.008	-0.008	-0.003	-0.005	-0.006
		(0.024)	(0.024)	(0.003)	(0.007)	(0.007)
	Flesch-Kincaid Grade Reading Level	-0.044	-0.044	**0.022**	**0.046**	**0.043**
		(0.050)	(0.050)	(0.008)**	(0.018)**	(0.015)**
Candidacy Requirements						
	Word Count	*0.190*	*0.190*	**0.010**	**0.025**	**0.023**
		(0.030)**	(0.030)**	(0.003)**	(0.006)**	(0.005)**
	Flesch-Kincaid Grade Reading Level	*0.088*	*0.088*	*-0.019*	*-0.039*	*-0.038*
		(0.039)*	(0.039)*	(0.006)**	(0.013)**	(0.012)**
Definitions						
	Word Count	**-0.074**	**-0.074**	*-0.012*	*-0.025*	*-0.021*
		(0.015)**	(0.015)**	(0.005)*	(0.011)*	(0.010)*

Flesch-Kincaid Grade Reading Level	**-0.311**	**-0.311**	-0.010	-0.021	-0.019
	(0.042)**	(0.042)**	(0.006)	(0.012)	(0.010)
Legislator salary	0.000	0.000	-0.000	-0.000	-0.000
	(0.000)**	(0.000)**	(0.000)	(0.000)	(0.000)
State population by seat	-0.000	-0.000	-0.000	-0.000	-0.000
	(0.000)**	(0.000)**	(0.000)	(0.000)*	(0.000)**
Number of incumbents	-0.001	-0.001	-0.000	0.000	0.000
	(0.001)*	(0.001)*	(0.000)	(0.000)	(0.000)
Chamber type	-0.557	-0.557	-0.007	-0.017	-0.021
House=1, Senate = 0	(0.041)**	(0.041)**	(0.004)*	(0.007)*	(0.006)**
Term Limit Dummy	0.191	0.191	0.025	0.058	0.052
	(0.036)**	(0.036)**	(0.002)**	(0.006)**	(0.005)**
1998	0.000	0.000	0.000	0.000	0.000
	(0.000)	(0.000)	(0.000)	(0.000)	(0.000)
2000	-0.069	-0.069	0.000	-0.001	0.003
	(0.004)**	(0.004)**	(0.001)	(0.001)	(0.001)*
2002	0.108	0.108	0.010	0.032	0.033
	(0.006)**	(0.006)**	(0.001)**	(0.002)**	(0.002)**
2004	0.040	0.040	0.039	0.090	0.083
	(0.003)**	(0.003)**	(0.001)**	(0.003)**	(0.002)**

	2006	-0.054	-0.054	0.024	0.060	0.054
		(0.004)**	(0.004)**	(0.001)**	(0.003)**	(0.003)**
	2008	-0.072	-0.072	0.026	0.064	0.058
		(0.004)**	(0.004)**	(0.001)**	(0.002)**	(0.002)**
	2010	0.070	0.070	0.019	0.050	0.047
		(0.007)**	(0.007)**	(0.001)**	(0.003)**	(0.003)**
	2012	0.116	0.116	0.024	0.058	0.055
		(0.005)**	(0.005)**	(0.002)**	(0.003)**	(0.002)**
	2014	-0.084	-0.084	0.024	0.054	0.051
		(0.009)**	(0.009)**	(0.001)**	(0.003)**	(0.002)**
	2016	-0.082	-0.082	0.015	0.040	0.036
		(0.010)**	(0.010)**	(0.001)**	(0.003)**	(0.002)**
	Constant	2.148	2.148	0.024	0.008	0.007
		(0.239)**	(0.239)**	(0.053)	(0.117)	(0.098)
sigma	Constant	0.518	0.518	0.039	0.087	0.078
		(0.014)**	(0.014)**	(0.002)**	(0.004)**	(0.004)**
N		903	903	903	903	903

MAIN INDEPENDENT VARIABLES

Variables	Conceptualization	Operationalization	Data Source
Pre-Bank Contribution Statutes	Complex language can add a transaction cost akin to a learning curve. It might increase the time, effort and learning required to comply with the statute.	These components include the Flesch-Kincaid Grade Reading level which gives us a measure of what US grade level should be able to comprehend the legislation. (Online-Utility.org).	http://www.online-utility.org/english/readability_test_and_improve.jsp
Definition Statutes	Because not all states have contribution statutes, definitions were also collected to test them for complexity.	Same components as Pre-Bank contributions were collected.	http://www.online-utility.org/english/readability_test_and_improve.jsp
Candidate Filing Statutes	Requirements for candidates to run for office including what they would first encounter as a candidate. Does not include dollar amounts/filing fees etc.	States requirements for candidates to file for office such as the candidate declaration/nomination, oath affidavit, or declaration filing.	http://www.online-utility.org/english/readability_test_and_improve.jsp
Flesch Kincaid Grade level :	US Grade Level	Index of US grade level necessary to comprehend the legislation	http://www.online-utility.org/english/readability_test_and_improve.jsp
Word Count	Number of words in the statute.		http://www.online-utility.org/english/readability_test_and_improve.jsp
Total Seats	Total number of legislative seats in each state legislature. How many contested seats there are in each election year.	This is the number of seats up for contestation in that state/year. It is not the number of seats in the institution.	www.followthemoney.org
Chamber Type	This designates whether the election was in either the	1-Senate, 0-House	www.followthemoney.org

	Senate or House chamber for each state legislature		
Legislative Professionalism - Salary	Legislative salary is theorized to incentivize individuals to run if the leg is more professional (higher pay).	Salary base amount (not including per diems or vouchers or other expenses).	NCSL, "2016 Survey: State Legislative Compensation, Session Per Diem, and Mileage," http://www.ncsl.org/research/about-state-legislatures/2016-legislator-compensation.aspx, Accessed January 19, 2017. State Legislative Compensation, Session Per Diem and Mileage
Term Limits		Term Limits Y or N; also Term limits repealed Y or N by year	NCSL
Strategic Factors - Incumbents	Strategic factors are the rational strategies on which candidates make a decision on whether or not to run.	The Institute considers anyone currently in its database as a state official an incumbent	www.followthemoney.org
Candidate decisions - survey	In order to investigate other potential factors affecting candidate decisions, need to talk to people who have run or not run for office to determine whether or not anything is missing	Survey 10 individuals. Ask questions based on Williams (2009), Maisel et al. (survey of judges as to why they ran or not.	Qualitative Interviews; Types of questions: http://ces.iga.ucdavis.edu/
Candidate Withdrawals	The number of candidates who filed to run, but then withdrew from the race.	The number of candidates who filed to run, but then withdrew from the race (not due to death or disqualification which are different categories).	www.followthemoney.org

Total Candidates	Sum of all candidates running	Total number of candidates running in that state's election	www.followthemoney.org

VARIABLE DESCRIPTIVE STATISTICS

Label	Obs	Unique	Mean	St. Dev	Min	Max
State	1067	50	25.55483	14.62128	1	50
Year	1067	11	2006.052	6.324931	1996	2016
Chamber type (state upper or state lower)	1067	2	0.505155	0.500208	0	1
Total number of candidates in an election	1065	338	139.0169	127.4998	0	1087
Total seats up for election in the chamber in that year	1000	81	65.556	58.70398	0	400
Total permanent seats in the chamber	1013	55	71.28233	55.10457	0	400
Number of incumbents	1008	171	58.13095	49.03454	0	466
Total Candidate Quantity/Number of seats available in that election	962	608	1.95188	0.666284	0	4.974
Total Candidate Quantity/Perm Chamber seats	962	608	1.95188	0.666284	0	4.974
Number of Withdrawn candidates	1017	25	1.512291	4.170823	0	49
No. of candidates withdrawn/total candidates running	958	14	0.010021	0.020275	0	0.13
No. of candidates withdrawn/total seats up	946	30	0.024472	0.050248	0	0.34
No. of candidates withdrawn/permanent chamber seats	962	27	0.020956	0.045518	0	0.34
Number of words in contribution statute	1067	50	1621.948	1165.626	184	6247
Flesch-Kincaid Grade Reading Level Contribution Statute	1067	48	14.18232	4.932572	6.6	31.8

Number of Words in CF statute definitions	1067	50	2662.23	1876.814	662	9883
Flesch-Kincaid Grade Reading Level CF Definitions	1067	50	16.58306	6.494551	5.02	36.15
Number of Words in candidacy requirement statutes	1067	50	2224.805	1220.696	483	5908
Flesch-Kincaid Grade Reading Level candidacy requirements	1067	49	11.01447	4.933929	5.37	30.22
Legislator salary	974	216	26189.32	22995.17	0	116098
State population by seat	958	955	3407341	4161368	194742.1	2.96E+07
Term Limit Dummy	1067	2	0.290534	0.454222	0	1

Bibliography

Abrams, B. A., and Settle, R. F. (2004). Campaign-finance Reform: A Public Choice Perspective. *Public Choice, 120*(3/4), 379–400.

Adams, J., Merrill III, S., Simas, E. N., and Stone, W. J. (2011). When Candidates Value Good Character: A Spatial Model with Applications to Congressional Elections. *The Journal of Politics, 73*(1), 17–30.

Ansolabehere, S., De Figueiredo, J. M., and Snyder, J. M. (2003). Why is there so little money in US politics? *The Journal of Economic Perspectives, 17*(1), 105–130.

Ansolabehere, S., and Gerber, A. (2008). Vote Fraud in the Eye of the Beholder: The Role of Public Opinon in the Challenge to Voter Identification Requirements. *Harvard Law Review, 121*, 1737–1774.

Assembly, N. C. G. *North Carolina General Statutes Ch. 22, § 163 278.13.*

Assy, R. (2011). Can the Law Speak Directly to Its Subjects? The Limitations of Plain Language. *Journal of Law and Society, 38*, 376–404.

Bachrach, P., and Baretz, M. S. (1963). Decisions and nondecisions: An analytical framework. *American Political Science Review, 57*, 632–642.

Banks, J. S. (1995). The design of institutions: an agency theory perspective. *Weimer, DL Institutional design*. Boston: Kluwer Academic Publishers, 17–36.

Banks, J. S., and Weingast, B. R. (1992). The political control of bureaucracies under asymmetric information. *American Journal of Political Science*, 509–524.

Bardwell, K. (2003). Campaign Finance Laws and the Competition for Spending in Gubernatorial Elections. *Social Science Quarterly, 84*(4), 811–825.

Baumgartner, F. R., Jones, B. D., and Mortensen, P. B. (2014). Punctuated equilibrium theory: Explaining stability and change in public policymaking. *Theories of the policy process, 8*, 59–103.

Bawn, K. (1997). Choosing Strategies to Control the Bureaucracy: Statutory Constraints, Oversight, and the Committee System. *Journal of Law, Economics, and Organization, 13*(1), 101–126.

Bimber, B. (1991). Information as a factor in congressional politics. *Legislative Studies Quarterly*, 585–605.

Black, G. S. (1972). A Theory of Political Ambition: Career Choices and the Role of Structural Incentives. *The American Political Science Review, 66*(1), 144–159.

Bozeman, B. (1993). A Theory of Government "Red Tape". *Journal of Public Administration Research and Theory: J-PART, 3*(3), 273–303.

Buchanan, J. M. (2003). Politics Without Romance. *Policy, 19*(3).

Buckley v. Valeo (The Supreme Court of the United States 1976).

Burden, B. C. (2007). Ballot Regulations and Multiparty Politics in the States. *www.apsanet.org*.
Cairney, P. (2012). Complexity theory in political science and public policy. *Political Studies Review, 10*(3), 346–358.
Calvert, R. L., McCubbins, M. D., and Weingast, B. R. (1989). A Theory of Political Control and Agency Discretion. *American Journal of Political Science, 33*(3), 588–611.
Colander, D., and Kupers, R. (2014). *Complexity and the art of public policy: Solving society's problems from the bottom up*: Princeton University Press.
Crawford, S. E. S., and Ostrom, E. (1995). A Grammar of Institutions. *American Political Science Association, 89*(3), 582–600.
Crow, P. (1988). Plain English: what counts besides readability? *Journal of Business Communication, 25*(1), 87–95.
Drometer, M., and Rincke, J. (2013). Electoral Competition and Endogenous Barriers to Entry. *European Journal of Political Economy, 34*, 253–262.
Endersby, J. W. (1993). Rules of Method and Rules of Conduct: An Experimental Study on Two Types of Procedure and Committee Behavior. *Journal of Politics, 55*(1), 218–236.
Eom, K., and Gross, D. A. (2007). Democratization Effects of Campaign Contribution Limits in Gubernatorial Elections. *Party Politics, 13*(6), 695–720.
Eshbaugh-Soha, M. (2006). The Conditioning Effects of Policy Salience and Complexity on American Political Institutions. *The Policy Studies Journal, 34*(2), 223–243.
Fabrigar, L. R., and Wegener, D. T. (2012). *Exploratory Factor Analysis*. New York: Oxford.
Ferejohn, J., and Shipan, C. (1990). Congressional Influence on Bureaucracy. *Journal of Law, Economics, and Organization, 6, Special Issue*, 1–20.
Flesch, R. (1948). A New Readability Yardstick. *Journal of Applied Psychology, 32*(3), 45–51.
Fox, R. L., and Lawless, J. L. (2004). Entering the Arena? Gender and the Decision to Run for Office. *American Journal of Political Science, 48*(2), 264–280.
Fox, R. L., and Lawless, J. L. (2005). To Run or Not to Run for Office: Explaining Nascent Political Ambition. *American Journal of Political Science, 49*(3), 642–659.
Frooman, H. (1981). Lawyers and Readability. *Journal of Business Communication, 18*(4), 45–51.
Fry, E. (1968). A Readability Formula That Saves Time. *Journal of Reading, 11*(7), pp. 513–516, 575–578.
Geyer, R., and Rihani, S. (2010). *Complexity and Public Policy*. New York: Routledge.
Gibbons, J. (1994). *Language and the Law*. Harlow, Essex, UK: Longman Group UK Limited.
Goidel, R. K., Gross, R. A., and Shields, T. G. (1999). *Money Matters: Consequences of campaign finance reform in US House elections.*: Rowman and Littlefield.
Gormley Jr, W. T. (1986). Regulatory issue networks in a federal system. *Polity, 18*(4), 595–620.
Gormley Jr, W. T. (2007). Public policy analysis: Ideas and impacts. *Annu. Rev. Polit. Sci., 10*, 297–313.
Gramm–Leach–Bliley Act (GLBA), US Congress (1999).
Green, D. P., and Krasno, J. S. (1988). Salvation of the Spendthrift Incumbent: Reestimating the Effects of Campaign Spending in House Elections. *American Journal of Political Science, 32*(4), 884–907.
Gross, D. A., and Goidel, R. K. (2003). *The States of Campaign Finance Reform*. Columbus: The Ohio State University
Gross, D. A., Goidel, R. K., and Shields, T. G. (2002). State Campaign Finance Regulations and Electoral Competition. *American Politics Research, 30*(2), 143–165.
Hamm, K. E. (1980). U.S. State Legislative Committee Decisions: Similar Results in Different Settings. *Legislative Studies Quarterly, 5*(1), 31–54.
Hamm, K. E., and Hogan, R. E. (2008). Campaign Finance Laws and Candidacy Decisions in State Legislative Elections. *Political Research Quarterly, 61*(3), 458–467.
Hammond, T. H., and Knott, J. H. (1996). Who Controls the Bureaucracy? Presidential Power, Congressional Dominance, Legal Constraints, and Bureaucratic Autonomy in a Model of Multi-Institutional Policy-Making Author. *Journal of Law, Economics, and Organization, 12*(1), 119–166.

Harshberger, S., and Davis, E. (2001). Federal Campaign Finance Reform: The Long and Winding Road. *National Civic Review, 90*(2), 125–136.

Haynes, P. (2008). Complexity Theory and Evaluation in Public Management. *Public Management Review, 10*(3), 401–419.

Heckman, J. J., and Smith, J. A. (2004). The determinants of participation in a social program: Evidence from a prototypical job training program. *Journal of Labor Economics, 22*(2), 243–298.

Heidelberg, R. L. (2016). The Power of Knowing the Rules. *American Review of Public Administration, 46*(6), 734–750.

Hogan, R. E. (2000). The costs of representation in state legislatures: Explaining variations in campaign spending. *Social Science Quarterly, 81*(4), 941–956.

Hogan, R. E. (2001). Campaign War Chests and Challenger Emergence in State Legislative Elections. *Political Research Quarterly, 54*, 815.

Hogan, R. E. (2004). Challenger Emergence, Incumbent Success and Electoral Accountability in State Legislative Elections. *The Journal of Politics, 66*(4), 1283–1303.

Hollada, J. L., Zide, M., Speier, W., and Roter, D. L. (2017). Readability Assessment of Patient-Centered Outcomes Research Institute Public Abstracts in Relation to Accessibility. *Epidemiology, July*, 37–38.

Holmes-Rovner, M., Stableford, S., Fagerlin, A., Wei, J. T., Dunn, R. L., Ohene-Frempong, J., Rovner, D. R. (2005). Evidence-Based Patient Choice: a Prostate Cancer Decision Aid in Plain Language. *BMC Medical Informatics and Decision Making, 5*(16).

Huber, J., Shipan, C. R., and Pfahler, M. (2001). Legislatures and Statutory Control of Bureaucracy. *American Journal of Political Science, 45*(2), 330–345.

Huber, J. D., and Shipan, C. R. (2000). The costs of control: Legislators, agencies, and transaction costs. *Legislative Studies Quarterly*, 25–52.

Hunt, B. (2002). Plain Language in Legislative Drafting: Is It Really the Answer? *Statute Law Review, 23*(1), 24–46.

Jacobs, A. M., and Matthews, J. S. (2017). Policy Attitudes in Institutional Context: Rules, Uncertainty, and the Mass Politics of Public Investment. *American Journal of Political Science, 61*(1), 194–207.

Johnson, T. (2013). Institutional Design and Bureaucrats' Impact on Political Control. *Journal of Politics, 75*(1), 183–197.

Kaufmann, W., and Feeney, M. K. (2014). Effect of Outcome Favourability on Red Tape Perceptions. *Public Administration, 92*(1), 178–191.

Kazee, T. A. (1983). The Deterrent Effect of Incumbency on Recruiting Challengers in US House Elections. *Legislative Studies Quarterly, 8*(3), 46480.

Kimball, D. C., Kropf, M., Moynihan, D., and Silva, C. L. (2013). The Policy Views of Partisan Election Officials. *UC Irvine Law Review, 551*, 551–574.

Kirk, J., and Miller, M. L. (1986). *Reliability and validity in qualitative research*. Beverly Hills: Sage Publications.

Klijn, E.-H. (2008). Complexity theory and public administration: What's new? Key concepts in complexity theory compared to their counterparts in public administration research. *Public Management Review, 10*(3), 299–317.

Kopczuk, W., and Pop-Eleches, C. (2007). Electronic filing, tax preparers and participation in the Earned Income Tax Credit. *Journal of Public Economics, 91*, 1351–1367.

Krepel, T. (1986). The Characteristics of Complex Policy Proposals. *Planning and Changing*, 44–50.

Kroft, K. (2008). Takeup, social multipliers and optimal social insurance. *Journal of Public Economics, 92*, 722–737.

Kulesza, C., Witko, C., and Waltenburg, E. (2016). Reform Interrupted? State Innovation, Court Decisions, and the Past and Future of Campaign Finance Reform in the States. *Election Law Journal, 2*, 143–159.

La Raja, R. J. (2008). *Small change: Money, political parties, and campaign finance reform*. Ann Arbor: University of Michigan Press.

LaRaja, R. (2005). Will the BCRA Strengthen the Political System? Negative: BCRA Is Not Improving the Political System. *Journal of Policy Analysis and Management, 24*(3), 599–610.

Lazarus, J. (2008). Incumbent Vulnerability and Challenger Entry in Statewide Elections. *American Politics Research, 36*(1), 108–129.

Lee, D. J. (2012). Taking the Good with the Bad: Cross-Cutting Effects of Ballot-Access Requirements on Third Party Electoral Success. *American Politics Research, 40*(2), 267–292.

Leete, B. A. (1981). Plain Language Legislation: A Comparison of Approaches. *American Business Law Journal, 18*, 511–524.

Legislatures, N. C. o. S. (Producer). NCSL. *National Conference of State Legislatures*. Retrieved from http://www.ncsl.org/legislatures-elections/legislator/staffinformation

Levine, M. D., and Hyde, M. S. (1977). Incumbency and the Theory of Political Ambition: A Rational-Choice Model. *The Journal of Politics, 39*(4), 959–983.

Lewis-Beck, M. S., Bryman, A., and Liao, T. F. (2004). *The Sage encyclopedia of social science research methods.* Thousand Oaks, CA: Sage.

Ley, P., and Florio, T. (1996). The Use of Readability Formulas in Health Care. *Psychology, Health and Medicine, 1*(1), 7–28.

Long, J. S., and Freese, J. (2006). *Regression Models for Categorical Dependent Variables Using Stata.* College Station, TX: Strata Press.

Lowi, T. (1972). Four Systems of Policy, Politics, and Choice. *Public Administration Review, 32*(4), 298–310.

LP, S. C. (2015). Stata Statistical Software: Release 14. College Station, TX: Strata Corp LP.

Lukes, S. (2005). *Power: A Radical View*. New York: Palgrave Macmillan.

Macey, J. R. (1992). Organizational Design and Political Control of the Administrative Agencies. *Journal of Law, Economics and Organization, 8*(1), 93–110.

Maestas, C. D., Fulton, S., Maisel, L. S., and Stone, W. J. (2006). When to Risk It? Institutions, Ambitions, and the Decision to Run for the US House. *American Political Science Review, 100*(2), 195–208.

Maestas, C. D., and Rugeley, C. R. (2008). Assessing the "Experience Bonus" Through Examping Strategic Entry, Candidate Quality and Campaign Receipts in US House Elections. *American Journal of Political Science, 52*(3), 520–535.

Maisel, L. S., and Stone, W. J. (1997). Determinants of Candidate Emergence in US House Elections: An Exploratory Study. *Legislative Studies Quarterly, 22*(1), 79–96.

Malbin, M., Corrado, A., and La Raja, R. (2005). Will the Bipartisan Campaign Reform Act of 2002 Strengthen the Political System? *Journal of Policy Analysis and Management, 24*(3), 599–610.

Malbin, M. J., and Gais, T. L. (1998). *The Day After Reform: Sobering Campaign Finance Lessons from the American States*. Albany, NY: Rockefeller Institute Press.

March, J. G., and Olsen, J. P. (1984). The New Institutionalism: Organizational Factors in Political Life. *American Political Science Review, 78*(3), 734–749.

March, J. G., and Olsen, J. P. (1989). *Rediscovering Institutions*. New York: Free Press.

Markell, D. L. (2006). Understanding citizen perspectives on government decision-making processes as a way to improve the administrative state. *Environmental Law*, 651–708.

Masson, M. J., and Waldron, M. (1994). Comprehension of Legal Contracts by Non-Experts: Effectiveness of Plain Language Redrafting. *Applied Cognitive Psychology, 8*(1), 67–85.

Mayhew, D. R. (1974). *Congress: The Electoral Connection*: New Haven, CT: Yale University.

McCubbins, M., Noll, R., and Weingast, B. (1987). Administrative Procedures as Instruments of Political Control. *Journal of Law, Economics and Organization, 3*, 342–277.

McKelvey, R. D., and Ordeshook, P. C. (1984). An Experimental Study of the Effects of Procedural Rules on Committee Behavior. *The Journal of Politics, 46*(1), 182–205.

McLaughlin, G. H. (1969). SMOG Grading - A New Readability Formula. *Journal of Reading, 12*(8), 639–646.

Miller, G. J. (2005). The Political Evolution of Principal-Agent Models. *Annual Review of Political Science, 8*, 203–225.

Moe, T. (1989). The Politics of Bureaucratic Structure *Can the Government Govern?* Washington, DC: The Brookings Institute.

Moe, T. (1990). Political Institutions: The Neglected Side of the Story. *Journal of Law, Economics and Organization, 6 (Special Issue)*, 213–253.

Moe, T. (1991). Politics and the Theory of Organizations. *Journal of Law, Economics, and Organization, 7 (Special Issue)*, 106–129.

Moncrief, G. F., Squire, P., and Jewell, M. F. (2001). Who Runs for the Legislature?

Montjoy, R. S. (2010). The Changing Nature...and Costs...of Election Administration. *Public Administration Review, 70*(6), 867–875.

Mooney, C. Z. (1992). Putting it on paper: The content of written information used in state lawmaking. *American Politics Quarterly, 20*(3), 345–365.

Moynihan, D., and Herd, P. (2010). Red Tape and Democracy: How Rules Affect Citizens Rights. *The American Review of Public Administration, 40*(6), 654–670.

Moynihan, D., Herd, P., and Harvey, H. (2014). Administrative Burden: Learning, Psychological, and Compliance Costs in Citizen-State Interactions. *Journal of Public Administration Research and Theory, 25*, 43–69.

Moynihan, D. P., Herd, P., and Ribgy, E. (2016). Policymaking by Other Means: Do States Use Administrative Barriers to Limit Access to Medicaid? *Administration and Society, 48*(4), 497–524.

Online-Utility.org (Producer). Online-Utility.org. *Online-Utility.org*. Retrieved from http://www.online-utility.org/english/readability_test_and_improve.jsp

Ostrom, E. (2007). Institutional Rational Choice: An Assessment of the Institutional Analysis and Development Framework. In P. Sabatier (Ed.), *Theories of the policy process* (pp. 21–64). Cambridge: Westview Press.

Petelin, R. (2010). Considering Plain Language: Issues and Initiatives. *Corporate Communications: An International Journal, 15*(2), 205–216.

Peters, B. G. (2012). *Institutional Theory in Political Science*. New York: The Continuum International Publishing Group.

Pierson, P. (2000). Increasing Returns, Path Dependence, and the Study of Politics. *American Political Science Review, 94*(2), 251–267.

Politics, I. o. M. i. S. (Producer). FollowtheMoney. *Institute on Money in State Politics*. Retrieved from www.followthemoney.org

Powell, R. T. (2000). The Impact of Term Limits on the Candidacy Decisions of State Legislators in US House Elections. *Legislative Studies Quarterly, 25*(4), 645–661.

QI4. (2014). In M. J. M. Shepherd (Ed.).

QI5. (2016). In M. J. M. Shepherd (Ed.).

QI6. (2016). In M. J. M. Shepherd (Ed.).

QI7. (2016). In M. J. M. Shepherd (Ed.).

QI11. (2014). In M. J. M. Shepherd (Ed.).

QI12. (2014). In M. J. M. Shepherd (Ed.).

QI13. (2014). In M. J. M. Shepherd (Ed.).

Randazzo, K. A. (2008). Statutory Constraint on the Seventh Circuit: Examining Congressional Influence. *Southern Illinois University Law Journal, 32*, 683–698.

Randazzo, K. A., Waterman, R. W., and Fine, J. A. (2006). Checking the Federal Courts: The Impact of Congressional Statutes on Judicial Behavior. *The Journal of Politics, 68*(4), 1006–1017.

Redish, J. G. (2000). Readability Formulas Have Even More Limitations than Klare Discusses. *ACM Journal of Computer Documentation, 24*(3), 132–137.

Ringquist, E. J., Worsham, J., and Eisner, M. A. (2003). Salience, complexity, and the legislative direction of regulatory bureaucracies. *Journal of Public Administration Research and Theory, 13*(2), 141–164.

Root, J., and Stableford, S. (1999). Easy to Read Consumer Communications: A Missing Link in Medicaid Managed Care. *Journal of Health Politics, Policy and Law, 4*(1), 1–26.

Rudd, R., Kaphingst, K., Colton, T., Gregoire, J., and Hyde, J. (2004). Rewriting Public Health Information in Plain Language. *Journal of Health Communications, 9*(3), 195–206.

Sabatier, P., and Whiteman, D. (1985). Legislative decision making and substantive policy information: Models of information flow. *Legislative Studies Quarterly*, 395–421.
Sabatier, P. A., and Weible, C. M. (2014). *Theories of the Policy Process*. Boulder, CO.
Scheibal, W. J. (1986). The Effectiveness of Plain English Laws:A Legal Perspective. *Journal of Business Communication, 23*(3), 58–63.
Schultz, D. (2002). States and Campaign Finance Reform. *National Civic Review, 91*(2), 205–210.
Scott, P. G., and Pandey, S. K. (2000). The Influence of Red Tape on Bureaucratic Behavior: An Experimental Simulation. *Journal of Policy Analysis and Management, 19*(4), 615–633.
Senate, U. (2009). *Plain Writing Act of 2009* (111–102).
Senate, U. (2010). *Plain Writing Act of 2010 124 STAT. 2862*. Washington, DC.
Severence, L., Greene, E., and Loftus, E. (1984). Toward Criminal Jury Instructions that Jurors Can Understand. *The Journal of Criminal Law and Criminology, 75*(1), 198–233.
Shepsle, K. A., and Weingast, B. R. (1984). When do rules of procedure matter? *The Journal of Politics, 46*(1), 206–221.
Shepsle, K. A., and Weingast, B. R. (1994). Positive Theories of Congressional Institutions. *Legislative Studies Quarterly, 19*(2), 149–179.
Squire, P. (1989). Challengers in US Senate Elections. *Legislative Studies Quarterly, 14*(4), 531–547.
Squire, P. (1995). Candidates, Money, and Voters. Assessing the State of Congressional Elections Research. *Political Science Quarterly, 48*(4), 891–917.
Stableford, S., and Mettger, W. (2007). Plain Language: A Strategic Response to the Health Literacy Challenge. *Journal of Public Health Policy, 28*(1), 71–93.
Stone, W. J., Maisel, L. S., and Maestas, C. D. (2004). Quality Counts: Extending the Strategic Politician Model of Incumbent Deterrence. *American Journal of Political Science, 48*(3), 479–495.
Strach, K. (2012). NC Board of Elections Campaign Finance Division. In M. J. Shepherd (Ed.).
Stratmann, T. (2005). Ballot access restrictions and candidate entry in elections. *European Journal of Political Economy, 21*, 59–71.
Stratmann, T., and Aparicio-Castillo, F. J. (2006). Competition Policy for Elections: Do Campaign Contribution Limits Matter? *Public Choice, 127*, 177–206.
Sullivan, R. (2001). The Promise of Plain Language Drafting. *McGill Law Review, 47*, 97–128.
Teisman, G. R., and Klijn, E.-H. (2008). Complexity Theory and Public Management. *Public Management Review, 10*(3), 287–297.
Thompson, J., and Moncrief, G. F. (1998). Exploring the "Lost World" of Campaign Finance. In J. A. Thompson and G. F. Moncrief (Eds.), *Campaign Finance in State Legislative Elections* (pp. 3–19). Washington, DC: Congressional Quarterly Inc.
Uslaner, E. (1993). *The Decline in Comity in Congress*: The University of Michigan Press.
Van Boom, W. H., Desmet, P., and Van Dam, M. (2016). "If It's Easy to Read, It's Easy to Claim" – The Effect of the Readability of Insurance Contracts on Consumer Expectations and Conflict Behaviour. *Journal of Consumer Policy, 39*, 187–197.
Wiengast, B. R. (1984). The congressional–bureaucratic system: a principal agent perspective (with applications to the SEC). *Public Choice, 44*(1), 147–191.
Witko, C. (2005). Measuring the Stringency of State Campaign Finance Regulation. *State Politics and Policy Quarterly, 5*(3), 295–310.
Witko, C. (2007). Explaining increases in the stringency of state campaign finance regulation, 1993–2002. *State Politics and Policy Quarterly, 7*(4), 369–393.
Wolfe, B., and Scrivner, S. (2005). The Devil May Be in the Details: How the Characteristics of SCHIP Programs Affect Take-Up. *Journal of Policy Analysis and Management, 24*(3), 499–522.
www.plainlanguage.gov (Producer). Improving Communication from the Federal Government to the Public. *www.plainlanguage.gov*. Retrieved from www.plainlanguage.gov
Wydick, R. (1978). Plain English for Lawyers. *California Law Review, 66*(4), 727–765.
Zetterberg, P. (2008). The Downside of Gender Quotas? Institutional Constraints on Women in Mexican State Legislatures. *Parliamentary Affairs, 61*(3), 442–460.
(2015). *Medical Writing, 24*(1).

Index

About the Author

Mary Jo McGowan Shepherd received her BA in political science from UNC Charlotte, an MA in international relations from Baylor University, and a PhD in Public Policy from UNC Charlotte. She received the Graduate Dean's Distinguished Dissertation Award for outstanding contribution to the field of social sciences in 2016 from the UNC Charlotte Graduate School. She researches institutions, elections administration, and complexity and teaches in the Department of Political Science and Public Administration at UNC Charlotte.

www.ingramcontent.com/pod-product-compliance
Ingram Content Group UK Ltd.
Pitfield, Milton Keynes, MK11 3LW, UK
UKHW041628031026
15587UKWH00001B/148

9 781498 535069